Social Welfare in Germany and Britain
Origins and Development

This account of the development of the social welfare systems of two major industrial countries by one of West Germany's most prominent social historians represents a timely contribution on the nature and future of the Welfare State to the ongoing debate. It covers the period from the late nineteenth century to the present and is genuinely comparative. The book was written in the hope that an analysis of the roots, principles and history of the organisation of social welfare might provide a better understanding of the issues and tasks of our time.

Gerhard A. Ritter, born in 1929 in Berlin, studied at the universities of Tübingen, Berlin and at St Antony's College, Oxford. He is Professor of Modern History at the University of Munich, was Chairman of the Association of German Historians (1976–80) and has been a member of the Bavarian Academy of Science since 1980. He has been Visiting Professor at a number of universities: Washington, St Louis (1965), Oxford (1965/6, 1971), California, Berkeley (1971/2) and Tel Aviv (1973). He has published widely in the field of German and British social and political history.

Social Welfare in Germany and Britain

Origins and Development

GERHARD A. RITTER

Social Welfare in Germany and Britain
Origins and Development

Translated from the German by
KIM TRAYNOR

BERG
Leamington Spa / New York

Berg Publishers Ltd
24 Binswood Avenue, Leamington Spa,
Warwickshire CV32 5SQ, UK

175 Fifth Avenue, New York 10010,
NY, USA

English translation © Berg Publishers Ltd 1986
Originally published as *Sozialversicherung in Deutschland
und England, Entstehung und Grundzüge im Vergleich.*
Translated from the German by permission of the publishers,
C. H. Beck Verlag, München.
© 1983 C. H. Beck Verlag, München

British Library Cataloguing in Publication Data

Ritter, Gerhard Albert
  Social welfare in Germany and Britain.
  1. Great Britain—Social policy
  I. Title II. Sozialversicherung in Deutschland
und England. *English*
  361.6′1′0941   HN385

  ISBN 0–907582–49–4

Library of Congress Cataloging-in-Publication Data
Ritter, Gerhard Albert.
  Social welfare in Germany and Britain.

  Translation of: Sozialversicherung in Deutschland und England.
  Bibliography: p.
  Includes index.
  1. Social security—Germany—History. 2. Social security—Great
Britain—History. I. Title.
HD7179.R5813 1986   368.4′00941   85–23030
ISBN 0–907582–49–4

Printed in Great Britain by The Camelot Press, Southampton

Contents

Tables

Figure

Foreword

The modern social security systems of the Western industrialised nations arose essentially in response to the social consequences of industrialisation. Their step-by-step replacement of traditional welfare methods reflected the demands of a working class which was making itself increasingly heard in the last three decades of the nineteenth century. From the time of their introduction onwards, these systems also increasingly performed the role of legitimising political authority and stabilising the existing social and economic order.

Social security today guarantees collective safeguards against the social consequences of capitalist methods of industrial production. However, the optimistic assumption which prevailed during the 1950s and 1960s in the Federal Republic of Germany and other industrial countries, that constantly rising social expenditure would neither undermine economic competitiveness nor overburden the wage-earner and tax-payer has recently been seriously shaken. The decline in the birth rate and increased life expectancy, the reduction in the length of the working-day and average working life, the massive rise in the cost of health services and, above all, the economic recession have inevitably led to an intensive discussion on the 'limits of the welfare state' (*Sozialstaat*).

In 1979,[1] 11 million West Germans, representing 26 per cent of the

---

1. *Statistisches Jahrbuch für die Bundesrepublik Deutschland*, 1981, pp. 94f. The West German government's Statistisches Bundesamt includes in its definition of 'persons whose main means of support is primarily derived from a pension or similar source

electorate, derived their main means of support primarily from pensions or similar sources of income. At present around 90 per cent of West Germany's population is entitled to social security benefits and in 1976 the amount paid out on old-age pensions alone reached a figure equivalent to 73 per cent of total federal government expenditure.[2] In Great Britain the National Health Service goes even further in extending its benefits to all citizens.

In 1980, according to figures supplied by the International Labour Office, West Germany spent 23.8 per cent of its Gross Domestic Product on its state system of social security. This figure was well above the corresponding figures for the United Kingdom (1979/80 = 17.7) and those for Japan (1979/80 = 10.9) and the United States (1979/80 = 12.7), but lower than those for France (1980 = 26.8), the Netherlands (1980 = 28.6) and Sweden (1980 = 32).[3]

After the experiences of the Depression and the Second World War, from the late 1940s until about 1973, the number of persons covered by social security rapidly grew in all industrial countries. This increase was accompanied by a corresponding rise in the average amount of expenditure on benefits for the individuals covered and, hence, the overall costs of social security systems. From about the mid-1970s, however, a less uniform picture has emerged. An expansion of social benefits outpacing economic growth has continued undiminished in

of income' not only old-age pensioners and pensioned civil servants, but anyone whose main source of income is unearned.

2. Hans Günter Hockerts, 'Sicherung im Alter: Kontinuität und Wandel der gesetzlichen Rentenversicherung 1889–1979', in Werner Conze and M. Rainer Lepsius (eds.), *Sozialgeschichte der Bundesrepublik Deutschland: Beiträge zum Kontinuitätsproblem*, Stuttgart 1983, pp. 276–323, esp. p. 296.

3. International Labour Office, *The Cost of Social Security: Eleventh International Inquiry, 1978–1980*, Geneva 1985, pp. 57–9. With 54.8 per cent of the total receipts in financing social security in 1979/80 the share of public authorities was significantly higher in the United Kingdom than in the Federal Republic of Germany (28.9 per cent in 1980). This was made up in Germany by higher contributions of employers (34.2 to 26.5 per cent in the UK) and of insured persons (34.0 to 15.8 per cent in the UK). The rest of the money came from other sources (*Cost of Social Security*, pp. 80, 82).

4. Ibid., pp. 56–9. For the growing share of the Gross Domestic Product claimed by social security costs in thirteen European countries (outside the Eastern Bloc) since 1949, see e.g. P. Flora *et al.*, *State, Economy and Society in Western Europe, 1815–1975*, Vol. 1, *The Growth of Mass Democracies and Welfare States*, p. 456, Frankfurt, London and Chicago 1983. Compared with the International Labour Office, the Federal Republic of Germany employs a much broader definition of social benefits in its official statistics. For example, it includes indirect benefits such as tax concessions, housing benefits and direct benefits of employers and employees. According to this definition, social expenditure in the German Empire, the Weimar Republic and the Federal Republic has risen from approx. 2 per cent of the GNP in 1914 and 10 per cent in the 1920s to approx. 20 per cent in 1960 and a third of the GNP since 1975.

Spain, Denmark, Sweden, France and Poland. In countries such as West Germany, the United Kingdom and the USA (and even the Soviet Union), on the other hand, the share of the Gross Domestic Product spent on social security appears to have stopped rising,[4] (although absolute figures on expenditure continue to rise). It would be wrong at this stage, however, to conclude that this development signifies a reversal in the long-term trend by which the welfare state has expanded.

This short study, which compares factors behind the growth of the German and British state welfare systems and their basic character before the First World War, is primarily intended as an historian's contribution to illuminating the historical problem concerning the formation of the modern welfare state. It can also offer a modest contribution to the present-day discussion on social security systems, though only very indirectly. Nevertheless, a retrospective look at the past may show that overcoming the 'crisis of the welfare state', insofar as this is not economically determined, depends far less on perfecting the large bureaucratic machinery created for its administration than on a fresh appreciation of the ideas of mutual support and providing relief through institutions other than the state, both of which played a much greater and more effective role in the period when social insurance first emerged. By stressing personal responsibility and support within the family or smaller communities, more attention might be devoted to the old, the sick, the unemployed and those with large families. This might also help counter the bureaucratic anonymity with which individuals are treated within the social security system. In the area of social services especially, which, alongside cash benefits, deserve more emphasis, community care and help within small groups have proved more intimate and more effective than large institutions responsible for redistributing wealth. The element of solidarity among the insured could be strengthened by reviving the idea of self-administration, which would in turn improve the collective control that is necessary for the successful functioning of the welfare state and the prevention of its abuse.

The reader will have no difficulty in recognising the fact that the

---

In 1983 social expenditure amounted to 533.9 billion marks or 31.9 per cent. This lay well below the GNP share of social benefits which averaged about 33 per cent in the years 1975 to 1982. The federal government has forecast social expenditure at 624.7 billion marks or 29.9 per cent of the projected GNP for 1987 (Detlev Zöllner, 'Landesbericht Deutschland', in Peter A. Köhler and Hans F. Zacher (eds.), *Ein Jahrhundert Sozialversicherung in der Bundesrepublik Deutschland, Frankreich, Großbritannien, Österreich und der Schweiz*, Berlin 1981, pp. 45–179; Johannes Brakel, 'Sozialbudget 1983: Fallende Tendenz', in *Bundesarbeitsblatt* 4 (1984), pp. 9–13, 106–114;

sections on Germany are more closely based on my own researchers than
those on Britain. I hope, however, that the comparative method I have
adopted will contribute to a deeper understanding not only of the
German social security system before the First World War but also the
specific character of the British system in the same period.

Comparative studies always face the problem that neither the
categories employed in national statistics nor the meanings of basic
concepts are completely identical. Even the central concept of the
'welfare state' has an ambivalent ring to it in Germany. As well as
conveying its positive sense of a modern, democratic *Sozialstaat*, it also
carries conscious echoes from the period of absolutism when it signified
state 'welfare' for citizens subject to a strict form of social control
exercised by a paternalistic government and its administrative institutions or *Polizey*. In Britain, on the other hand, the concept of the
'welfare state',[5] which appeared in the 1940s and gained currency
during the period of the Labour governments between 1945 and 1951,
and which was used during the Second World War in conscious
contrast to the 'power states' of the European dictators,[6] assumed an
unequivocally positive meaning. It implied not only the guarantee of
an acceptable minimum living standard and state welfare against
social risks but also the long-term realisation of egalitarian and democratic principles in the treatment of citizens. Since the mid-1950s, the
initially very broad popular consensus which helped establish the welfare
state during the period of austerity in the 1940s has been shaken. The
affluent society has witnessed growing criticism of the degree of state
intervention in social and economic affairs and the accompanying
restriction of the individual's right to self-determination, although the
modern welfare state has not been connected with the older welfare
policies of absolutist states, as has been the case in West Germany.

The same problem encountered in the use of concepts also arises
when comparisons are made between important political and social
institutions which are deeply rooted in the history of the countries
involved. Despite such problems, it is, nevertheless, worthwhile undertaking a comparative study of Germany and Britain since both countries were mutually influenced to a significant degree as regards the

---

idem, 'Sozialbudget: Neuberechnung 1983', in *Bundesarbeitsblatt* 4 (1985), pp. 5–7,
133–9.

5. *See* Asa Briggs, 'The Welfare State in Historical Perspective', in *Archives Européennes
de Sociologie* 2 (1961), pp. 221–58, esp. pp. 221, 227–32; Norman Furniss and
Timothy Tilton, *The Case for the Welfare State: From Social Security to Social Equality*,
Bloomington and London 1977, esp. p. X, pp. 18–20).

6. Maurice Bruce, *The Coming of the Welfare State*, London 1961, p. IX.

development of government intervention and social policy. Moreover, the choice of countries in this study enables us to analyse two main types of social security system.

This study originated in researches carried out on the history of the German working class and German labour movement which were supported by the Friedrich-Ebert-Stiftung and the Stiftung Volkswagenwerk. Not least, it grew out of personal interest dating back to the early 1950s in the relationship of the state to the working class and the labour movements of Germany and England during the period of industrialisation. The manuscript of the original German edition was completed in May 1982. In the last three years, partly in connection with the centenary of the introduction of social insurance and partly in the wake of the fresh debate on the 'crisis of the welfare state', a whole range of publications has appeared in West Germany on the history of social insurance and social policy before 1914. I have made use of these recent studies in revising my book for this English edition.

I am indebted especially to Klaus Tenfelde and Hans Günter Hockerts for reading the original draft of the German manuscript and suggesting various improvements. Special thanks are also due to Hans Gerhard Husung for providing me with statistical material on the working of the National Insurance Act of 1911 and Herbert Loebe for helping me in the preparation of the tables.

Allmannshausen, February 1985   Gerhard A. Ritter

CHAPTER 1

The Social Question and Social Insurance in Europe in the Late-Nineteenth Century

Although its roots were much older, the discussion concerning the so-called 'social question' in Central, Northern and Western Europe assumed a new topicality around a hundred years ago. The term was mainly understood to refer to the problem posed by the workers; that is, the integration of the industrial workers into the existing social and political order. It was also increasingly taken to mean the preservation of the traditional middle class, comprising artisans and small tradesmen. That this discussion took on new life from the late 1870s onwards was due in the first place to the serious economic depression after 1873, which shook beliefs in the self-regulating capacity of the market and the ability of the individual to protect himself by his own devices against poverty, economic hardship and exploitation. The depression also gave rise to fears of a threat to public order through acts of desperation by a populace suffering increasingly from unemployment and the impoverishing effects of the crisis. The deep disquiet of the aristocracy and the middle class on account of the Paris Commune of 1871, which raised the spectre of revolution, also played its part.

This double challenge posed by the crisis of industrial capitalist society and the gradual emergence of a potentially revolutionary proletariat set in motion and strengthened those forces in society which hoped to defuse potential conflict by a policy of concrete social reforms.

Alongside the Churches, these were middle-class social reformers, who often stood in close social and intellectual contact with the higher reaches of the civil service and helped awaken a kind of social conscience through their criticisms of Manchester liberalism. These reformers made a decisive contribution to identifying social problems and to some extent worked out detailed suggestions for their solution. Apart from the development of social insurance schemes, which before 1914 were typically referred to by the general term of workers' insurance, the development of workmen's protection was a prominent feature of this reformist policy towards labour. Serious consideration was also given at an early stage to the problem of balancing competing interests and regulating conflict in the newly emerged industrial society through the creation of suitable institutions to represent the antagonists.

Social insurance, as a new form of welfare which gradually took over from the traditional system of poor relief, more suited to a relatively stable agrarian society, increasingly defined the discussion of the social question in Europe from the 1880s onwards. The reasons for this must be seen in the first place in the process of social and economic change which was stimulated by population growth, industrialisation, urbanisation and internal migration. There were certainly many determining factors behind the new forms of social change and widespread social and economic distress, which were conceptualised as 'the social question': the dissolution of a society based on traditional estates and a system of guilds; the departure of more and more people from the security of village life; the overcoming of the previously often-imposed celibacy of the humbler sections of the community;[1] the disintegration of the traditional family as a productive unit involving the whole household[2] and the accompanying loss of the family's function as a provider of relief in times of distress; the breakdown of the household community of employer and employees in traditional crafts and in the countryside; the development of a capitalist labour market, in which

1. On restrictions governing the subject's freedom to marry and conditions governing the right of domicile and settlement in nineteenth-century Germany, *see* Wolfgang Köllmann, 'Bevölkerung und Arbeitskräftepotential in Deutschland 1815–1865: Ein Beitrag zur Analyse der Problematik des Pauperismus', in Köllmann, *Bevölkerung in der industriellen Revolution: Studien zur Bevölkerungsgeschichte Deutschlands*, Göttingen 1974, pp. 61–98, 267–71, esp. pp. 96–8; Antje Kraus, ' "Antizipierter Ehesegen" im 19. Jahrhundert: Zur Beurteilung der Illegitimität unter sozialgeschichtlichen Aspekten', in *Vierteljahrschrift für Sozial- und Wirtschaftsgeschichte* 66 (1979), pp. 174–215; Klaus-Jürgen Matz, *Pauperismus und Bevölkerung: Die gesetzlichen Ehebeschränkungen in den süddeutschen Staaten während des 19. Jahrhunderts*, Stuttgart 1980.
2. For this concept of pre-industrial society, *see* Otto Brunner, 'Das "ganze Haus" und die alteuropäische "Ökonomik"', in idem *Neue Wege der Verfassungs- und Sozialgeschichte: Vorträge und Aufsätze*, Göttingen 1956, pp. 33–61.

wage levels were determined by the market rather than the workers' needs, and in which the employer's paternalism lost its traditional and legal basis; the emergence of an industrial proletariat; the increased danger of accidents at work caused by machines; industry's lack of interest in older workers and the growing dependence of work opportunities on an economy subject to fluctuations in the economic cycle. All these factors played an essential part in defining the problem. Nevertheless, social insurance, especially that administered by the state, did not come about simply as the result of society reaching a specific stage of economic and social development. Had this been the case, it would not have been Germany but rather Great Britain, Belgium, Switzerland and France – in that order – which would have been the countries first to develop systems of state-administered social insurance.[3]

If we enquire into what in the first place determined the timing of Germany's new social insurance, its content and form, several quite different determining factors deserve mention; for example, the particular character of the dominant political and social traditions at the time, the specific type of political constitution, the strength and prestige of the state bureaucracy, the existing constellation of social, economic and political forces, the timing and extent of the workers' political mobilisation, the vitality and flexibility of traditional forms of poor relief administered by the state, local authorities, Churches and privately run charity organisations, as well as the tradition of self-help. To these must be added the position and influence of the empirical social sciences; that is, their ability to identify areas of social risk and calculate the costs involved in providing for relief through a system of social insurance. The concept of insurance, which made considerable headway at this time, was particularly important. Following on from

3. *See* Wolfram Fischer, 'Wirtschaftliche Bedingungen und Faktoren bei der Entstehung und Entwicklung von Sozialversicherung', in Hans F. Zacher (ed.) *Bedingungen für die Entstehung und Entwicklung von Sozialversicherung. Colloquium der Projektgruppe für Internationales und Vergleichendes Sozialrecht der Max-Planck-Gesellschaft*, Berlin 1979, pp. 91–102. The 'functionalist' view, which sees social insurance as the inevitable result of a certain stage being reached in socio-economic development, is also rejected by Alber in his comparative study. The fact that the dualistic constitutional monarchies — which he regarded as authoritarian and which denied their Parliaments any say in the formation of government — took the lead in this field over the parliamentary democracies is explained in terms of their greater need to take the initiative through a 'social policy from above' in order to defend the system against the workers' political mobilisation. This policy attempted to compensate for the growing lack of legitimacy in the political sphere and integrate the workers into bourgeois society without guaranteeing them equal rights of participation (*see* Jens Alber, *Vom Armenhaus zum Wohlfahrtsstaat: Analysen zur Entwicklung der Sozialversicherung in Westeuropa*, Frankfurt and New York 1982, pp. 130f., 149f., 163f., 195f.).

its early forerunners, especially marine insurance, it became widely
prevalent in the course of the eighteenth and nineteenth centuries,
initially in the fields of shipping, fire, livestock insurance and storm
damage. Gustav Schmoller, one of Germany's leading economists and
social scientists of the late-nineteenth and early-twentieth centuries,
saw:

> the triumph of insurance in every conceivable area as one of the age's great
> advances in social progress. It was an entirely logical development that
> insurance should spread from the upper classes to the lower classes; that it
> had to try, as far as possible, to eliminate poverty; and that the older
> charitable relief funds for the workers were more and more constructed on
> the sound principle of insurance.[4]

Based on contributions from the employers and the employees and
subsidies from the state, social insurance borrowed essential elements
from three earlier forms of collective subsistence outside of the work of
religious bodies and other charitable institutions: the system of mutual
benefit societies as practised by the guilds, corporations and journeymen associations, the employer's obligation to provide his servants and
clerical workers with protection as laid down in the Prussian General
Law Code (*Allgemeines Landrecht*) of 1794 and the provision of poor relief
by the state and local authorities. The joint liability of the insured, the
employer and the state, as incorporated in social insurance, mainly
differed from earlier systems of social security in that, unlike the
provision of the guilds, it was not restricted to the members of any one
occupation but instead took in a wider range of groups. In contrast to
the personal obligations placed on the employer during the feudal
period, it was not, moreover, based on paternalistic principles. Another
way in which it differed from the traditional care of the poor was in the
insured person's individual legal right to claim benefits, free from any
political or social discrimination. While previous forms of welfare had
been mainly local in character, even though the framework of the law
concerning poor relief could be defined by general laws, social insurance was distinctly based on legislation of a national character and, in
many cases, national institutions. Unlike the traditional system of poor
relief, which stressed the individual's personal blame for his hardship,
it placed firmly in the foreground those general factors which produced
crises in the life of the individual, for which he himself could not be held

---

4. Gustav Schmoller, 'Vier Briefe über Bismarcks sozialpolitische und volkswirtschaftliche Stellung und Bedeutung', in idem, *Charakterbilder*, Munich and Leipzig
   1913, pp. 27–76, esp. p. 57.

responsible. It differed from earlier forms of private insurance in that it provided security, not against predicaments arising from 'natural' causes but against those resulting from 'social' factors. In terms of its contributions and benefits, it took differing social criteria into account and aimed to take in specific sections of the population on a comprehensive scale, including those who would have been turned down by private insurers as 'bad risks' or else forced to pay much higher contributions. Social insurance treated these people no differently from those regarded as 'good risks'.

There is no doubt that the state-run social insurance schemes which appeared in other European countries outside Germany and several non-European countries at the end of the nineteenth and beginning of the twentieth centuries owed a great deal to the German model of a relatively comprehensive and viable compulsory workers' insurance created during the 1880s.[5] To quote Schmoller once more, Germany's social insurance legislation was not, therefore, 'a change for the better purely in terms of Germany's social policy, but possessed a world-wide historical significance'.[6] Certainly, alongside the more or less full-scale adoption of the German model, as happened in the case of Austria, Hungary and Luxembourg (which was still part of the German Customs Union [*Zollverein*]),[7] alternative solutions could be worked out,

5. I cannot go along with Alber's view that the influence of Germany's social insurance on other countries was minimal (*Vom Armenhaus zum Wohlfahrtsstaat* pp. 134–46). Alber measures its influence in terms of how long it took other countries to respond to Germany's example and what type of welfare programmes they introduced. According to his findings, only a few countries followed Germany's legislation soon after its introduction, and barely half of the insurance systems he refers to adopted the German idea of compulsory insurance. In my opinion, the question of its influence abroad cannot be decided solely or even mainly in terms of the time gap or the voluntary or compulsory nature of the insurance. Rather, it seems to me necessary to investigate the concrete legislative processes in individual countries in order to decide the extent to which these were possibly influenced by Germany's example.

6. Ibid., p. 56.

7. Dr Georg Zacher (ed.), *Die Arbeiter-Versicherung im Auslande*, 5 vols., Berlin 1900–08 (individual issues appeared from 1898 onwards), see esp. vol. 1, no. VII, 'Die Arbeiterversicherung in Österreich', 1899; no. VIII, 'Die Arbeiterversicherung in Ungarn', 1899; vol. 2, no. XIV, 'Die Arbeiterversicherung in Luxemburg', 1901. Addenda to these issues appeared in vols. 3, 4 and 5 (nos. VIIa, VIIIa, XIVa and VIIIb). Zacher, who was at the Reichsversicherungsamt between 1890 and 1905 before being appointed a director of the Kaiserliches Statistisches Amt, provides a good general overview of social insurance around 1900. Volumes 4 and 5 of his work also deal with social insurance in the United States (XVII) and Australian and New Zealand workers' insurance, which was especially influential in helping shape the British system (XVIII). *See also* Peter A. Köhler and Hans F. Zacher, 'Die Sozialversicherung im Europa der Jahrhundertwende', in *Die Sozialgerichtsbarkeit* 28 (1981), pp. 420–32.

often on the basis of a critical analysis of Germany's example. This was the case at first in the countries of Western Europe and Scandinavia.[8] Alongside the German model of compulsory state insurance schemes, state-funded voluntary insurance schemes, based mainly on the liberal principle of encouraging self-help, were widespread in Europe long before 1914. The support of governments for voluntary schemes was especially prevalent and effective in the case of sickness insurance. That attempts were made to deal with old-age insurance by means of voluntary insurance schemes in France (up to 1910), Italy (up to 1919) and Belgium (up to 1924), was probably connected with the fact that Catholicism, with its principle of subordinating the state's role and stressing that of the family when dealing with social problems, was especially strong in these countries. However, this did not prevent Catholic countries such as Austria and Luxembourg from also introducing compulsory insurance before 1914.

The German government and its higher civil service were fully aware of the German model's influence abroad, as was the German labour movement in the years leading up to 1914.[9] Its imitation by other countries, whose insurance systems were keenly studied in Germany, was, for example, greatly advertised from 1889 onwards at international conferences on workers' insurance and through the dissemination of an extensive literature on Germany's social insurance system.[10]

8. *See* Stein Kuhnle, 'The Growth of Social Insurance Programs in Scandinavia: Outside Influences and Internal Forces', in Peter Flora and Arnold Heidenheimer (ed.), *The Development of Welfare States in Europe and America*, New Brunswick and London 1981, pp. 125–50. Kuhnle concludes that, apart from Norway, the insurance laws which were eventually passed in Scandinavia departed from the German principle of compulsory insurance and were basically determined by other models, i.e. original, home-grown concepts. At the same time, he stresses the fact that Germany's example was of great importance in stimulating public discussion and legislative activity.

9. For instance, even the Social Democrat leader, August Bebel, recognised Germany's pioneering role in the field of social insurance. In a Reichstag speech of 3 April 1889 he predicted that other countries would follow its example:

  I believe, that once other European countries follow this path, which I am aware was first taken by the German Empire before all other European states — and it is inevitable that this example will be followed — there is no doubt in my mind that the more these countries realise that they have to make much greater sacrifices in this area for genuine cultural tasks [*Kulturaufgaben*] and as a result will be limited in terms of what they can spend on other areas. . . . To the extent that countries realise they have to solve these tasks and make the appropriate sacrifices, the more we will see a reduction in the presently oppressive expenditure for military purposes and armaments. [*Stenographische Berichte über die Verhandlungen des Reichstags*, VII. Legislaturperiode, IV. Session, (*Sten. Berichte des Reichstags*, VII, IV) vol. 2, p. 1222].

10. For conferences on workers' insurance, *see* Dr Tonio Bödiker, *Die Arbeiterversicherung in den Europäischen Staaten*, Leipzig 1895, pp. 235–7. During the world exhibition

At the great international exhibitions around the turn of the century great stress was laid on exhibiting information on the German system. For example, at the world exhibition in St Louis in 1904 a special display was mounted, entitled 'Workers' Insurance in the German Empire'. Later transferred to the University of Harvard as a permanent exhibit, it contained, among other things, around a thousand photographs intended to illustrate Germany's latest accident prevention measures.[11] According to the report of the government official in charge, only the German section in the exhibits on insurance succeeded in 'illustrating a social insurance system based on a unified concept', which, as he saw it, had made 'a significant contribution towards solving the social problem in our century'. In comparing the systems of the different countries represented, two basically differing approaches distinctly emerged:

the one is rooted in the traditional conviction that only the greatest measure of freedom for the individual can develop the best and most efficient re-

---

held in Paris from 9–14 September 1889, the first Congrès des Accidents founded a 'Comité permanent des Accidents'. A conference held two years later in Berne expanded its programme to include social insurance. The Comité published a bulletin intended to give an overview of all existing and proposed legislation on workers' insurance, as well as relevant academic studies on the subject. To spread the message concerning Germany's social insurance the Reichsversicherungsamt sponsored a publication by Dr Zacher entitled 'Leitfaden zur Arbeiterversicherung des Deutschen Reiches', Berlin 1893, which appeared in German, French and English versions at the world exhibition held in Chicago. Ordered in bulk, it cost only 10 pfennig per copy and by 1895, 100,000 copies had already been sold. Similar publications appeared at other world exhibitions.

11. The catalogue for the world exhibition in St Louis gives a good idea of what the display contained: *Die Arbeiterversicherung des Deutschen Reichs für die Weltausstellung in St Louis 1904 dargestellt vom Reichs-Versicherungsamt und Kaiserlichen Statistischen Amt in Berlin. Katalog und Führer . . .* , ed. by G. A. Klein. A selection of the ninety-one statistical tables compiled by the Reichsversicherungsamt and displayed at St Louis in German, English and French versions was published in *Atlas und Statistik der Arbeiterversicherung des Deutschen Reichs: Beiheft zum Reichs-Arbeitsblatt Juni 1904. Hrsg. vom Kaiserlichen Statistischen Amt, Abteilung für Arbeiterstatistik. Bearb. im Reichs-Versicherungsamt*, Berlin 1904. Five further aspects of Germany's social insurance were dealt with specially for the exhibition in Ludwig Lass, 'Entstehung und soziale Bedeutung'; G. A. Klein, 'Statistik der Arbeiterversicherung'; Konrad Hartmann, 'Unfallverhütung und Arbeitshygiene'; Bielefeldt, 'Arbeiterversicherung und Volksgesundeit'; and Friedrich Zahn, 'Arbeiterversicherung und Volkswirtschaft'. These articles were published as one volume entitled, *Die deutsche Arbeiterversicherung als soziale Einrichtung: Im Auftrage des Reichs-Versicherungsamtes dargestellt für die Weltausstellung in St Louis 1904*, Berlin 1904. This book was also available in an English version. The standard work on social insurance by Prof. Dr Ludwig Lass at the Reichsversicherungsamt and Prof. Dr Friedrich Zahn at the Kaiserliches Statistisches Amt, *Einrichtung und Wirkung der Deutschen Arbeiterversicherung*, Berlin 1904, was also issued in a revised 3rd edition 'for the world exhibition in St Louis 1904'.

sources of the nation, and thus the nation itself, to the full. The other proceeds from the more recent view of society, which does not see the modern civilised state [*Kulturstaat*] as a collection of separate individuals, but as a finely structured organism. According to this view, there must be an 'organic' solution to the social problem, but one which must not be left to the free play of social and economic forces. . . . The experiences and exhibits of all the countries which have no compulsory insurance provide proof of the fact that any system of voluntary insurance against the partial or total loss of employment as a result of occupational diseases, industrial accidents, premature disablement and the effects of old age, founded on the workers' own initiative and sense of self-help, usually only affects the élite of workers; leaving the vast majority of wage-earners and those precisely in most need of assistance in the same condition of lethargy and helplessness as before.[12]

According to Tonio Bödiker, the first head of the German government's Imperial Insurance Office (Reichsversicherungsamt) and whose study of 'Workers' Insurance in Europe' was published in 1895, workers' insurance was similar in the 'moral sphere' to steam power and electricity 'in the material sphere'. It was 'a benevolent principle of great import . . . and an integral part of mankind's cultural progress'. The idea that Germany's system of social insurance should spread to other countries was not something called for mainly out of the desire to maintain the competitiveness of German industry. In contrast, some large-scale industrialists were even of the opinion that industry would eventually benefit from social legislation. It was, as Bödiker saw it, an international obligation dictated by 'the common interests of the propertied classes of all countries. Naturally, the German nation, finding itself in the centre of Europe, had an interest in seeing that such obligations were carried out, just as every man expected his next-door neighbour to avoid setting his own house on fire, or, at least, extinguish it once started'.[13]

The spread of social insurance was virtually regarded as a civilising mission designed to bring about greater unity among the world's nations. This was the opinion of Friedrich Zahn, head of the Bavarian Statistical Office, speaking in 1912, not long after the introduction of Britain's system of national insurance. He believed that the increasing 'similarity of social policy in the civilised world' was laying a 'new basis' for 'the solidarity of nations' in the shape of 'international law on workers' insurance', and that this was effectively promoting the 'productive and revitalising powers of the various nations'.[14]

12. 'Amtlicher Bericht des Reichskommissars', Berlin 1906, pp. 515 ff., reprinted in Zacher, *Arbeiter-Versicherung*, vol. 5, no. XIX, Gesammelte Aufsätze über die Arbeiterversicherung im In- und Auslande, pp. 143–5.
13. Bödiker, *Arbeiterversicherung*, pp. III, 238.

Whereas at the time of Germany's introduction of social insurance there was hardly any discussion of the view that the workers' productivity could be raised in the interests of industry and, therefore, of the nation as a whole, this consideration was to play an important part later when the German system was presented to the rest of the world. We find a typical example of this if we return to the report of the official in charge of Germany's contribution to the world exhibition of 1904. He rejected as 'economically unsound' the view, commonly held in America, that the spending of millions on 'the sick, crippled, diseased and weak' obstructed 'the process of natural selection' and that 'a nation could become great and powerful only if all its inferior elements were eliminated'. This view overlooked the fact 'that every productive energy in the nation involved a more or less substantial investment in terms of educational and training costs, and that this expenditure could only be recouped subsequently through the worker's productivity. It followed that if the utilisation of this resource was prematurely terminated, the nation incurred an economic loss'.[15] An even more concrete statement intended to justify the considerable costs which workers' insurance would incur was supplied by a German writer in 1913, when he stated that 'the victory in international competition has always gone to the highest paid and most qualified labour force'.[16]

According to the findings of a comprehensive study on 'Workers' Insurance Abroad', published in 1907, some twenty years after the introduction of social insurance in Germany, eight of the fourteen countries studied had accident insurance administered by the state. Four countries had compulsory sickness insurance schemes. Compulsory old-age and disablement insurance covering the vast majority of workers still existed only in Germany. In other countries employers were generally held liable in cases of industrial injury. There were also general legal regulations governing voluntary sickness, old-age and disablement insurance, which were in some cases supported by the state, as well as support for the elderly in distress, financed exclusively by the state and independent of traditional forms of poor relief.[17]

According to another study of fourteen countries in Western, Cen-

---

14. Friedrich Zahn, 'Belastung durch die deutsche Arbeiterversicherung', in *Zeitschrift für die gesamte Versicherungswissenschaft* 12 (1912), pp. 1127–60, esp. p. 1160.
15. Zacher, *Arbeiter-Versicherung*, vol. 5, no. XIX, p. 145.
16. Ludwig Stephinger, *Versicherung und Gesellschaft*, Jena 1913, p. 27.
17. *See* table in 'Die Arbeiterversicherung in Deutschland und im Auslande', in Zacher, *Arbeiter-Versicherung*, vol. 5, no. XIX, pp. 186–93. The tables of the fourteen European countries mentioned in the text refer to Germany, Austria, Hungary, Italy, France, Belgium, Great Britain, Norway, Sweden, Denmark, Finland, Spain, the Netherlands and Luxembourg.

tral, Southern and Northern Europe, in 1914 thirteen had state-administered accident insurance, twelve had sickness insurance and nine provided some form of relief for older workers, either through a system of insurance or public relief administered independently of traditional poor laws. Of these insurances eighteen were compulsory: eight covered accidents, five sickness and five old-age pensions. Outside of Germany, old-age pension insurance was only introduced after 1910 and, as was the case in France, sometimes did not function very effectively. Alongside fourteen further systems of state-administered and, in many cases, state-funded insurances, Denmark and Britain had old-age pension schemes administered by the state and based on social welfare principles.[18] Three countries had voluntary unemployment insurance. Only Great Britain had a system of compulsory unemployment insurance, first introduced in 1911, though admittedly restricted to relatively few workers. Thus it can be seen that in the thirty years following the introduction of Germany's social insurance the idea of insurance against accident, sickness, old age and disablement had become widespread throughout Western and Central Europe. In the course of this development earlier schemes of a voluntary nature were gradually replaced by compulsory insurance for broad sections of the population. Even the more advanced principle of embracing the whole population through a system of social security for all citizens, rather than the members of specific occupations, already existed before the First World War, when Sweden introduced its national system of old-age pensions in 1913. Introduced by other Scandinavian countries during the inter-war period, a national insurance system leading to old-age pensions for the whole population was also subsequently adopted by Great Britain, the Netherlands and Switzerland and was sometimes extended to cover sickness insurance. The present study does not attempt to provide by means of general hypotheses a comparative analysis of the emergence of social insurance throughout the world or even in Europe. This is not only beyond the capacity of a single individual but requires much more detailed advance research than is at present available.[19] The present enquiry will therefore

18. Alber, *Vom Armenhaus zum Wohlfahrtsstaat*, pp. 28, 142 f. Unlike Zacher's study, Alber's does not deal with Hungary and Spain, but includes Iceland and Switzerland.

19. A comparative approach is taken by the research project, promoted by the Projektgruppe für Internationales und vergleichendes Sozialrecht der Max-Planck-Gesellschaft and sponsored by the Fritz Thyssen-Stiftung, entitled 'Ein Jahrhundert Sozialversicherung: Bismarcks Sozialgesetzgebung im eupropäischen Vergleich'. Its first findings have already been published by Hans F. Zacher and Peter A. Köhler (*see* Select Bibliography). Next to Gaston V. Rimlinger's pioneer-

concentrate on a comparative analysis of the development and character of the new systems of social welfare which emerged at significant intervals in Germany and Great Britain between 1880 and 1914.

Germany's social insurance system had a considerable influence on developments abroad. In the case of Austria, for example, a system of social insurance, which borrowed heavily from Germany's example, was introduced in the 1880s. However, it departed from Germany's version in several important respects. Its political motives in Austria tended to have more of an anti-liberal than an anti-socialist bias; there it functioned as a device to shore up a monarchy torn by nationalist antagonisms and held together a heterogeneous coalition of political forces during the 1880s. Also, Austria's social insurance did not include any old-age and disablement insurance for workers. This was introduced only in 1939 after the country's annexation by Germany ('*Anschluss*').[20] But while its social insurance essentially followed the German pattern, its comparatively progressive measures for the protection of workers in middle-sized and large-scale firms, as introduced in amendments to its Commercial Law Code (*Gewerbeordnung*) in 1883 and 1885,[21] placed Austria ahead of other countries. These changes in the law led to the prohibition of Sunday work and working on public holidays. They also imposed substantial restrictions on the use of female and child labour and provided for an average working-day of eleven hours maximum. In Germany, on the other hand, where Bismarck initially stood in the way of any major attempts at government intervention in the field of labour conditions, legal controls on the working hours of adult male workers were rejected right up to the revolution of 1918–19.

This constructive policy towards labour in Austria was the product of a bureaucracy which, from the time of enlightened despotism, had been educated in the tradition of reform from above. It was carried out by a conservative authoritarian government composed mainly of civil

---

ing study on *Welfare Policy and Industrialisation in Europe, America and Russia*, New York 1971, Alber's study *Vom Armenhaus zum Wohlfahrtsstaat* deserves mention. This was written as part of a research project entitled 'Historische Indikatoren der westeuropäischen Demokratien', which was sponsored by the Stiftung Volkswagenwerk.

20. For the development of Austria's social insurance system, *see* esp. Herbert Hofmeister, 'Landesbericht, Österreich', in Köhler and Zacher (eds.), *Ein Jahrhundert Sozialversicherung*, pp. 445–730, esp. pp. 514–88; Kurt Ebert, *Die Anfänge der Modernen Sozialpolitik in Österreich: Die Taaffesche Sozialgesetzgebung für die Arbeiter im Rahmen der Gewerbeordnungsreform (1879–1885)*, Vienna 1975. For a detailed comparative analysis of Germany's accident insurance law of 1884 and Austria's accident insurance law of 1887, *see* Bödiker, *Arbeiterversicherung*, pp. 44–63.

21. *See* Ebert, *Anfänge*, pp. 115–61, 176–249.

servants and led by Graf Taaffe in alliance with a parliamentary majority of Slav and German-clerical composition. In contrast to Germany's social insurance legislation of the same period, Austria's was distinctly directed against big business and finance capitalism, though it provided protective legislation for artisans and small shop-keepers. However, although the typical wage-earning groups of pre-industrial society — servants, journeymen, cottage industry workers and agricultural labourers — were excluded, the legislation was in no way intended to help bring about any emancipation of Austria's numerically very weak industrial proletariat, which was to be won over to the concept of a Christian state based on traditional estates and earlier pre-industrial ideals. On the contrary, through the use of the Habsburg state's traditional policing methods and its withholding of the franchise, the political and trade union activities of the proletariat were even more successfully suppressed here than in Germany during the period of Bismarck's anti-Socialist law. In addition to the effects of the economic crisis after 1873, a policy of brutal persecution led to the numerical weakening and internal disintegration of the Austrian social-ists. It produced an organisational split within their ranks as they grew more and more radical and in some cases resorted to political terrorist methods. The Austrian Social Democratic Party was only able to recover from this split when its two wings reunited in 1889.[22]

In contrast, the development of social insurance in France revealed strong parallels with Britain's example of a welfare system initially based mainly on voluntary forms of insurance. In the case of France, the German model tended to make the idea of compulsory insurance less attractive. As in Britain, the strength of liberal political and economic ideas long delayed the creation of a compulsory welfare system administered by the state. But, unlike Britain, there were also major differences: a deep-rooted individualism, the considerably weaker development of workers' self-help organisations and solid opposition to the idea of levying compulsory contributions.[23] This opposition, which can only be understood against the background of France's econ-

---

22. For an account of how Austrian labour policy vacillated between brutal harassment and constructive state-aid during the 1880s and its effects on the political labour movement, *see* Hans Rosenberg, *Grosse Depression und Bismarckzeit, Wirtschaftsablauf, Gesellschaft und Politik in Mitteleuropa*, Berlin 1967, pp. 227–52.

23. *See* Yves Saint-Jours, 'Landesbericht Frankreich', in Köhler and Zacher (eds.), *Ein Jahrhundert Sozialversicherung*, pp. 181–268, esp. pp. 199–224; Irene Bourquin, '*Vie Ouvrière*' und Sozialpolitik: Die Einführung der 'Retraites ouvrières' in Frankreich um 1910. *Ein Beitrag zur Geschichte der Sozialversicherung*, Berne etc. 1977; Henri Hatzfeld, *Du paupérisme à la securité sociale: essais sur les origines de la securité sociale en France 1850–1940*, Paris 1971.

omic structure, in which small-scale businesses dominated, was shared by employers and unions alike; the latter being very much under the sway of syndicalist ideas. In addition, France's version of state-administered social insurance was very limited, right up to 1930, in terms of the groups it embraced and the risks it covered.[24] A law of 1910 on workers' and peasants' insurance largely failed to come into effect owing to its rejection by the groups which the new measures were to affect. The delay in the introduction of a comprehensive system of social insurance in France can be explained, not least, by the absence of any system of public relief. Apart from the care of orphans and the mentally ill, France's provisions for the poor were not subject to compulsory legal controls by the state.[25] The impetus provided by intensive contemporary discussions on the need to reform the traditional poor-relief system, which proved so necessary to the development of social insurance in Germany and Great Britain,[26] was, therefore, missing to a considerable extent.

In the case of Great Britain, information on the emergence and early development of social insurance and the attendant problems faced by British social policy has been comparatively easier to obtain. Here there has been a long uninterrupted tradition of historical inquiry into the system of poor relief, which has continued down to the present.[27] Studies of the origins of the welfare state have also occupied a central

24. No provision was made for unemployment insurance. After 1898, employers were made liable for industrial injury and this was first linked to compulsory accident insurance only in 1946.
25. On the French system of poor relief, *see* Maurice Block, 'Frankreich', in A. Emminghaus (ed.), *Das Armenwesen und die Armengesetzgebung in europäischen Staaten*, Berlin 1870, pp. 601–35; Rudolf Schwander, *Die Armenpolitik Frankreichs während der grossen Revolution und die Weiterentwicklung der französischen Armengesetzgebung bis zur Gegenwart*, Strassburg 1904; Dr Uhlhorn and E. Münsterberg, 'Geschichte der öffentlichen Armenpflege', in *Handwörterbuch der Staatswissenschaften*, 3rd edn, vol. 2, Jena 1909, pp. 6–30, esp. pp. 26f. Laws of 1893, 1904 and 1905 extended obligatory legal provision to the sick in need, abandoned, maltreated and neglected children, the elderly poor over the age of seventy and the infirm and incurable.
26. Maurice Block, in his well-informed contemporary account of Germany's social insurance system emphasises the fact that the legal provision of poor relief, which did not exist in France, smoothed the way in Germany for the introduction of social insurance: Maurice Block, *Les assurances ouvrières en Allemagne*, Paris 1895. Bismarck also pointed out the fact that France had no compulsory legal provision for the poor in his speech defending the first draft of Germany's accident insurance law (text of speech in Bismarck, *Gesammelte Werke*, 2nd edn, vol. 12, Berlin 1929, pp. 236–49, esp. p. 245).
27. Sydney and Beatrice Webb's classic study, *English Poor Law History, Part II: The Last Hundred Years* (2 vols., London 1929; reprint edn by W. A. Robson, London 1963), which forms vols. VIII and IX of the Webbs *English Local Government*, has had a great influence on modern research. A short summary of recent research findings can be found in Michael E. Rose, *The Relief of Poverty, 1834–1914*, London 1972.

place in historical and social science research since the Second World War.[28] On the basis of this literature, therefore, and taking into account the wealth of contemporary sources, this study intends only to shed light on what was specific to the British system and the factors behind its introduction by comparing it with developments in Germany, which were keenly followed in Britain at the time. In Germany, on the other hand, a great deal of research had to be done.

Only in recent years has research into this area begun to turn its attention in Germany to the history of poverty and the poor in the nineteenth and twentieth centuries, a subject which offers wide scope for inquiry.[29] What is even more astonishing is the continued lack of systematic research into what Schmoller called 'the greatest enduring social action' of Bismarck's life-time; that is, his creation of social insurance legislation for the working class.[30] The original intention of publishing a substantial documentary and narrative history on the subject under the auspices of the Historische Reichskommission in Munich, never achieved completion, owing to the forced emigration of the scholar commissioned for it, Hans Rothfels, after the Nazis came to power in 1933.[31] Parts of Rothfels' research did appear in two important articles he wrote, as well as in his valuable study on 'Theodor Lohmann and the Period of Struggle in Social Policy' and in a volume on

---

28. Of the many studies on this area, two notable accounts are Bentley B. Gilbert's important study of the Liberal government's social reforms of 1906–11, *The Evolution of National Insurance in Great Britain: The Origins of the Welfare State*, London 1966, and Jose Harris' brilliant analysis of the emergence of a state policy on the problems of unemployment and regulating the labour market, i.e. *Unemployment and Politics: A Study in English Social Policy, 1886–1914*, Oxford 1972.

29. Cf. recent studies by Christoph Sachße and Florian Tennstedt, *Geschichte der Armenfürsorge in Deutschland: Vom Spätmittelalter bis zum Ersten Weltkrieg*, Stuttgart 1980; Kathleen M. Pearle, 'Poverty, Charity and Poor Relief in Imperial Germany, 1873–1914', Phil. diss., State University of New York and Stony Brook 1980; Rüdeger Baron, 'Die Entwicklung der Armenpflege in Deutschland vom Beginn des 19. Jahrhunderts bis zum Ersten Weltkrieg', in Rolf Landwehr and Rüdeger Baron (eds.), *Geschichte der Sozialarbeit: Hauptlinien ihrer Entwicklung im 19. und 20. Jahrhundert*, Weinheim and Basle 1983, pp. 11–71; Bernd Balkenhol, *Armut und Arbeitslosigkeit in der Industrialisierung, dargestellt am Beispiel Düsseldorfs, 1850–1900*, Düsseldorf 1976; Lisgret Militzer-Schwenger, *Armenerziehung durch Arbeit: Eine Untersuchung am Beispiel des württembergischen Schwarzwaldkreises, 1806–1914*, Tübingen 1979; Matz, *Pauperismus*, esp. pp. 45–9, 261–4, as well as the fourth volume of the *Jahrbuch der Sozialarbeit*, ed. by Christoph Sachße and Florian Tennstedt, Reinbek bei Hamburg 1981, which traces the history of social work in Germany from the late Middle Ages to the Weimar Republic. Among the older literature the *Schriften des deutschen Vereins für Armenpflege und Wohltätigkeit* (later renamed *Deutscher Verein für öffentliche und private Fürsorge*) are worth consulting.

30. Schmoller, 'Vier Briefe', in *Charakterbilder* p. 56.

31. For research done before 1945, cf. Walter Vogel, *Bismarcks Arbeiterversicherung: Ihre Entstehung im Kräftespiel der Zeit*, Braunschweig 1951, pp. 3–6.

Bismarck's concept of the state, which appeared as early as 1925 and included several previously unpublished documents.[32]

After 1938 a plan also existed to publish a collection of documents, comprising several volumes, on the emergence of Germany's social insurance system. This project was connected with the plans of the German Labour Front (Deutsche Arbeitsfront – DAF) to create a national system of health care and old-age provision.[33] Apart from the documentary collection, it was also to consist of a detailed survey and a number of case studies, and was intended to lend respectability to the DAF's undertaking by establishing its historical legitimacy. However, this publication also failed to materialise.[34] Finally, towards the end of the Second World War, Walter Vogel, in charge of social policy documents at the official government archives in Potsdam, (Reichsarchiv), produced a study on 'Bismarck's Workers' Insurance', which was also based on previously unpublished sources. He was encouraged in this project by the government's Ministry of Labour (Reichsarbeitsministerium), which had rejected the DAF's plans. His book, which appeared in 1951 attempted to show what effect public ideas and public opinion, as well as 'Bismarck's close advisors, in and out of office', had had in influencing the social insurance, especially the accident insurance law of 1884.[35] But, however valuable Vogel's study is, it does not provide a detailed analysis of the process by which the whole German social insurance system emerged in the 1880s. This is also beyond the scope of the present inquiry. It remains a task for future research to deal with the subsequent development of Germany's social insurance and shed light on such topics of interest as the

32. Hans Rothfels, *Theodor Lohmann und die Kampfjahre der staatlichen Sozialpolitik (1871–1905): Nach ungedruckten Quellen*, Berlin 1927; *see also* his 'Prinzipienfragen der Bismarckschen Sozialpolitik' (1929), reprinted in idem, *Bismarck: Vorträge und Abhandlungen*, Stuttgart 1970, pp. 166–81, idem, 'Bismarck's Social Policy and the Problem of State Socialism in Germany', in *Sociological Review* 30 (1938), pp. 81–94, 288–302; idem. (ed.), *Otto von Bismarck, Deutscher Staat. Ausgewählte Dokumente*, Munich 1925. In the later edition which appeared under the title *Bismarck und der Staat* thirteen documents were left out and fifty-two others added to from the Friedrichsruh edition of Bismarck's works.

33. *See* Wolfgang Scheur, *Einrichtung und Maßnahmen der sozialen Sicherheit in der Zeit des Nationalsozialismus*, Wirtschafts- und sozialwiss. Diss., Cologne 1967, esp. pp. 155–72; Karl Teppe, 'Zur Sozialpolitik des Dritten Reiches am Beispiel der Sozialversicherung', in *Archiv für Sozialgeschichte* 17 (1977), pp. 195–250, esp. pp. 237–48.

34. The main editor on this project, Rudolf Craemer, who died in 1941, wrote a short book for the Arbeitswissenschaftliches Institut der Deutschen Arbeitsfront (DAF) entitled *Bismarcks Erbe in der Sozialversicherung*, which the DAF published in Berlin in 1940.

35. Vogel, *Arbeiterversicherung*, p. 4.

background to the German government's insurance code (*Reichsversicherungsordnung*) of 1911 or the provision of insurance for white-collar workers in the same year.[36] The latter was undoubtedly connected with the rise and growth of white-collar demands and would throw considerable light on the German government's official social policy aims. More important still would be an analysis of the extremely varied and lasting effects of social insurance.[37] While the present study is the first attempt to treat this question systematically, it cannot, of course, be regarded as exhaustive. It remains for future research to deal with these interesting problems.

What this brief study intends to do is to develop lines of enquiry and criteria on which the historian can base his judgements. It is not an attempt to provide a definitive assessment. It also tries to give an impression of the available wealth and abundance of source material on which future studies might be based. This is to be found not only in official archives but also in statistical studies from the period, in literature from the social sciences, economics, insurance and medicine, in the publications of local labour organisations and several other important periodicals of the time, which contain detailed discussions on different aspects of the 'social question'.

36. A brief account of the emergence of the *Reichsversicherungsordnung* (though not of the introduction of white-collar workers' insurance) can be found in Karl Erich Born, *Staat und Sozialpolitik seit Bismarcks Sturz: Ein Beitrag zur Geschichte der innenpolitischen Entwicklung des Deutschen Reiches, 1890–1914*, Wiesbaden 1957, pp. 238–42. On the background to the introduction of the *Reichsversicherungsordnung, see* the documents in Peter Rassow and Karl Erich Born (eds.), *Akten zur staatlichen Sozialpolitik in Deutschland, 1890–1914*, Wiesbaden 1959, pp. 412–38. For useful summaries on the history of Germany's social insurance, *see* Horst Peters, *Die Geschichte der sozialen Versicherung*, 3rd edn, Sankt Augustin 1978; Detlev Zöllner, 'Landesbericht Deutschland', in Köhler and Zacher (eds.), *Ein Jahrhundert Sozialversicherung*, pp. 45–179. The book by the Social Democrat and trade unionist, Friedrich Kleeis is still an interesting account. For a long time employed as an auditor of the local sickness insurance offices and an official of a workers' secretariat, he had personal experience of the everyday practice of social insurance: Friedrich Kleeis, *Die Geschichte der sozialen Versicherung in Deutschland*, Berlin-Lichterfelde 1928; reprint ed. by Dieter Dowe with an introduction by Florian Tennstedt, Berlin and Bonn 1981.
37. Florian Tennstedt, 'Sozialgeschichte der Sozialversicherung', in Maria Bloehmke (ed.), *Handbuch der Sozialmedizin*, Stuttgart 1976, vol. 3, pp. 385–492, contains many interesting points, particularly on the significant role of social insurance in the development of medical services.

CHAPTER 2

The State and Social Insurance in Germany before 1914

Any discussion of Germany's social insurance must begin by inquiring into the reasons for its exceptionally early appearance. Among these, the following deserve particular emphasis:

1. The idea that the state had a special role and function in promoting social welfare and exercising social control was based on a long tradition in Germany. It derived, not least, from the earlier feudal view that, as long as the subject fulfilled his obligations towards the appropriate authority, he had a right to expect adequate provision of his material needs. In older political and administrative theories the term 'police' (*Polizey*) covered, among other things, social welfare and the guarantee of public order.[1] Throughout the nineteenth century, neither conservative groups nor considerable sections of the bureaucracy and the employers ever fully discarded the old authoritarian and paternalistic traditions from the time of earlier forms of state welfare. Even liberal thinkers, like Robert von Mohl, tried to combine the new late-eighteenth-century ideal of a state based on legal norms (*Rechtsstaat*) with the traditional concept of state welfare, according to which the

---

1. Lothar Gall, *Bismarck: Der weisse Revolutionär*, 3rd edn, Frankfurt am Main 1980, p. 86. For an account of the concept of *Polizeiwissenschaft*, originating in the sixteenth century as the administrative theory and political science of the older German territorial state, especially its application in the eighteenth and early nineteenth centuries, *see* Hans Maier's classic study, *Die ältere deutsche Staats- und Verwaltungslehre*, 2nd edn, Munich 1980.

state and its 'police' were responsible for the well-being of its citizens.[2]

The social sciences in Germany, whose origins lay in the period before the 1848 Revolution, also eventually took the view that the general guarantee of civil rights could not provide a basis for solving the problems conceptualised as the 'social question'. These were seen as the product of relationships in an industrial society based on new means of production. Instead, an active 'social policy' was required. The state had to intervene in the social process and seek to balance the claims of competing interests through an administration geared to social needs.[3]

2. As a result of the country's relatively late industrialisation, Germany's political liberalism was greatly influenced by the higher civil service and its close social allies, the liberal professions, at the expense of the commercial classes and industrial bourgeoisie. The former groups certainly did not view uninhibited economic growth, industrialisation and urbanisation as positive developments. In particular, they feared the uncontrollable growth of the urban population and the emergence of a potentially revolutionary proletariat.[4] As a result, the idea that the middle classes should educate the lower strata of the community towards the ideal of self-help by actively supporting savings associations (*Sparvereine*) and benefit societies (*Unterstützungsvereine*) found widespread acceptance during the early period of German liberalism. At a relatively early stage, German liberals also appealed directly to the state to do justice to its function as protector of property and guarantor of the social order by carrying out a policy of sweeping social reforms aimed at improving the material and moral condition of the lower classes.

2. Robert Mohl, *Die Polizei-Wissenschaft nach den Grundsätzen des Rechtsstaates*, 2 vols., Tübingen 1832/33; cf. also Erich Angermann, 'Die Verbindung des "polizeistaatlichen" Wohlfahrtsideals mit dem Rechtsstaatsgedanken im deutschen Frühliberalismus: Eine Studie über die Verwaltungslehre Robert v. Mohls', in *Historisches Jahrbuch* 74 (1954), pp. 462–72.

3. *See* Eckart Pankoke, *Sociale Bewegung — Sociale Frage — Sociale Politik: Grundfragen der deutschen 'Socialwissenschaft' im 19. Jahrhundert*, Stuttgart 1979, esp. pp. 15f., 101ff., 135ff., 157ff., 194ff.

4. *See* James J. Sheehan, *German Liberalism in the Nineteenth Century*, Chicago and London 1978, esp. pp. 28–34, 87f.; Donald G. Rohr, *The Origins of Social Liberalism in Germany*, Chicago and London 1963. On the ambivalent attitude of German Liberals towards social changes produced by the free market, unrestricted geographical mobility, industrialisation and urbanisation, *see also* the contemporary debate on poverty, dealt with in an excellent collection of well-chosen sources by Carl Jantke and Dietrich Hilger (eds.), *Die Eigentumslosen: Der deutsche Pauperismus und die Emanzipationskrise in Darstellungen und Deutungen der zeitgenössischen Literatur*, Freiburg and Munich 1965.

The first attempt to create a rallying point for social reform efforts was made by the Central Association for the Welfare of the Working Classes (Centralverein für das Wohl der arbeitenden Klassen), founded in 1844 at the instigation of the King of Prussia. However, this body, which attempted to combine the efforts of both the state and middle-class reformers, had no real or effective impact on the design of German social policy. It was regarded with too much suspicion by senior members of the bureaucracy. Disturbed by the appearance of communist and socialist tendencies in the Association's local branches, as well as the workers' emancipatory demands for active participation in carrying out reforms, they completely withheld support for the groups involved.[5] Nevertheless, in its early phase the Central Association provided the crucial impetus behind the founding of the science of social statistics in Germany,[6] and its plans for a General Prussian Institute for the Care of the Aged (Allgemeine Preussische Altersversorgungsanstalt)[7] stressed at a relatively early juncture the state's responsibility for its citizens' social welfare.

3. Ideas such as these were expressions of an attempt to adapt the older concept of state welfare to the new social conditions created by economic freedom, industrialisation and urbanisation. They were in keeping with the administrative practice of a powerful and confident bureaucracy which had developed its own distinctive traditions.[8]

5. On the Central Association's founding and early effectiveness, *see* Jürgen Reulecke, *Sozialer Frieden durch soziale Reform: Der Centralverein für das Wohl der arbeitenden Klassen in der Frühindustrialisierung*, Wuppertal 1983. *See also* Heinz Richard Schneider, *Bürgerliche Vereinsbestrebungen für das "Wohl der arbeitenden Klassen" in der preussischen Rheinprovinz*, Phil. diss., Bonn 1967; Joseph Hansen (ed.), *Rheinische Briefe und Akten zur Geschichte der politischen Bewegung, 1830–1850*, vol. 1 (1830–45), Essen 1919, pp. 674–911, and the new edition of *Mittheilungen des Centralvereins für das Wohl der arbeitenden Klassen (1848–1858)*, 5 vols., ed. by Wolfgang Köllmann and Jürgen Reulecke, Hagen 1980.

6. *See* Jürgen Reulecke, 'Pauperismus, "social learning" und die Anfänge der Sozialstatistik in Deutschland', in Hans Mommsen and Winfried Schulze (eds.), *Vom Elend der Handarbeit: Probleme historischer Unterschichtenforschung*, Stuttgart 1981, pp. 358–72, esp. pp. 363–5.

7. *See* the detailed discussions and plans of the Central Association between 1849 and 1850, in *Mittheilungen*, vol. 1, pp. 457–503, 533–7, 564–6, 577–81, 628–32; vol. 2, pp. 647–710, 722–4.

8. On the emergence of the modern state bureaucracy, the political and social attitudes of its prominent civil servants and its relationship to other social groups in Prussia up to the end of the period of the Stein-Hardenberg reforms, *see* the pioneering study by Hans Rosenberg, *Bureaucracy, Autocracy and Aristocracy: The Prussian Experience 1660–1815*, Boston 1966, which has still not had sufficient attention paid to it by German researchers. *See also* Franz-Ludwig Knemeyer, *Regierungs- und Verwaltungsreformen in Deutschland zu Beginn des 19. Jahrhunderts*, Cologne and

Owing its rise in power and influence to Europe's strong mercantilist and bureaucratic traditions, it did not hold back throughout the nineteenth century from intervening in social and economic affairs, even in the face of *laissez-faire* liberalism, which gained considerable ground in Germany.[9]

Germany's tradition of state intervention, which, in contrast to Great Britain, gave the country its lead in creating the modern style of bureaucratic welfare state, was considerably strengthened by the experience of the 1848 Revolution. Confronted by the threat of an advancing proletariat, the politically weak middle classes increasingly showed themselves content with their limited political gains. The more this attitude prevailed during the revolutionary period, the more the German federal states were subsequently given a free hand in savagely suppressing any radical or social democratic tendencies in the post-revolutionary period. The larger states, particularly Prussia, tried to soften this policy of repression by applying palliative social policy measures. Thus, although, from 1850 onwards the individual German states introduced repressive laws against associations, and the German Confederation applied its reactionary decree of 1854 against the labour movement,[10] these measures were accompanied by a series of social reforms, which, as far as content was concerned, were probably only reluctantly carried out. There were improvements in the protection of child labour, for which a law of 1839 on the employment of youth had already paved the way,[11] and the prohibition of the 'truck-shop' system (i.e. the complete or partial payment of wages in goods) provided workers with greater protection against being swindled by employers.

Berlin 1970; Bernd Wunder, *Priviligierung und Disziplinierung: Die Entstehung des Berufsbeamtentums in Bayern und Württemberg (1780–1825)*, Munich and Vienna 1978.

9. Thus, Reinhart Koselleck, in his book *Preussen zwischen Reform und Revolution: Allgemeines Landrecht, Verwaltung und soziale Bewegung von 1791 bis 1848*, Stuttgart 1967, p. 630, mentions that the Prussian government was 'almost constantly' compelled 'especially in the 1820s and 1840s' to 'bring to an end the acute situation of distress by means of emergency relief works, road construction, the free distribution of wheat and seedlings, controls on bread prices, tax allowances or salt donations'. *See also* Hanns Hubert Hofmann, *Adelige Herrschaft und souveräner Staat: Studien über Staat und Gesellschaft in Franken und Bayern im 18. und 19. Jahrhundert*, Munich 1962.

10. *See* Frolinde Balser, *Sozial-Demokratie 1848/49–1863: Die erste deutsche Arbeiterorganisation 'Allgemeine deutsche Arbeiterverbrüderung' nach der Revolution*, 2 vols., Stuttgart 1962, vol. 1, pp. 237–336, 441–79.

11. *See* Günther K. Anton, *Geschichte der preussischen Fabrikgesetzgebung bis zu ihrer Aufnahme durch die Reichsgewerbeordnung*, ed. with an introduction by H. Bülter, Berlin 1953, pp. 74–6. Measures to protect children also existed in Bavaria, Bremen and Baden. For Bavaria, *see* Joachim Kermann, 'Vorschriften zur Einschränkung der industriellen Kinderarbeit in Bayern und ihre Handhabung in der Pfalz: Ein Beitrag zur Entwicklung der bayerischen Arbeiterschutzgesetzgebung im 19. Jahrhundert', in *Jahrbuch für westdeutsche Landesgeschichte* 2 (1976), pp. 311–74.

Finally, the appointment of the first factory inspectors,[12] although at first relatively ineffective, created a new form of state control over working conditions.[13]

Based on earlier laws of 1845 and 1849, the 1854 Prussian law on benefit funds (*Unterstützungskassengesetz*)[14] was particularly significant. Through the use of local community statutes and, where necessary, higher administrative decrees, workers, journeymen and apprentices could be forced to join local funds and employers made to pay a subsidy amounting to half of the insured member's contributions. By introducing a compulsory levy on the employer, which had no parallel in the history of European social legislation, together with its provision for insured members to participate in the independent management of the funds (based on their share of contributions), this law, intended to reduce the financial costs of poor relief, anticipated the sickness insurance law of 1883. Certainly, the number of citizens directly affected was still very limited. In 1860 the law covered only 427,190 members of benefit funds.[15] Domestic workers, day-labourers and agricultural labourers were still excluded and there was still no old age and disablement provision. As a rule, funds were organised on an occupational basis and, in the big cities especially, covered only journeymen in the various craft occupations. Intent on maintaining the separate identity of the various branches within the handicrafts industry, the journey-

---

12. See Alphons Thun, 'Beiträge zur Geschichte der Gesetzgebung und Verwaltung zu Gunsten der Fabrikarbeiter in Preussen', in *Zeitschrift des Königlich Preussischen Statistischen Bureaus* 17 (1877), pp. 59–94, esp. pp. 90–2; *see also* his 'Die Fabrikinspektoren in Deutschland', in *Jahrbuch für Gesetzgebung, Verwaltung und Volkswirtschaft im Deutschen Reich* (Schmollers Jahrbuch), Neue Folge, 5 (1881), pp. 55–77, esp. pp. 56–9. In 1853 a total of only three factory inspectors were appointed for the administrative districts of Düsseldorf, Arnsberg and Aix-la-Chapelle. Between 1874 and 1878 the number of factory inspectors in Prussia was increased from three to fifteen. Outside of Prussia, only Saxony had full-time inspectors. Baden employed inspectors on a part-time basis. The situation changed only when optional inspection was replaced by compulsory inspection through an amendment to the Commercial Code in 1878. Nevertheless, the actual growth of factory inspection did come about after Bismarck's fall from office in 1890 (*see* Stephan Poerschke, *Die Entwicklung der Gewerbeaufsicht in Deutschland*, Jena 1911, and Wolfgang Bocks, *Die badische Fabrikinspektion. Arbeiterschutz, Arbeiterverhältnisse und Arbeiterbewegung in Baden 1879 bis 1914*, Freiburg and Munich 1978).
13. See Heinrich Volkmann, *Die Arbeiterfrage im preussischen Abgeordnetenhaus, 1848–1869*, Berlin 1968, esp. pp. 39–59. For the history of the ban on the truck-shop system in Prussia, *see* Anton, *Geschichte*, pp. 155ff. For Bavaria, *see* Horst Hesse, *Die sogenannte Sozialgesetzgebung Bayerns Ende der sechziger Jahre des 19. Jahrhunderts: Ein Beitrag zur Strukturanalyse der bürgerlichen Gesellschaft*, Munich 1971.
14. Volkmann, *Arbeiterfrage*, pp. 63–77.
15. These members included 170,487 factory workers. According to a survey of 1861, which may well have employed a different definition of the term 'factory worker', the total number of factory workers in Prussia amounted to 378,521 (ibid., p. 76).

men were even more keen to establish separate funds from those of the much-despised factory workers. From the insurance point of view, the latter were regarded as poorer risks.[16]

Finally, the 1854 law on miners' provident societies (*Knappschafts-gesetz*) was of central importance in influencing the design of Germany's later social insurance legislation of the 1880s. The older provident societies for miners, which had 'given cohesion to the old style of community based on estates',[17] had been financed by contributions from both employers and employees. The new law made the miners' societies the basis of Germany's new system of workers' insurance, administered in public law. It gave miners free medical treatment and provided them with security against the financial effects of enforced unemployment resulting from sickness, accident, disablement or old age. In the event of a miner's death, his dependent widow and orphans could claim assistance. The motives behind this constructive policy towards labour between 1849 and 1855 were very similar to those behind the social insurance laws of the 1880s. It was not so much aimed at relieving social distress as an attempt to counter the proletariat's threat to the political and social order through the use of preventive measures.

4. There has been a great deal of discussion in recent years on the entire process of social and political modernisation. It has often been argued that Germany's relatively late industrialisation gave the country a considerable advantage. Not least, it allowed Germany's industrial take-off to begin from, so to speak, a higher plateau, benefiting as it did from the experiences of countries which had already undergone the process.[18] To put it crudely, according to this view, economic backwardness stimulated social progress. A more detailed examination of

16. *See* Wilfried Reininghaus, 'Das erste staatlich beaufsichtigte System von Krankenkassen: Preussen 1845–1869. Das Beispiel der Regierungsbezirke Arnsberg und Minden', in *Zeitschrift für Sozialreform* 29 (1983), pp. 271–96, esp. pp. 277f.

17. Klaus Tenfelde, *Sozialgeschichte der Bergarbeiterschaft an der Ruhr im 19. Jahrhundert*, 2nd edn, Bonn 1981, p. 282. On the law governing provident societies and the development of the miners' provident movement after 1854, cf. Tenfelde, pp. 282–91, and Wolfram Fischer, 'Das wirtschafts- und sozialpolitische Ordnungsbild der preussischen Bergrechtsreform 1851–1865', in *Zeitschrift für Bergrecht*, 102 (1961), pp. 181–9.

18. An excellent discussion of the question — also widely debated by contemporaries — as to why other countries, especially the German Empire, caught up with Great Britain economically, while the latter still enjoyed its exceptional lead as the foremost industrial nation in the middle of the nineteenth century, is contained in David S. Landes, *The Unbound Prometheus: Technological Change and Industrial Development in Western Europe from 1750 to the Present*, Cambridge University Press 1969, esp. pp. 326–58.

this argument would soon produce conflicting evidence and would, for example, modify the view, already mentioned, that the fears felt by Germany's authoritarian state were a dominant factor. Rather than follow up this particular argument, it seems to me more revealing to concentrate on Germany's economic and social situation from about 1870 onwards, since it was this that provided the crucial background to the development of Germany's social policy.

The impact of the rise of the labour movement and the economic crisis after 1873 upon the social question

The overall policy of suppressing the workers' emancipatory demands during the period before and after the 1848 Revolution was temporarily suspended during the 1860s. While general liberalising tendencies allowed permanent political parties to take shape, the specific factors at work during the Prussian constitutional conflict of the early 1860s led Bismarck, as Prussian Prime Minister, to toy with the idea of pulling the carpet from under the feet of the Liberal opposition by attempting to win over the workers' loyalty to the concept of a 'social monarchy'. Bismarck entered into an exchange of ideas with the brilliant founder of the General German Workers' Association (Allgemeiner Deutscher Arbeiterverein), Ferdinand Lassalle.[19] While he took a great interest in Lassalle's ideas, their influence on his actual policy has, however, probably been overestimated. The audience granted by the King of Prussia to a deputation of Silesian weavers, demanding the monarchy's intervention to prevent their wages sinking, certainly made an impression on contemporaries. But this, together with a royal loan to set up a cooperative for weavers dismissed by their employers, remained an isolated episode.[20] No substantial progress was made, either on the question of benefit funds or in the field of workmen's protection.[21] On the other hand, the advent of universal, direct and equal parliamentary male suffrage, which Bismarck, despite liberal reservations, had introduced in the North German Confederation in 1866–67 and later the

19. *See* Gustav Mayer (ed.), *Bismarck und Lassalle, ihr Briefwechsel und ihre Gespräche*, Berlin 1928; Shlomo Na'aman, 'Lassalles Beziehungen zu Bismarck — ihr Sinn und Zweck. Zur Beleuchtung von Gustav Mayers "Bismarck und Lassalle" ', in *Archiv für Sozialgeschichte* 2 (1962), pp. 55–85.
20. Adolf Richter, *Bismarck und die Arbeiterfrage im preussischen Verfassungskonflikt*, Stuttgart [1934], pp. 51–91.
21. Volkmann, *Arbeiterfrage*, pp. 177–83.

Empire, laid the necessary basis for the subsequent growth of the initially divided Social Democrats into a party based on widespread popular support. Similarly, the law governing freedom of association (*Koalitionsrecht*), as grounded in the Confederation's Commercial Code of 1869 and later adopted by the Empire as a whole – though diluted by strict measures to prevent enforced unionisation[22] — laid the crucial foundations for the growth of the initially divided trade union movement.

By the late 1860s there was a discernible strain on relations between the state and organised labour. This followed the founding of the Social Democratic Party in 1869, with its distinctly anti-Prussian stance and rejection of Bismarck's policies, including his solution for uniting Germany while excluding Austria. It was also a result of the Social Democrats' openly professed allegiance to the First International, which had adopted a radical programme at Basle in September 1869, demanding the immediate nationalisation of all land. Following the critical anti-government stance adopted by both of Germany's two main workers' parties during the Franco-Prussian War, especially as regards the annexation of Alsace-Lorraine, and Bebel's declaration of support for the Paris Commune in his Reichstag address on 25 May 1871,[23] the state's latent emnity was transformed into outright hostility. Repressive measures were immediately taken against Germany's socialist parties and trade unions.

At the same time, the speculative fever which accompanied the Empire's founding period, together wih the acute housing shortage, especially felt in the big cities, led to a deepening of the social and economic divisions in German society. These problems were com-

---

22. The relevant passage (para. 153) of the Commercial Code reads as follows:

> Whosoever induces or attempts to induce others to take part in such arrangements [para. 152] or secure their compliance by physical coercion, threats, social pressure [*Ehrverletzung*] or ostracisation, or hinders or similarly attempts to hinder others from withdrawing from such arrangements, is liable to be imprisoned for a period of up to three months, except in cases where a severer sentence is applicable in accordance with the criminal law of the land.

23. *See* Bebel's speech before the Reichstag on 25 May 1871, (*Sten. Berichte des Reichstags*, I, I, vol. 2, pp. 920f.). According to a statement Bismarck made in his Reichstag speech of 17 September 1878, during the debate on the proposed anti-Socialist law, Bebel's speech had brought about a change in his own position on the social question: 'From that moment on, I was fully convinced of the danger threatening us . . . the Commune's proclamation to the people was like a shaft of light which brought the point home and from then on I recognised an enemy in social democratic elements, against whom the state and society find themselves in a position of self-defence' (Bismarck, *Gesammelte Werke*, vol. 11, pp. 602–12; ibid., pp. 601f.).

pounded by the numerous strikes which took place in the period between 1869 and 1874[24] and which were widely viewed by the middle classes and the political authorities as a threat to the existing social and economic order. The serious economic crisis which began in 1873–74 and became particularly severe during 1879 added mass unemployment and a worsening situation of widespread social distress to the picture. These events and developments, which put a damper on the middle classes' almost euphoric belief in progress, led to renewed public awareness of the 'social question', followed by intense public discussion of social reform.

Several distinct schools of thought can be discerned in the ensuing debate on reform, which was often carried out in public with considerable acrimony. For example, in terms of the ideas they put forward, the state socialism of men like Johann Karl Rodbertus and Hermann Wagener can be safely assigned to the conservative camp. The latter belonged for a time to the circle of Bismarck's closest social policy advisors.[25] On the opposite side, however, Germany's organised labour movement, united in 1875, was by no means committed to Marxist views on the subject. It wavered between support of state socialism and an adherence to Utopian beliefs. The idiosyncratic ideas of the Berlin economist, Eugen Dühring, were for a time well received in the ranks of the Social Democratic Party.[26]

Groups belonging to the Christian-Social movement were also particularly active in seeking solutions to the social question. Their main motive was to prevent the workers drifting away from Christianity and

24. *See* on this wave of strikes, the social forces providing its impetus, together with its aims and its effects on employers' attitudes, public opinion and the government, Lothar Machtan, 'Zur Streikbewegung deutscher Arbeiter in den Gründerjahren (1871–1873)', in *Internationale wissenschaftliche Korrespondenz zur Geschichte der deutschen Arbeiterbewegung* 14 (1978), pp. 419–42; '"Im Vertrauen auf unsere gerechte Sache . . ." Streikbewegungen der Industriearbeiter in den 70er Jahren des 19. Jahrhunderts', in Klaus Tenfelde and Heinrich Volkmann (eds.), *Streik: Zur Geschichte des Arbeitskampfes in Deutschland während der Industrialisierung*, Munich 1981, pp. 52–73; idem. *Streiks im frühen deutschen Kaiserreich*, Frankfurt and New York 1983 and idem, *Streiks und Aussperrungen im Deutschen Kaiserreich. Eine sozialgeschichtliche Dokumentation für die Jahre 1871 bis 1875*, Berlin 1984.

25. *See* Wolfgang Saile, *Hermann Wagener und sein Verhältnis zu Bismarck: Ein Beitrag zur Geschichte des konservativen Sozialismus*, Tübingen 1958.

26. *See* Dieter Dowe and Klaus Tenfelde, 'Zur Rezeption Eugen Dührings in der deutschen Arbeiterbewegung in den 1870er Jahren', in *Wissenschaftlicher Sozialismus und Arbeiterbewegung: Begriffsgeschichte und Dühring-Rezeption*, Trier 1980, pp. 25–58. For a summary of the development of the German Social Democrats' Party theory, *see* Susanne Miller, *Das Problem der Freiheit im Sozialismus: Freiheit, Staat und Revolution in der Programmatik der Sozialdemokratie von Lassalle bis zum Revisionismusstreit*, 5th edn, Bonn-Bad Godesberg 1977.

the Church. Taking up the social policy ideas of the Bishop of Mainz, von Ketteler, young Catholic priests, nicknamed the 'red chaplains', won the wide support of laymen for their view that the workers' own representative associations were the best means of restoring the industrial worker's human dignity, threatened as it was by industrial society, exploitation, materialism and liberalism. This movement, which had strong support among the miners of the Ruhr and in the area around Aix-la-Chapelle and Krefeld,[27] adopted a clearly hostile attitude, not only towards the state (at the height of the *Kulturkampf* during the 1870s), but towards the official spokesmen for Catholic interests in the Centre Party. The Centre was eventually able to integrate these groups into its mainstream following the adoption of a motion introduced by a Ketteler's nephew, Count Ferdinand von Galen, to subscribe to a detailed programme in support of workmen's protection. Through the work of Franz Hitze, it also succeeded in gaining control over the growth of Catholic working men's associations and began to place more emphasis on social policy. In keeping with the principle of relegating the state's influence to a subordinate role, the Centre stressed that of the Christian family, the local community and the need to return to a corporative form of society, structured around the principle of different professions and trades.

The Protestant Church could derive from Luther's teaching the belief that the Christian authorities were responsible for the welfare of the state's subjects. The idea of establishing a Christian association of the needy in society with a view to defusing tensions caused by the social question were based on the arguments of Johann Hinrich Wichern, founder of the so-called 'Inner Mission', and on the social policy views of the conservative Christian politician, Victor Aimé Huber. Towards the end of the 1870s, however, the desire to inoculate the workers against Social Democratic atheism and republicanism saw efforts to solve the social question assume a new political dimension. This was first seen after 1882 in the growth of Protestant workers' societies and in Pastor Rudolf Todt's setting up of a Central Association for Social Reform on the Basis of Religion and the Constitutional Monarchy' (1877–81). But the attempt to woo the workers away from the Social

27. Tenfelde, *Sozialgeschichte*, pp. 464ff.; Herbert Lepper, 'Kaplan Franz Eduard Cronenberg und die christlich-soziale Bewegung in Aachen 1868–1878', in *Zeitschrift des Aachener Geschichtsvereins* 79 (1968), pp. 57–148; *Sozialer Katholizismus in Aachen. Quellen zur Geschichte des Arbeitervereins zum hl. Paulus für Aachen und Burscheid 1869–1878(88)*, ed. with an introduction by Herbert Lepper, Mönchengladbach 1977.

Democrats and win them over to Germany's conservative 'social monarchy' by creating a Christian-Social workers' party, only a few weeks after the Association's founding, was a failure. Under the influence of Court Chaplain Stoecker, this party, in which anti-Semitic ideas played an increasing part, became more and more a rallying point for the urban petty bourgeoisie, suffering from the pressures of big business and the effects of the economic crisis.[28]

The founding of the Social Policy Association (Verein für Sozialpolitik) in 1872 was particularly symptomatic of the change taking place in the social and political climate during the 1870s. Founded in response to the *laissez-faire* ideology of the Manchester school of economics, as espoused by the German National Economic Congress, it consciously took its approach to economic questions from the tradition of the earlier 'historical' school of national economic studies. While it aimed at providing, through scholarly investigation, the scientific data on which a policy of social reform could be based, it also set out to exert a direct influence on public opinion, the bureaucracy and the framing of social policy legislation. The university academics who largely made up the Association were soon dubbed *Kathedersozialisten* (academic socialists) by their opponents, and the name stuck. Yet the Association produced a number of widely differing views on social policy, which reflected its members' politics, whether of a conservative, liberal or state-socialist hue. The economist Gustav Schmoller, who played a critical part in the early years and subsequent development of the Association, regarded the state as the 'greatest moral agency for the education of mankind'.[29] He believed that a solution to the social

28. For the social policies of German Protestantism, *see* Günter Brakelmann, *Kirche und Sozialismus im 19. Jahrhundert: Die Analyse des Sozialismus und Kommunismus bei Johann Hinrich Wichern und bei Rudolf Todt*, Witten 1966; Hans Brandenburg, *Adolf Stoecker: Ein Kämpfer um Volk und Kirche*, Lahr-Dinglingen 1958; Siegfried Kaehler, 'Stoeckers Versuch, eine christlich-soziale Arbeiterpartei in Berlin zu begründen (1878)', in Paul Wentzcke (ed.), *Deutscher Staat und deutsche Parteien: Festschrift für Friedrich Meinecke*, Munich and Berlin 1922, pp. 227–65; Fritz Einicke, 'Die Stellung der evangelischen Arbeitervereine zur sozialen Frage', Wirtschafts- und sozialwiss. Diss. (MS), Cologne 1950; Bruno Feyerabend, '*Die evangelischen Arbeitervereine: Eine Untersuchung über ihre religiösen, geistigen, gesellschaftlichen und politischen Grundlagen und über ihre Entwicklung bis zum ersten Weltkrieg*, Wirtschafts- und sozialwiss. Diss., Frankfurt 1955; Klaus Erich Pollmann, *Landesherrliches Kirchenregiment und soziale Frage: Der evangelische Oberkirchenrat der altpreussischen Landeskirche und die sozialpolitischen Bestrebungen der Geistlichen nach 1890*, Berlin and New York 1973.

29. Although the Social Policy Association was not formally constituted until 13 October 1873, *see* the manifesto set out in Gustav Schmollers opening speech at its founding meeting in Eisenach on 6 October 1872: Ständiger Ausschuss (ed.), *Verhandlungen der Eisenacher Versammlung zur Besprechung der sozialen Frage am 6. und 7. Oktober 1872*, Leipzig 1873, p. 4.

question could be found if only the monarchical state, from a position above class differences, would pursue an active social policy committed to the principle of social justice. Here Schmoller was consciously harking back to the idealised traditions of eighteenth-century Prussian mercantilism. The Liberal Lujo Brentano also believed in the idea of justice and a social equilibrium between all classes. But, greatly influenced by Britain's example, he supported the idea of an emancipatory social policy in which the conscious promotion of workers' self-help organisations occupied a central place.[30] The mainly Protestant, pro-governmental social reformers in the Association did, however, agree on one point. The solution to Germany's social problems and conflicts could not be left simply to the social groups directly affected. Instead, bourgeois society, with the help of the state, was called upon to play an active part[31] in dispelling the danger of an 'impending social revolution',[32] combating the deepening of class differences and integrating the proletariat into the social and political system.[33]

If the founding of the Central Association for the Welfare of the Working Classes was essentially a response to the widespread impoverishment experienced in Germany during the period before the 1848 Revolution, the Social Policy Association was mainly a response to the challenge of the Social Democrats. The publications of the *Kathedersozialisten*, together with their influence on the bureaucracy at ministerial level (still to be investigated by detailed research), significantly contributed to creating a favourable climate for social reform among Germany's political and bureaucratic élites during the following decades.

The attempt to undermine support for the Social Democrats by carrying out a policy of concrete reforms was also the ultimate motive behind Germany's social insurance legislation in the 1880s. Bismarck wanted to revive his policy towards labour from as early as the autumn of 1870 onwards. Tough repressive measures were to be applied against

---

30. For Brentano's ideas, *see* James J. Sheehan, *The Career of Lujo Brentano: A Study of Liberalism and Social Reform in Imperial Germany*, Chicago and London 1966, esp. pp. 74–84.

31. *See* Rüdiger vom Bruch, 'Streiks und Konfliktregelung im Urteil bürgerlicher Sozialreformer 1872–1914', in Tenfelde and Volkmann (eds.), *Streik*, p. 254.

32. Opening speech by Schmoller at the meeting in Eisenach in October 1872, in *Verhandlungen*, p. 1.

33. Gustav Schmoller, 'Die soziale Frage und der preussische Staat', reprinted in idem, *Zur Sozial- und Gewerbepolitik der Gegenwart: Reden und Aufsätze*, Leipzig 1890, pp. 37–63; quotation from p. 62. This essay occasioned a vehement attack on Schmoller and the *Kathedersozialisten* by Treitschke in an article entitled, 'Der Socialismus und seine Gönner', which appeared in the *Preussiche Jahrbücher* of 1874.

the socialist labour movement, and, if possible, enforced at an international level with the help of foreign governments. At the same time, these measures were to be accompanied by state intervention in the social process in order to redress what, to Bismarck's mind, were the workers' justifiable grievances.[34] In a letter of 21 October 1871 to the Prussian Minister for Trade, Graf von Itzenplitz, Bismarck demanded that the government 'should, via legislation and the administration, go some way towards meeting the demands of the working classes . . . as long as this is compatible with the general interests of the state'. At the same time, the government would have to act 'to contain agitation threatening the state, as far as possible by means of proscriptive and punitive measures; though without damaging the healthy state of public life'.[35]

He argued against objections that by paying heed to social grievances he would simply be assisting the socialist cause. On 17 November 1871 he said that Germany's socialist movement was not yet dominated by the International. This 'was evidenced by the divisions between the party founded by Lassalle and Bebel and Liebknecht's, which was affiliated to the International'. He went on to say that the state's intervention would indeed succeed in 'reconciling the majority of workers to the existing state and would restore harmony between the interests of workers and employers. . . . I regard it as self-evident that in this matter we cannot ignore burning issues such as working hours, wages, the housing shortage and the like'.[36]

As a result of Bismarck's initiatives, a conference of experts on social policy was held towards the end of 1871. One year later Hermann Wagener chaired a conference of delegates from Germany and Austria-Hungary. On the one hand, it proposed that steps be taken to suppress the socialist workers' movement by tightening up the laws on compulsory unionisation and curtailing those on freedom of association, the press and freedom of assembly. At the same time, it considered new measures for workers' protection, the setting up of labour exchanges, the introduction of accident insurance legislation and state support for existing sickness insurance funds.[37] But, apart from two laws on benefit funds introduced in 1876, appropriate measures either never got beyond the draft stage or were dropped by Bismarck, who gradually

34. Rothfels, *Lohmann*, p. 27.
35. Heinrich von Poschinger (ed.), *Aktenstücke zur Wirthschaftspolitik des Fürsten Bismarck*, 2 vols., Berlin 1890–91, vol. 1, p. 161.
36. Ibid., pp. 166f.
37. *See* Richard Lipinski (ed.), *Dokumente zum Sozialistengesetz. Materialien nach amtlichen Akten*, 1928, pp. 13–17.

changed his views on the socialist danger and the need to find a
solution to social problems. The first of the two laws to be passed
placed under state supervision any workers' insurance funds seeking
privileged legal status as 'registered' benefit funds (*eingeschriebene Hilfskassen*). These were permitted in law as alternatives to the compulsory
funds administered by the local authorities (*örtliche Zwangskassen*). The
latter were the subject of the second law — an amendment to the
Commercial Code. Before registration could be granted to voluntary
funds, these funds were required to end any formal connection with a
trade union, accept non-union members, give up their local character
by creating a centralised fund and limit themselves to providing only
sickness benefits. This last condition conflicted with the previous
practice of trade unions, whose benefit arrangements were often of
much wider scope. Some of these union funds continued to exist and
provide their members with supplementary benefits or death benefits.
The attempt to use the law to curb the activities of the unions proved
unsuccessful. In fact, it had the opposite effect, since the registered
benefit funds strengthened the tendency of the trade unions to evolve a
more centralised organisation. At the same time, they used the funds to
recruit new members, thus strengthening their organisational basis.
They also saw the possibility of using them as cover organisations
which could take the union's place in the event of proscription.[38]

The law on benefit funds (*Hilfskassengesetz*) was only hesitatingly
accepted. It did not in fact lead to an increase in the number of workers
becoming members of benefit funds. It had the opposite effect from that
intended by the state authorities, because it helped the unions, and to
some extent the Social Democrats, to survive the period of proscription
under the anti-Socialist law. The slight improvements which took place
in the existing provisions for workers' protection by a further change in
the Commercial Code in 1878 proved relatively insignificant. Although
a considerable number of government studies and statistics appeared
on the condition of industrial workers, little progress was made in the
field of social policy during the 1870s. There were various reasons for
this. During this period Bismarck was preoccupied with other problems.
There was also, doubtless, passive opposition from the Prussian govern-

38. *See* Gunnar Stollberg, 'Die gewerkschaftsnahen zentralisierten Hilfskassen im
    Deutschen Kaiserreich', in *Zeitschrift für Sozialreform* 29 (1983), pp. 339–69, esp.
    pp. 342, 346; Florian Tennstedt, *Vom Proleten zum Industriearbeiter: Arbeiterbewegung
    und Sozialpolitik in Deutschland 1800 bis 1914*, Cologne 1983, pp. 306ff.; idem, 'Die
    Errichtung von Krankenkassen in deutschen Städten nach dem Gesetz betr. die
    Krankenversicherung der Arbeiter vom 15. Juni 1883: Ein Beitrag zur Frühge-
    schichte der gesetzlichen Krankenversicherung in Deutschland', in *Zeitschrift für
    Sozialreform* 29 (1983), pp. 297–338, esp. pp. 299–309.

ment's ministers, a majority of whom remained committed to *laissez-faire*. At this stage the Reichstag also was still rejecting repressive measures against the workers and the labour movement. As long as measures to secure the existing order were lacking, there was in the view of the ruling élite no reason to establish a new system of social security.

In 1875 Bismarck was still describing himself to Schmoller as a *Kathedersozialist*, only he 'simply didn't have the time' to make anything of it.[39] But, at the very latest from the time of the Gotha Congress of 1875, when the Lassallean and Eisenach factions united to form the Socialist Workers' Party of Germany (Sozialistische Arbeiterpartei Deutschlands), his hopes of winning over at least part of the socialist-influenced working-class evaporated. He felt that the findings of government investigations into female and child labour and working conditions for apprentices, journeymen and factory workers,[40] which he had commissioned in 1873, did not warrant any essential improvements in workers' protection or increased factory inspection. Influenced by the effects of the economic crisis and moving away from his earlier critical stance towards employers on labour questions, he tended more and more to the view, from the mid-1870s onwards, that rigorous measures against the socialists and support of the employers' interests was the best way to revive the economy, create jobs and thus improve the workers' social conditions. Such a view was bound to lead to a more limited version of the constructive policy towards labour which he had previously pursued, reducing it simply to welfare measures, which were later to form the basis of his social insurance legislation.

Bismarck's view of the growing socialist threat was very much reinforced by the Social Democrats successes in the Reichstag elections of January 1874 and January 1877. In the latter election the party, on the strength of its half-million voters, admittedly won only 9.1 per cent of the vote, giving it twelve of the Reichstag's 397 seats. But, its 38-per-cent share of the total vote in the Kingdom of Saxony, a predominantly industrial area, made it the strongest party there with seven of the state's twenty-three seats. In Berlin and Hamburg it registered further substantial gains with a 39.2-per-cent and 40-per-cent

---

39. Schmoller, 'Vier Briefe', in *Charakterbilder*, p. 41.
40. *Ergebnisse der über die Frauen- und Kinder-Arbeit in den Fabriken auf Beschluss des Bundesraths angestellten Erhebungen*, compiled by the Imperial Chancellery (Reichskanzleramt), Berlin 1877; *Ergebnisse der über die Verhältnisse der Lehrlinge, Gesellen und Fabrikarbeiter auf Beschluss des Bundesraths angestellten Erhebungen*, compiled by the Imperial Chancellery Berlin 1877.

share of the respective votes.[41] It thus became perfectly clear that the Social Democrats had extended their original basis of support from the economically backward centres of the cottage industry and were becoming the dominant political force in Germany's Protestant urban and industrial areas.

It is well known that Bismarck used the two assassination attempts on the Emperor in May and June 1878 to introduce legislation suppressing both the Socialist Party, which he viewed as a kind of 'enemy within',[42] and the free trade unions. The move was also designed to ensure a Reichstag majority for the conservative change of course which now took place in domestic politics and foreign-trade policy. It is, however, revealing that soon after the second assassination attempt various government ministries issued directives calling for tougher action to be taken against socialist tendencies among officials and workers employed by the state, while, at the same time, departments receiving these directives were urged to help eliminate 'the spirit of discontent and growth of the socialist movement' by 'sympathetically dealing with the question of wage-levels, working hours', the provision of workers' housing and the extension of welfare arrangements.[43] On 11 September 1878, Otto Graf zu Stolberg-Wernigerode, Bismarck's deputy in the Prussian Cabinet (Staatsministerium) took the view (in a memorandum, almost certainly sanctioned by Bismarck in advance),[44] that 'the prospective emergency legislation' to suppress the Social Democratic movement 'by no means completed the task of applying persistent and salutary state counter-measures against the dangers resulting from the socialist movement, which was an evil to be tackled at the roots'. In the course of the Cabinet's intense discussion, the ministers present discussed a whole range of possible options available to the government as 'counter-measures' apart from further repression. It was suggested that the system of benefit funds be enlarged in scope and organisation, that the law covering employers' liability be amended

41. *See* Gerhard A. Ritter unter Mitarbeit von Merith Niehuss, *Wahlgeschichtliches Arbeitsbuch: Materialen zur Statistik des Kaiserreichs 1871–1918*, Munich 1980, esp. pp. 38, 69, 89, 95.

42. Bismarck's Reichstag speech of 9 October 1878 in defence of the second draft bill of the anti-Socialist Law (*Gesammelte Werke*, vol. 12, pp. 1–15, ibid. p. 9).

43. *See* Ordinance of the Prussian Minister of Trade to the Chairmen of the Royal Commissariats of Railways (Königliche Eisenbahn-Commissariate) of 3 June 1878, Staatsarchiv Münster, Oberpräsidium Münster 2693 I, folio 9f.; Ordinance of the Prussian Minister of Trade to the Presidents of Administrative Districts (*Regierungspräsidenten*) of 14 June 1878, ibid., fos 18f.

44. Written opinion of the Vice-President of the Prussian State Ministry of 11 September 1878, Geheimes Staatsarchiv, Berlin-Dahlem, Rep. 84a, vol. 10771, pp. 329–35.

and that legal provision be made for adult education for workers, apprentices and shop assistants. Further proposals included increasing indirect taxes at the same time as reducing direct taxes and local tax rates. There was also a proposal to establish a pro-government workers' press. This press would replace the socialists' banned party newspapers with one which would put forward the workers' interests in a conciliatory manner.[45] In similar vein, the regular reports on the state of the socialist movement, requested by the federal states and local authorities during the period of the anti-Socialist law, soon included additional sections with detailed accounts of the government's 'welfare arrangements' for the workers.

The motives and main characteristics of Germany's social insurance legislation in the 1880s

Official government statements constantly stressed the role of Germany's social insurance legislation in positively complementing the anti-Socialist law. Thus, in a royal speech of 15 February 1881, the draft bill for an accident insurance law was described as 'supplementing the legislation designed to counter Social Democratic activities'.[46] Similarly, in a celebrated royal message of 17 November 1881,[47] the main sections of which were edited by Bismarck, the theme was taken up again. The 'redress of social problems is not simply to be sought by repressing Social Democratic excesses, but equally by positively promoting the workers' welfare'.

Germany's social insurance was intended to innoculate those workers who had not yet succumbed to Social Democratic propaganda. It was also meant to cure those already 'infected' by causing a split

45. See *inter al.* the written opinions of the Prussian Minister for Religious Affairs, the Minister of Finances, the Minister of Trade, the Minister for War, the Minister for Agriculture, the Minister of the Interior and the President of the Imperial Chancellery (Reichskanzleramt), Karl Hofmann (ibid. vol. 10771).

46. Royal speech at the opening of the new session of the Reichstag, obviously written by Bismarck, in whose *Gesammelte Werke* it appeared. The speech was read out by Stolberg-Wernigerode, who also held the post of Vice-Chancellor (Bismarck, *Gesammelte Werke*, vol. 12, pp. 186f.).

47. For the background to the Emperor's message, *see* Florian Tennstedt, 'Vorgeschichte und Entstehung der Kaiserlichen Botschaft vom 17. November 1881', in *Zeitschrift für Sozialreform* 27 (1981), pp. 663–729. The same issue contains the complete text of the statement and facsimile passages of the parts of the draft referring to workers' insurance, which were heavily reworked by Bismarck (ibid. pp. 730–5, 711ff.).

between them and their leaders — the latter being viewed by Bismarck as a lost cause — with the aim of generally bringing the workers closer to the state. Thus the preamble to the first draft of the accident insurance law of 8 March 1881 stated that it was not just 'a humanitarian and Christian obligation . . . but essential to the preservation of the state' that 'the unpropertied classes, which were at once the most numerous and least educated among the population', be shown by means of 'directly tangible advantages' that 'the state does not exist merely out of necessity or is simply created for the protection of the better–situated classes in society', but is a benevolent 'institution also serving their needs and interests'.[48]

Bismarck, who was impressed by Napoleon III's system of old-age pension funds, hoped that substantial pay-outs of state benefits to the workers would help bring about their reconciliation with the state. The tide of revolution would be stemmed as a conservative mentality spread among those expecting a pension. 'Whoever has a pension to look forward to in his old age', he remarked to the writer Dr Moritz Busch on 21 January 1881, 'is much more contented and more easily taken care of than the man who has no prospect of any'. He realised that the implementation of his plans would certainly incur considerable expenditure, but, he continued:

'the contentment of the unpropertied classes . . . was well worth the great expense involved. . . . As a country with one of the lowest tax rates, we can afford a great deal in this respect. And if we use the result [of introducing a tobacco monopoly or increasing taxes on luxuries] to safeguard the future of our workers, whose insecurity is the main cause of their hatred for the state, we are only guaranteeing our own future. That is a good investment for us as well. It enables us to thwart a revolution which could break out fifty years from now, or even ten — a revolution which, even if it was successful for only a few months, would directly and indirectly run up quite different costs from our pre-emptive strategy in terms of its disruption of business and trading'.[49]

Eight years later, Bismarck managed to win the support of the Reichstag's Conservative majority for the passage of a disablement and old-age insurance law in Parliament, but only after a fervent appeal, in which he returned to the theme of strengthening a conservative and patriotic mentality by means of old-age pensions:

48. *See* 'Begründung zum Entwurf eines Gesetzes betr. die Unfallversicherung der Arbeiter', in *Sammlung sämtlicher Drucksachen des Reichstags*, IV. Legislaturperiode, IV. Session 1881, vol. 1, no. 41, p. 17.
49. Busch's diary entry recording his conversation with Bismarck, in Bismarck, *Gesammelte Werke*, vol. 8, Berlin 1926, p. 396.

I lived in France long enough to realise that the attachment most Frenchmen feel towards their government . . . and thus, ultimately, to their country, is essentially connected with the fact that most Frenchmen are in receipt of a state pension, albeit amounting to little, often very little. . . . . People there say, if the state comes to any harm, I'll lose my pension; and even if it's only 40 francs per annum, they don't want to lose it, and so have a vested interest in the state. . . . . If we had 700,000 small-time pensioners, drawing their pension from the state from precisely those social classes, which otherwise have little to lose and mistakenly believe they could gain a great deal from change, I would regard that as extremely advantageous. Even if they only stand to lose from between 115 to 200 marks, the cash keeps them sufficiently afloat. However little it may be, it keeps them on their feet.

Such pensions would teach 'even the common man' to look upon 'the Empire as a benevolent institution'.[50]

Bismarck's view of humanity and his concept of politics were coloured by his belief that, irrational behaviour aside, people's politics were governed by their material interests. For this reason, political considerations took first priority when it came to improving the workers' social security. This explains why the industrial workers, who were the most influenced by the Social Democrats and the trade unions, became the first target group of his social insurance legislation, and not the agricultural labourers, domestic servants and cottage industry workers, who were incorporated only later. The hardship experienced by the latter groups was in most cases much worse and their social situation much more oppressive. Certainly, the political motive which was doubtless present in the choice of groups to be included was to some extent complemented by the fact that the industrial workers, who enjoyed relatively steady and well-paid work compared with other lower-paid workers, were more likely to be able to afford regular insurance contributions. It is no coincidence that whenever social insurance has been introduced in developing countries it has almost always been applied at first to industrial workers and not the very poor.[51]

Even in Germany's case, the social insurance laws should not be interpreted simply as a strategy to resist the growth of the labour movement and exercise social control over the workers within the framework of the existing social and political order. One has also to take into account the economic and social factors which shaped the legislation.

50. Speech of 18 June 1889 in *Sten. Berichte des Reichstags*, VII, IV, vol. 3, 1831–36, 1834.
51. Detlev Zöllner, *Öffentliche Sozialleistungen und wirtschaftliche Entwicklung: Ein zeitlicher und internationaler Vergleich*, Berlin 1963, esp. pp. 74–81.

Bismarck argued that 'socialist and democratic activities' were to a great extent responsible for the economic crisis, in that socialism reduced the German worker's efficiency and will to work, thus reducing the country's economic competitiveness *vis-à-vis* France.[52] The Chancellor also stated that the general lack of confidence in the economy's future, which he again blamed on the socialists, deterred employers from investing and this led in turn to even more unemployment.[53] This argument can only be interpreted as an attempt to find a scapegoat for the economic depression and mobilise the employers in the struggle against the Social Democrats. It was hardly a serious attempt to find a realistic explanation for the causes of the economic crisis after 1873.

On the other hand, there is no doubt that Germany's concrete social problems led to a strong build-up of pressure for reform. While the risk of accidents was greatly increasing as a result of the growing numbers of industrial workers[54] and the more widespread use of machines, the statute of 1871 covering accident liability (*Reichshaftpflichtgesetz*) was generally felt to be extremely unsatisfactory. Apart from the railways, which had to accept full liability for industrial injury where it could not be demonstrated that factors outside their control or the insured party were to blame, mine-workers, factory workers, quarrymen and navvies (journeymen, agricultural labourers and other groups were not covered at all) could only claim compensation under this law if they could prove that the employer or one of his representatives was culpable.[55] It was often exceptionally difficult to furnish proof of this kind, for, if another worker was at fault, the employer could not be held liable. It was also extremely difficult, if not impossible, when attempting to produce proof of technical negligence, to establish the state of a work-place or equipment at the time before an accident took place. Potential witnesses refused to speak out in their evidence because they feared the consequences of civil or criminal actions in which they were to blame, or because they feared dismissal by their employer. There were also cases where a firm's bankruptcy, which could easily follow on

52. Bismarck's Reichstag speech on 9 February 1876 in Bismarck, *Gesammelte Werke*, vol. 11, pp. 425–37, esp. p. 433.
53. Reichstag speech of 9 October 1878 in ibid. vol. 12, pp. 1–15, ibid. p. 9.
54. The risk of accident was considerably greater in the industrial sector compared with the agricultural sector. Thus the employers' occupational associations in the industrial sector paid out on average 15.28 marks for each insured member in 1913, whereas the figure for the occupational associations in agriculture was only 2.41 marks (*Amtliche Nachrichten des Reichsversicherungsamts* 31 (1915), pp. 14f.).
55. *See* Ernst Wickenhagen, *Geschichte der gewerblichen Unfallversicherung: Wesen und Wirken der gewerblichen Berufsgenossenschaften*, 2 vols., Munich and Vienna 1980, vol. 1, pp. 21–7.

from a major disaster involving injury and loss of life, led to claims for compensation not being met. These were cases where the employer had failed to cover himself for liability with a private insurance company. In view of the highly unfavourable legal position for the injured party, the private insurers were happy, for their part, to allow a court action to take place, before paying out compensation. Contrary to its intended purpose, the law on liability for industrial accidents led to an intensification of conflict between many employers and employees as a result of acrimonious court cases which often dragged on for years.[56] In all, according to contemporary estimates, less than 20 per cent of registered accidents in the areas of industry covered by the law — and by no means all accidents were registered — resulted in compensation being paid out.[57] Since, as a rule, payments could not be made until the courts had given a ruling on the case, the injured party or the bereaved dependants often found themselves already in conditions of abject poverty.

When initial plans to extend the principle of employers' liability for accidents at work[58] failed on account of opposition from both Bismarck

56. For the weaknesses in the liability law, see *Jahresbericht der* [preussischen] *Fabriken-Inspektoren für 1877*, pp. 13, 30f., 73f., 85, 98f., 128f., 219–21, 265; 1878, pp. 51, 235f.; 'Begründung zum Entwurf eines Gesetzes betreffend die Unfallversicherung der Arbeiter', in *Sammlung sämtlicher Drucksachen des Reichstags*, IV, IV, vol. 1, no. 41. 1881, pp. 19–22; T. Bödiker, *Die Unfall-Gesetzgebung der europäischen Staaten*, Leipzig 1884, pp. 12–16; Hans Michael v. Heinz, *Entsprechungen und Abwandlungen des privaten Unfall- und Haftpflichtversicherungsrechts in der gesetzlichen Unfallversicherung nach der Reichsversicherungsordnung*, Berlin 1973, pp. 29–33.

57. A. von Miaskowski, 'Zur Geschichte und Literatur des Arbeiterversicherungswesens in Deutschland', in *Jahrbücher für Nationalökonomie und Statistik*, Neue Folge, 4 (1882), pp. 474–96, esp. p. 477; Kleeis, *Geschichte*, p. 84. The significance of the change in law brought about by the accident insurance legislation of 1884 and subsequent amendments can clearly be seen, for example, in the fact that according to accident statistics for 1897 no less than 80 per cent of industrial accidents would not have qualified for compensation under the terms of the previously existing law (Lass and Zahn, *Einrichtung*, p. 60).

58. Some firms had already taken out insurance before 1884, not only against the risk of liability but all types of accident. According to statistics compiled on behalf of the government by T. Bödiker at the Imperial Office of the Interior ('Die Unfall-Statistik des Deutschen Reichs nach der Aufnahme vom Jahre 1881', in *Monatshefte zur Statistik des Deutschen Reichs für das Jahr 1882*, ed. by the Kaiserliches Statistisches Amt, vol. 53 of *Statistik des Deutschen Reichs, Ergänzungsheft*, Berlin 1882, p. 21) in which the first ever systematic attempt was made to convey information on accidents, their consequences, the differing incidence of risk in different branches of industry and occupations, the costs to firms and the government of introducing accident insurance and the extent of existing insurance. Figures for 1881 were as follows: of 1,957,548 workers listed by the statistics, 548,503 or 28 per cent were covered against all types of accident, 309,370 or 15.8 per cent against accidents involving employers' liability, 978,474 or 50 per cent had no cover. In the case of 37,919 workers, or 2 per cent, it is noted that only some of the workers (e.g.

and the employers,[59] the accident insurance provisions subsequently introduced steered clear of the problem of demonstrating culpability. Bismarck's original intention was to give the government a major share in running the scheme, but this failed to materialise. The accident insurance law, which levied employers only, excluded private insurers and effectively transferred the employer's individual risk to employers' associations based on occupational membership and categories of risk. At the same time, the accident insurance law, as opposed to the law on employers' liability, limited the claims of injured parties in cases of total disablement to only two-thirds of previous earnings.

Since the accident insurance law did not replace the Empire's liability laws, private insurers offered a 'new' form of liability insurance for those areas of risk where no cover was available;[60] for better-paid salaried employees, the self-employed and the personnel of small firms, who were not initially covered by the new law. Insurers also extended cover against claims for damages to new areas of business, such as the medical profession, chemists, hotel owners, hauliers and the like.

In 1880 Germany's existing sickness insurance provisions only covered about 5 per cent of the population.[61] Benefits remained inadequate, since in most cases loss of earnings was only partly compensated for, free medical treatment was not guaranteed and often sick or disabled workers were excluded. Because of their often relatively small membership, the older insurance funds were sometimes unable to cope with the financial burden placed on them by the long-term illness of an individual member. Their local character and the fact that their membership was based on specific occupations also meant that they could not do justice to the geographical and occupational mobility of their members.[62] Contrary to the government's expectations, the law on benefit funds of 7 April 1876 did not lead to a substantial increase in the number of citizens insured. On the contrary, in Prussia the total number of benefit funds, including newly established and partly adapted 'registered benefit funds', dropped from 5,239 to 4,901 and their

---

machine-workers, engine stokers, etc.) were insured. No figures are available in the case of 82,922 workers, or 4.2 per cent.

59. *See* Rothfels, *Lohmann*, pp. 49–51.
60. *See* Hans-Peter de Longueville, 'Die Entwicklung der Haftpflichtversicherung in Deutschland. Ein Beispiel für Produktinnovation im Versicherungsbereich', in Friedrich-Wilhelm Henning (ed.), *Entwicklung und Aufgaben von Versicherungen und Banken in der Industrialisierung*, Berlin 1980, pp. 29–62, esp. pp. 44–7.
61. Tennstedt, 'Sozialgeschichte der Sozialversicherung', in Blohmke (ed.), *Handbuch*, p. 386.
62. *See* Florian Tennstedt, *Sozialgeschichte der Sozialpolitik in Deutschland, vom 18. Jahrhundert bis zum Ersten Weltkrieg*, Göttingen 1981, p. 166.

membership fell from 869,204 to 839,602.[63] According to an estimate made by Theodor Lohmann in 1881, only about half of Germany's industrial workers, who formed the target group for the sickness insurance law of 1883 (later extended to other groups) were insured against sickness through a benefit fund.[64]

Germany's existing provisions for old age and disablement were even worse. Apart from civil servants with pension rights, a small number of employees insured through their own firms and mine-workers belonging to provident societies, most old and disabled people had next to no cover. This problem was made worse as the incidence of occupational diseases[65] (not covered by accident insurance) increased, and the average age of workers in industry, which showed little interest in elderly or partly disabled workers, decreased. Thus, according to the occupational census of 1907, only 9.6 per cent of all male wage-earners in industry and handicrafts (10.2 per cent in transport and trade) were older than fifty years of age. In the agricultural sector, where much greater numbers of older workers were employed, the figure was, in contrast, 17.3 per cent.[66] The traditional importance of providing for the elderly within the family and at their place of birth began to dwindle rapidly, since the great extent of internal migration in Germany compared with other industrial societies — in 1907 only 42.4 per cent of Germans living in large cities had been born there[67] — became a lasting characteristic of the German labour market. During the early

---

63. See 'Begründung des Entwurfs eines Gesetzes, betreffend die Krankenversicherung der Arbeiter', in *Sten. Berichte des Reichstags*, V, II, 1882/83, vol. 5 (Anlagen), no. 14, pp. 40f.

64. See Florian Tennstedt, *Soziale Selbstverwaltung: Geschichte der Selbstverwaltung in der Krankenversicherung von der Mitte des 19. Jahrhunderts bis zur Gründung der Bundesrepublik Deutschland*, vol. 2, Bonn 1977, p. 21.

65. A wealth of material on occupational diseases can be found in the reports of factory inspectors, official investigations, research by social reformers and medical publications. Ludwig Hirt published a four-volume work as early as the 1870s on diseases among workers, 'Die Krankheiten der Arbeiter', Breslau 1871 and Leipzig, 1875 and 1878. This work included statistical details on the morbidity, mortality and life-expectancy of workers in different occupations.

66. *Berufs- und Betriebszählung vom 12. Juni 1907. Berufsstatistik, Abteilung X: Die berufliche und soziale Gliederung des deutschen Volkes*, compiled by the Kaiserliches Statistisches Amt, *Statistik des Deutschen Reichs* 211 (Berlin 1913), p. 187. The proportion of wage-earners over fifty years of age to the total number of wage-earners had scarcely changed since 1882 (agriculture, 17.77 per cent; industry, 9.55 per cent; trade and transport, 10.96 per cent). Percentages for 1882 are based on the absolute figures in *Berufsstatistik nach der allgemeinen Berufszählung vom 5. Juni 1882, Statistik des Deutschen Reichs*, Neue Folge, 2 (1884), pp. 109*f.).

67. Wolfgang Köllmann, 'Industrialisierung, Binnenwanderung und Soziale Frage: Zur Entstehungsgeschichte der deutschen Industriegroßstadt im 19. Jahrhundert', in his *Bevölkerung*, pp. 106–24, esp. p. 117.

1880s the annual volume of migration to and from the big cities of over 50,000 inhabitants was already calculated at a quarter of the urban population. After 1905 the figure climbed to as much as a third.[68]

The burden of providing for elderly workers (and their dependants), forced temporarily or permanently out of work through accidents, sickness, disablement, old age or seasonal and chronic unemployment, fell mainly on the existing system of poor relief. In 1881 an attempt was made to ascertain the extent of public relief in Germany before preparing the terms of the new social insurance legislation, but this proved unsuccessful. The findings were regarded as too unreliable to be published.[69] However, a further, more successful attempt was made in 1885, which produced the only comprehensive set of statistics available to us on the poor in Germany for the period before 1918. According to its figures, the number of people in receipt of poor relief in 1885 amounted to 3.4 per cent of Germany's population. The proportion of those supported by local area relief associations (*Ortsarmenverbände*) was 5.24 per cent in the cities, compared with the considerably lower figure for rural communities of 2.16 per cent. The following categories were given as reasons for providing relief:[70]

	per cent
Caused by accident:	
personal injury	2.1
injured breadwinner	0.3
death of breadwinner	0.9
Not caused by accident:	
death of breadwinner	17.2
illness of recipient or members of family	27.9
physical or mental disability	12.4
infirmity resulting from old age	14.8
Other reasons	
large family	7.2
unemployment	6.0
drink problem	2.0
work-shy	1.4
miscellaneous stated causes	7.7
causes not stated	0.1 .

68. *See* Dieter Langewiesche, 'Wanderungsbewegungen in der Hochindustrialisierungsperiode: Regionale, interstädtische und innerstädtische Mobilität in Deutschland 1880–1914', in *Vierteljahrschrift für Sozial- und Wirtschaftsgeschichte* 64 (1977), pp. 1–40, esp. p. 7.

69. Statistisches Bundesamt Wiesbaden (ed.), *Bevölkerung und Wirtschaft 1872–1972*, Stuttgart 1972, p. 26.

Among the fundamental reasons behind the introduction of Germany's social insurance were growing criticisms of the existing practice of placing the burden of running the system on the local authorities[71] and pressure from municipal councils to reduce the local rates for poor relief.[72]

Bismarck took the view that the payment of poor relief was not 'carried out everywhere according to the principle of fair distribution'.[73] He was concerned to relieve the financial burden on Germany's rural communities, which were feeling the negative effects of industrialisation, not least because of the numbers of workers returning to the countryside without means and no longer capable of work. Admittedly, the figures were exaggerated by contemporaries.[74] However, when disablement and old-age insurance was subsequently introduced, the very small pension amounts were justified on the basis that they were only intended to suffice for 'the most essential level of

---

70. 'Statistik der öffentlichen Armenpflege im Jahr 1885', in *Statistik des Deutschen Reichs*, Neue Folge, 29 (Berlin 1887), pp. 31*, 40*. An interesting interpretation of these statistics by a government official in the Kaiserliches Statistisches Amt is M. Schumann's 'Die Armenlast im Deutschen Reich', in *Jahrbücher für Nationalökonomie und Statistik*, Neue Folge, 17 (1888), pp. 594–630.

71. As an opponent of compulsory insurance, Lujo Brentano put forward the view in a widely read work that workers' wages should be sufficiently raised to enable them to pay their own insurance against six eventualities: to guarantee themselves a proper burial and the continuance of their children's education, as well as protection against old age, disablement, sickness and unemployment (*Die Arbeiterversicherung gemäß der bisherigen Wirtschaftsordnung*, Leipzig 1879, esp. pp. 102–10).

72. *See* Lujo Brentano, 'Die beabsichtigte Alters- und Invaliden-Versicherung für Arbeiter und ihre Bedeutung', in *Jahrbücher für Nationalökonomie und Statistik*, Neue Folge, 16 (1888), pp. 1–46, esp. pp. 15f., and the article by the Mayor of Altona, Adickes, 'Die Vertheilung der Armenlasten in Deutschland und ihre Reform', in *Zeitschrift für die gesammte Staatswissenschaft*, 27 (1881), pp. 235–91, 419–31, 727–822. Adickes' statistics on fifty-one Prussian towns and cities (pp. 422–31) show that compulsory contributions towards the cost of poor relief varied enormously. While they amounted to only 10 per cent of the entire direct taxes in some towns, in others, like Barmen, Altona, Krefeld, Dortmund, Duisburg, Mönchen-Gladbach, Bochum and Hagen, they amounted to almost 50 per cent of direct taxes and in some cases even more. A major reform in the way the costs of poor relief were distributed would have been necessary had social insurance legislation not been introduced.

73. Extract from the written justification (*Motive*) to the accident insurance law of early January 1881, based on corrections made in Bismarcks' own hand (Bismarck, *Gesammelte Werke*, vol. 6c, pp. 205f.)

74. On the small numbers of workers returning, *see* (for the western half of the Ruhr area) Heinz Reif, 'Soziale Lage und Erfahrungen des alternden Fabrikarbeiters in der Schwerindustrie des westlichen Ruhrgebietes während der Hochindustrialisierung', in *Archiv für Sozialgeschichte* 22 (1982), pp. 1–94, esp. 40–54. Reif is surely right in accounting for the small number of old workers returning to their place of birth in terms of the close ties to their previous place of work and the 'essentially more spartan poor relief of the less financially well-off rural authorities' (p. 89).

subsistence in places where it was possible to live cheaply'. Pensioners were, therefore, advised, 'where practicable, to take up residence in the countryside'. This meant they could contribute to 'increasing the rural population, besides bringing more money into the countryside along with the work they were still capable of'.[75] The improvement which the government hoped to see in the agricultural sector and in the situation of rural communities was apparently achieved at first.

According to available statistics on the occupation, sex, age and place of residence, of 90,491 men and 35,906 women in receipt of an old-age pension before 1 December 1891, 54.9 per cent of all male pensioners and 46.4 per cent of female pensioners had been employed in agriculture. In contrast, only 24.4 per cent of male pensioners and 14.4 per cent of female pensioners had been employed in industry and handicrafts. The respective figures for the trade and transport sector were 3.6 per cent and 2.2 per cent. If we compare these figures with the statistics from 1895 on occupations and professions, according to which, of every 100 employed men (or women), only 35.7 (41.9) were employed in agriculture, compared with 43.5 (23.1) in industry and handicrafts and 11.3 (8.8) in trade and transport, we can see a strong predominance of pensioners from the agricultural sector. This finding is confirmed if we look at the number of pensioners living in urban or rural communities. Whereas 27.9 per cent of Germany's total population lived in communities of more than 10,000 inhabitants as at 1 December 1890, one year later this was true of only 13.7 per cent of male and 17.1 per cent of female pensioners. At the same time, the statistics show that the pensions of workers previously employed in agriculture were far lower than those employed in other occupations, a fact accounted for by the below-average wages of the agricultural sector.[76] It can safely be assumed that the steady increase in the numbers of those receiving a disablement pension, compared with those receiving old-age pensions, led to a gradual decrease in the initially high concentration of pensioners in the countryside.

The close connection between social insurance and poor relief can

75. 'Denkschrift betr. Alters- und Invalidenversicherung', which together with the 'Grundzüge zur Alters- und Invalidenversicherung' was sent on 6 July 1887 to the governments of the various federal states except Prussia, and requested a reply (Reichsamt des Innern, no. 1086 II, Geheimes Staatsarchiv Berlin-Dahlem, Rep. 90, vol. 1263). The Grundzüge (Principles) and the Denkschrift (memorandum) were later published.

76. See 'Statistik der Altersrentenempfänger des Jahres 1891', in Amtliche Nachrichten des Reichs-Versicherungsamts: Invaliditäts- und Altersversicherung, 3rd yr, no. 3, 1 February 1893, pp. 26–45, esp. pp. 32–5. Occupational census for 1895 in Statistik des Deutschen Reichs, Neue Folge, 221 (1913), pp. 279, 132*f.

clearly be seen in the first draft of the accident insurance law, which came before the Federal Council (Bundesrat) on 15 January 1881. It proposed that the regional poor relief associations (*Landesarmenverbände*), or equivalent institutions, should, in the case of a worker earning less than 750 marks per annum, pay a third of the insurance premium. The remainder would be paid by the employer. In the case of workers earning over 750 marks the cost of the contributions was to be equally shared between employer and employee.[77] It had even been originally proposed to levy a third of the insurance premium on the local relief association (*Ortsarmenverband*) of the district in which a firm was based. However, in his memorandum to the meeting of the Prussian Cabinet on 21 December 1880, Bismarck's deputy, Otto Graf zu Stolberg-Wernigerode, rightly reminded the other ministers present that the regional associations would see their having to take on such a burden, as 'an unjustifiable imposition'. Furthermore, their involvement would 'from the outset invest the insurance with the character of poor relief, which it does not have, and which in the interests of the workers it must not have'.[78] As a result, the proposal had already been dropped from the draft laid before the Federal Council. During the ensuing discussions in the Federal Council and the Prussian National Economic Council (Volkswirtschaftsrat), founded in October 1880 as an advisory body of experts and interested parties, the draft underwent further changes. In the version now laid before the Reichstag, the imperial government was substituted for the regional poor relief associations. However, the official explanation of the bill still stated that 'in truth, the measures, which could be taken to improve the lot of the unpropertied classes, were but a further step towards developing the basic concept behind the state's provisions for the poor'.[79] In a similar vein, Bismarck, in defending government subvention, which was subsequently rejected by the Reichstag, partly on the grounds that it resembled poor relief,[80] explained in a speech on 2 April 1881 that the government was merely seeking permission 'to let the state take the place of the local authorities responsible for the care of the poor'. He explained in great detail how in this way the burden of poor relief

77. Extensive reprint of the bill's contents and its explanation in Schulthess' *Europäischer Geschichtskalender* 22 (1881), pp. 18–29.
78. Geheimes Staatsarchiv, Berlin-Dahlem, Rep. 90, vol. 1263.
79. 'Begründung zum Entwurf des Gesetzes betreffend die Unfallversicherung der Arbeiter', in *Sammlung sämtlicher Drucksachen des Reichstags*, IV, IV, vol. 1, p. 18.
80. *See* 'Bericht der XIII: Kommission über den Gesetzentwurf, betreffend die Unfallversicherung der Arbeiter', in *Sten. Berichte des Reichstags*, IV, IV, vol. 4 (Anlagen), no. 159, pp. 829–47, esp. p. 840: 'State aid will give disablement compensation the character of poor relief'.

might be removed from the 'communism of the local authorities' and transferred to 'the state's communism'; and he pointed also to the considerably lighter burden on those areas where the majority of workers were organised in miners' provident societies or similar associations.[81]

The draft bill for the sickness insurance law was also seen by its authors as a measure designed 'to improve the workers' economic condition' and 'relieve the public burden of the poor'.[82] The local authority sickness funds (*Gemeindekrankenkassen*), which were mainly modelled on Bavaria's system, in fact closely followed the older pattern of welfare for the sick. In contrast to other types of funds allowed by the sickness insurance law, these did not exist as separate corporate entities. Nor did they allow any participation by insured members in managing the fund. In many cases, they had to accept those workers rejected by other funds as unacceptable risks. The contributions to these local authority funds for the sick were low and, where necessary, supplemented by money from the local authority. For these reasons, their benefit payments stuck to the legally permitted minimum, whereas most other funds, which covered the vast majority of persons insured against sickness, voluntarily went beyond this.[83]

The concept, which formed the basis of Bismarck's views on the development and reform of poor relief, emerges even more clearly in the draft proposals for Germany's disablement and old-age insurance. After Bismarck's original plan of financing this insurance exclusively from government funds had failed[84] because of the Reichstag's rejection of a tobacco monopoly for the Empire, the 'Principles' of 1887, on which the insurance was to be based, still proposed that all male workers should pay standard contributions, regardless of income, and draw a pension whose amount would be calculated only on the length

81. Bismarck, *Gesammelte Werke*, vol. 12, pp. 236–49, esp. pp. 246f., 249.
82. 'Begründung des Entwurfs eines Gesetzes betreffend die Krankenversicherung der Arbeiter', in *Sten. Berichte des Reichstags*, V, II, vol. 5 (Anlangen), no. 14, p. 140.
83. Ibid., p. 143. 'This form of sickness insurance also merely represents an extension of existing arrangements. Already at present paragraph 29 of the law on residential in-maintenance of 6 June 1870 . . . obliges local area relief associations [*Ortsarmenverbände*] to provide medical treatment and board for sick domestic servants, shop assistants and apprentices for a period of six weeks without any claim on reimbursement'. In addition, a directive from the Prussian Minister of the Interior and the Prussian Minister of Trade of 26 November 1883 obliged the Prussian authorities to take steps to 'reduce to a minimum' the work of the local authority sickness funds (*Gemeindekrankenkassen*) — later abolished in 1911 — 'in cases where for specific reasons organised, self-managed sickness funds . . . could not be set up'. (Staatsarchiv Koblenz, Abt. 403, Nr. 8420).
84. *See* below, p. 52.

of the period of contributions. In order to justify the fact that no account would be taken either of the increased danger of disablement in certain occupations, or the differences in wage-levels between industry and agriculture, it was stated that 'the possibility of all workers leading a *modest* existence would be ensured and that in this respect there was no need to draw distinctions on the basis of a man's previous position in life'. Moreover, workers with a higher earning potential could secure themselves an additional pension by their own efforts.[85] Since it was believed that women could live more cheaply and would be less of a financial burden on the authorities, a contribution and pension amounting to two-thirds of the rate for men was thought to be adequate in their case. Similarly, anyone over the age of seventy who was still capable of work was to receive less than disabled workers. In the disablement and old age insurance, the government, the employer and the employee were each expected to pay a third share of the total contributions. As the economist and social reformer Lujo Brentano clearly spelled out in his penetrating analysis of the published 'Principles' behind the planned insurance system, the insured workers could only look forward to a pension amounting to whatever would be 'necessary to relieve the burden of costs on the previous system of poor relief. The idea that an old-age or disablement pension should be calculated according to a worker's previous living standards while in work, thus aiming at the ideal of providing the worker with a more humane existence by means of social insurance', was expressly rejected.[86] In Brentano's opinion, what was aimed at was merely an expedient reform of the poor rates, which no longer discriminated against the recipients of poor relief. At the same time, the reform realised the idea of 'state control' over the poor law 'in an almost exemplary fashion' and did justice to the interests of the local authorities, those paying taxes for the poor and those receiving poor relief. By removing the landowners' sole liability for providing relief in their manorial areas,[87] which was akin to their former obligation towards tied labour, Brentano maintained that such measures would also make the agricultural labourers less dependent.[88]

85. 'Denkschrift betr. Alters- und Invalidenversicherung', p. 13. Italics as in original memorandum. The idea of a standard pension put forward in the memorandum was criticised in the written opinion of Scholz, the Minister of Finance on 21 August 1887. Among other reservations, it was pointed out that prices were much higher in industrial areas compared with the countryside (Geheimes Staatsarchiv, Berlin-Dahlem, Rep. 90, vol. 1263).

86. Brentano, 'Alters- und Invaliden-Versicherung', in *Jahrbücher für Nationalökonomie und Statistik*, Neue Folge, 16 (1888), p. 29.

87. In 1890, 2,154,925 Germans lived in 17,495 autonomous manorial communities, which were mainly scattered throughout the area of Prussia east of the River Elbe

However, there was at first no general agreement to incorporate agricultural workers under the terms for disablement and old-age pensions. In the case of accident insurance they were included from 1 May 1889 by an amendment to the original statute. As regards sickness insurance, agricultural workers were completely incorporated only after 1 January 1914.[89] The Prussian Minister of Agriculture at first warned against the burdening of agricultural employers with contributions for disablement and old-age insurance[90] and in a statement laid before the Prussian Cabinet on 11 September 1887 Bismarck also toyed with the idea of restricting the new pensions scheme to the larger cities and industrial areas: 'It is a well-known fact that poor relief in the towns is less adequate than that paid out by the rural authorities. In the countryside, those who are unfit for work owing to old age or disablement are, as a rule, adequately protected against hardship. Death caused by malnutrition or suicides on account of hunger occur exclusively in the cities'.[91]

It is impossible to provide proof for such assertions. Bismarck was prone to exaggerate the extent of rural poor relief,[92] which in fact laid

---

and in Mecklenburg. These were autonomous administrations dominated by the local landowner, who was not only the main employer in the area but also the representative of the state. As such, he alone had to shoulder the burden of public poor relief for the inhabitants of his area (*see* Gerd Hohorst, Jürgen Kocka and Gerhard A. Ritter, *Sozialgeschichtliches Arbeitsbuch, vol. II. Materialien zur Statistik des Kaiserreichs 1870–1914*, 2nd edn, Munich 1978, pp. 47–9).

88. Brentano, 'Alters- und Invalidenversicherung', esp. pp. 33, 37f.

89. Insurance cover could be extended to agricultural labourers by means of local statutes and regional laws, though only limited use was made of this provision. The *Begründung* (official explanation) to the 1883 accident insurance bill still stated that the agricultural worker's

> need for sickness insurance . . . is not as urgent as that of industrial workers, since the family is maintained largely intact and the system of providing help through the family is much more accepted as the rule in the former's case compared with the latter. Similarly, the idea of helping one's neighbours is still of more general and much greater significance in rural areas than in the towns and areas with a predominantly industrial population. Like help provided within the family and the support widely provided by rural employers in cases of sickness, neighbourly help is, however, mainly given in the form of services and the donation of natural produce. To replace this form of mutual support by a system of sickness funds necessarily based on a money economy would, in the interests of best maintaining the natural economy most suited to rural conditions, appear undesirable; and not without harm in its moral effects. [*Steno. Berichte des Reichstags*, V, II, vol. 5 (Anlagen), no. 14, p. 142].

90. The Minister's written opinion of 27 July 1887 (Geheimes Staatsarchiv, Berlin-Dahlem, Rep. 90, vol. 1263). The Finance Minister argued for a cautious step-by-step approach, especially in areas of work involving particular risk to the workers and a greater erosion of their health, making the point that the costs imposed on the employer could 'limit his ability to compete and export his goods' successfully (written opinion of 21 August 1887, ibid.).

91. Written opinion printed in Bismarck, *Gesammelte Werke*, vol. 6c, pp. 364f.

down stringent rules for claimants and intentionally imposed degrading conditions on those in receipt of benefit. Yet they show how, when it came to working out the terms of Germany's disablement and old-age insurance, Bismarck viewed things in the traditional categories of poor relief, which he saw principally as a task for the nation and not the separate local authorities.

His celebrated statement in support of the 'right to work', made at length in a speech to the Reichstag on 9 May 1884, also has to be viewed in this light:

Give the worker the right to work, as long as he is still healthy. Give him work, as long as he is healthy. *Look after him when he is ill. Take care of him when he is old.* If you do this and don't shy away from the sacrifices involved or scream about state socialism the minute someone mentions 'care for the elderly' or when the state shows a bit more Christian charity towards the worker, then I believe that the supporters of the Wydener programme [from the Social Democrats who held their party congress in August 1880 at Schloß Wyden in Switzerland] will play their pied-pipes in vain, that the numbers joining them will decrease, as soon as the workers see that the governments of the Empire and federal states *and their legislatures* are seriously concerned for their well-being.[93]

This statement, which has often been interpreted as a major change of mind by Bismarck towards adopting a policy of state socialism, was expressly directed against the activities of the Social Democrats. It simply meant that, in keeping with the terms laid down in Prussia's General Law Code of 1794,[94] he recognised the community's obligation to clothe and feed, not just the worker incapacitated by old age or

---

92. *See* Sachße and Tennstedt, *Geschichte*, esp. pp. 250f. For Bismarck's idealised view of rural poor relief, *see* for example his speech of 18 May 1889 (*Sten. Berichte des Reichstags*, VII, IV, vol. 3, pp. 834f.).

93. *Sten. Berichte des Reichstags*, V, IV, vol. 1, p. 481. (Original italics.)

94. Bismarck believed his statement was entirely 'in keeping with Prussia's civil law' (ibid., p. 500). He referred to the first two paragraphs under the nineteenth heading in the second section of the General Law Code of 5 February 1794:

> 1. It falls to the state to make provision for the feeding and caring of citizens unable to provide their own upkeep or receive this from other private parties specifically liable for their provision under the law.
> 2. Those who only lack the means and opportunity to earn their keep and that of their dependents shall be given work suitable to their abilities and capacity.

> The Chancellor made no reference, however, to the third paragraph which reads as follows: 'Those who from indolence, love of idleness and other slovenly tendencies show no desire to earn the means for their keep, shall be allocated useful work under appropriate supervision by coercive legal means and punishments' (*see* Michael Stolleis [ed.], *Quellen zur Geschichte des Sozialrechts*, Göttingen 1976, p. 64).

illness but also the unemployed, when no work could be found for them. Here, too, one can see the connection which existed in Bismarck's thinking between traditional ideas of poor relief, the struggle against the Social Democrats and modern social insurance.

Despite this, Germany's social insurance not only extended the scope of benefits and the number of persons insured: it constituted a crucial and qualitative step forward in that it led to improved social conditions for the groups it affected. In contrast to traditional forms of poor relief, which imposed strict social control on recipients of benefits, involved their being disenfranchised and frequently left them feeling degraded by their acceptance of charity, it gave the insured party a legal right to claim relief in the event of accident, sickness, old age and disablement, independent of any means test.

To return to Bismarck's Reichstag speech of 2 April 1881, which is essential to our understanding of his thoughts on the subject of social insurance, the Chancellor went on to explain that the government's proposed accident insurance also aimed at generally 'keeping alive the sense of human dignity' that, as far as he was concerned, 'even the poorest German should retain'. This was desirable:

> so that he doesn't find himself simply a receiver of charity devoid of rights, but has some means of support [*peculium*], which no one has a right to, bar himself — means which more easily open the odd door which would otherwise be closed. This will ensure him better treatment in the house that takes him in, since he can take the extra money he brings into the household away again. . . . What defence does a weak cripple have against being thrown into a corner and left to go hungry? He has none! But, if he has even 100 or 200 marks to himself, then the landlord thinks twice before he troubles him. We've seen it happen with our war invalids. Even though they only receive five or six thalers per month, that is a fair sum for a poor man's budget in the countryside where the canny landlady thinks twice before she annoys or gets rid of the boarder who brings in the money.[95]

In fact, despite its general statements, the Prussian General Code of Law, like the Elizabethan Poor Laws in England, did not guarantee the right to work. It merely undertook the obligation to grant support to 'certain persons or corporations in exchange for compulsory forms of work' (Brentano, 'Alters- und Invaliden-Versicherung', in *Jahrbücher für Nationalökonomie und Statistik*, Neue Folge, 16 [1888], p. 9.).

95. Bismarck, *Gesammelte Werke*, vol. 12, p. 240. In Roman law a *peculium* was a special property which the master of a household gave to persons subject to his authority (wife and children) for their own independent administration and use, or the money a slaved saved through his own efforts, usually to buy his freedom. (See *inter al.* Harald Steindl, 'Dem Arbeiter ein "Peculium": Ein Rückblick auf die Anfänge der Sozialversicherungsgesetzgebung', in *Juristische Schulung* 21 (1981), pp. 871–5, esp. pp. 871f.)

No doubt the status enjoyed by a pensioner was a great deal better than that of someone living on local poor rates, especially as local authorities would try to recover all benefit payments from his relatives, who were legally obliged to support him. The pensioner could take with him whatever little money he received, whereas poor relief was tied to residence in one particular community and only granted after the claimant had totally used up his savings. Moreover, in the countryside, it was often paid out in kind.

Germany's social insurance legislation introduced measures against accident, sickness, old age and disablement, designed to prevent that social slide into pauperism which induced such a sense of shame in contemporaries dependent on poor relief. It transferred to the imperial government many of the social tasks previously undertaken by the country's local authorities and thus effectively broke down the strong degree of social control over recipients of local poor relief. In so doing, it furthered the process, already begun around the mid-nineteenth century, whereby a distinction was drawn between the treatment of the poor and that of the workers. Originally no such distinction had been made.[96] At the same time, it helped promote the view that poverty and the accompanying *de facto* loss of citizen's rights were no longer a stroke of fate which the individual and his family had to suffer helplessly. Thus, long before the German workers had won equal political rights, social insurance constituted a decisive step forward in the process of integrating into society those groups of workers who qualified for inclusion under the provisions of social insurance.

In the final analysis, the social insurance legislation of the 1880s should not be viewed simply against the background of the anti-Socialist law and contemporary social problems. It also owed a great deal to the main aims of Bismarck's economic and fiscal policies from the late 1870s onwards. These included finding new sources of tax revenue for the imperial government and establishing Prussia as a 'dominant railway power',[97] which would exert considerable influence over the running of Germany's economy by its effective control of freight charges.[98]

96. *See* Tennstedt, 'Sozialgeschichte der Sozialpolitik', in Blohmke (ed.), *Handbuch*, esp. pp. 87–91.

97. *See* Bismarck's letter of 12 June 1876 to the Minister of Trade, Achenbach, in Poschinger (ed.), *Aktenstücke zur Wirtschaftspolitik*, vol. 1, p. 232.

98. *See* the excellent article by Werner Abelshauser, 'Staat, Infrastruktur und regionaler Wirtschaftsausgleich in Preussen der Hochindustrialisierung', in Fritz Blaich (ed.), *Staatliche Umverteilungspolitik in historischer Perspektive: Beiträge zur Entwicklung des Staatsinterventionismus in Deutschland und Österreich*, Berlin 1980, pp. 9–58. Marx and Engels also followed the state's nationalisation of the railways with consider-

It can clearly be argued that Bismarck's protective tariff policy of 1879 and, even more, the fivefold increase in grain duties up to 1887, produced a rise in the cost of living for working-class families.[99] This more than outweighed the cost of social security to the employers and the subvention of pensions paid by the government.[100] Fierce condemnation of so-called 'bread profiteers' became one of the Social Democrats' most effective arguments in the long run. It played a vital part in laying bare the state in the eyes of the workers as one which favoured the partisan interests of the land-owning class, and it also made the task of integrating the workers into the social and political order all the more difficult.

In Bismarck's one-sided estimation, it was the foreign exporter and not the domestic consumer who bore the costs of the grain tariffs.[101] His tariff policy would 'protect the nation's work', help overcome the economic crisis and reduce unemployment. It was precisely the workers who would, therefore, benefit from this policy. Thus, in a highly confidential decree of 13 March 1879, issued as a commentary on economic and fiscal proposals, Bismarck informed the Prussian ambassador in Saxony, Karl Graf von Dönhoff, that 'the most effective way for the governments of the federal states to combat the impending

---

able interest. Eduard Bernstein produced detailed information at Engel's request concerning the development of stock exchange quotations on the most important nationalised railway companies (*see* Bernstein's letters to Engels of 26 October and 17 November 1882, in Helmut Hirsch (ed.), *Eduard Bernsteins Briefwechsel mit Friedrich Engels*, Assen 1970, pp. 140–3, 161–6).

99. According to Carl von Tyska's estimate, based on sources from 1905, in *Die Lebenshaltung der arbeitenden Klassen in den bedeutenden Industriestaaten: England, Deutschland, Frankreich, Belgien und die Vereinigten Staaten*, Jena 1912, pp. 46 and 66, the cost of basic food provisions was about 8 per cent higher in Germany than in Britain. This was largely a result of the government's protectionist measures. According to other contemporary sources, the duties on food products amounted to just over half the various duties on consumer items. Naturally enough, these mostly affected the poorer classes and accounted for about 5 per cent of family incomes below 1,200 marks (Volker Hentschel, *Wirtschaft und Wirtschaftspolitik im wilhelminischen Deutschland: Organisierter Kapitalismus und Interventionsstaat*, Stuttgart 1978, pp. 202f.).

100. The employers shouldered the entire costs of accident insurance and generally a third of sickness insurance contributions. In the case of individual companies' own internal sickness funds (*Betriebskrankenkassen*) the employer's share of contributions was often greater. In the case of the workers' independent funds (*freie Hilfskassen*) the employers' did not pay contributions. The imperial government paid 50 marks per annum on each old-age pension and disablement pension, the remainder of which was financed by equal shares of workers' and employers' contributions.

101. In his article entitled 'Bismarcks Herrschaftstechnik als Problem der gegenwärtigen Historiographie' (*Historische Zeitschrift* 234 [1982], pp. 561–99, esp. 578), Otto Pflanze shows that Bismarck put forward this argument not only in parliamentary speeches for public consumption but also during secret internal governmental discussions.

socialist danger, which threatens us from all sides, is to embark on a series of practical economic reforms'. He saw these 'as a necessary extension of the repressive measures we were obliged to take on account of last year's crimes and outrages'. He went on to say that:

> the effect of these repressive measures can only be of a partial and temporary nature, since the evil lies deeper than these manifestations. . . . I am convinced that the dreadful economic situation, as experienced by the whole community and not just certain individuals, is the main source of discontent among the workers and artisans — and it is not limited to the working classes. The governments' lack of money is also a contributory factor, in that it prevents us from paying the lower ranks of the civil service adequately, thus driving them, including even the police, the lower judiciary and the postal and telegraphic services, into the arms of the socialists. . . . What we really need in this case is a major economic and fiscal reform, or, to put it briefly, more sales, more money.[102]

According to another decree issued on the same day, his economic proposals 'were closely and inseparably connected with the imperial government's efforts to strengthen the monarchical and conservative principle, upon which the German Empire and its constituent parts are built, against impending internal and external threats'.[103] These quotations reveal very clearly the close connection which existed in Bismarck's thinking between preserving the monarchical system, the repressive policies of the authoritarian German states and the role of social and economic reforms.

From the mid-1870s onwards, right up to his dismissal in 1890, the idea of securing the Empire's finances and redistributing tax-burdens was a central feature of Bismarck's domestic policy, a fact which has not yet been sufficiently recognised by historians of the period. By increasing indirect taxes, Bismarck hoped to end the Empire's dependence on the matricular contributions of its federal states, the amounts of which were determined and approved on an annual basis by the Reichstag. He also hoped that this policy would reduce the Reichstag's influence and permit, for example in Prussia, the abolition of class-taxes, which weighed heavily on the lower classes. Rural landowners were also to be helped by abolishing the state tax on land and real

---

102. Highly confidential decree of 13 March 1879 to the Prussian ambassador to Saxony, Carl Graf von Dönhoff, Hamburger Bibliothek fü Sozialgeschichte und Arbeiterbewegung, Nachlass Schulz, Gesandtschaftsberichte Dresden' 5, pp. 44–6. Bismarck went on to say that 'if our parliamentary activities are to remain in line with realities, the protection of material interests in Parliament has to be more pronounced than is the case at present'.
103. Highly confidential decree of 13 March 1879 to Donhöff, ibid., pp. 46f.

estate. This was to be transferred to the local authorities in order to provide them with a new source of revenue.

Bismarck's strategy for fiscal policy failed, however, on account of opposition from both the Reichstag and, to a lesser extent, the Lower House of the Prussian Parliament. The former's opposition resulted in a compromise. The revenue from import duties and tobacco taxes, exceeding 130 million marks per annum, was to be transferred to federal state governments in accordance with the so-called Franckenstein clause introduced by the Centre Party. The Prussian Parliament effectively diluted his tax proposals for Prussia when the Lex Huene of 1885 stipulated that the imperial government's transfer payments to Prussia, which were above 15 million marks per annum, were to be passed on to the local communities.

Bismarck found it particularly impossible to form a Reichstag majority for the introduction of a tobacco monopoly for the Empire, as proposed in the royal message of 17 November 1881. This was intended to remove oppressive direct taxes on low wage-earners, while at the same time freeing local atuhorities from the costs of providing poor relief and schooling.[104] As a result, Bismarck's original plan of dispensing with workers' contributions and financing disablement and old-age insurance exclusively from government funds could not be put into effect. As early as mid-December 1880, after the Prussian National Economic Council had suggested replacing the originally proposed share of the relief associations (*Armenverbände*) in financing poorer workers' accident insurance benefits with government supplements, Bismarck put down in a memorandum the idea of introducing a tobacco monopoly for the purpose of financing accident, old-age and disablement insurance for the 'have-nots'.

> All those willing to insure themselves must be entitled to a state supplementary benefit. This is an idea taken from state socialism! Society as a whole must undertake to support those who own no property and endeavour to cover the costs involved by taxing foreign produce and luxury goods. The social and political significance of generally insuring the 'have-nots' is incalculable. The tobacco monopoly could bring in 100 million marks, which

104. Article 25 of the Prussian Constitution of 31 January 1850 stipulated that 'the local communities are to find the means for establishing, maintaining and enlarging elementary schools . . . which, in the case of a proven shortage of funds, will be supplemented by the state'. However, it was not until the laws of 14 June 1888 and 31 March 1889 that the payment of school rates, which previously accounted for up to 15 per cent of a schoolmaster's salary, were abolished in Prussia (Folkert Meyer, *Schule der Untertanen: Lehrer und Politik in Preussen, 1848–1900*, Hamburg 1976, pp. 101f.)

would be enough to produce that conservative mentality in the great mass of have-nots, which the right to a pension brings with it.[105]

In the summer of 1881, following the Reichstag's rejection of the first draft bill for accident insurance, Bismarck's plans took on even more concrete form. Now he no longer aimed at a voluntary insurance scheme involving state supplements, which would have been similar to the pension scheme of the French Caisse Nationale de Retraites pour la Vieillesse',[106] founded in 1850, but widely rejected by the workers. Instead, he aimed at an insurance system for which the imperial government alone would be responsible. During a meeting of the Prussian Cabinet on 15 August 1881, Bismarck proposed linking the issue of accident insurance and old-age provision for the poorer sections of the community with his plans for a tobacco monopoly. This already existed at the time in Austria and France. The Chancellor was hoping that by this tactic he would be able to create a Reichstag majority in favour of his proposed measures. He admitted that the plans for old-age insurance would 'by no means be perfect in the next parliamentary session, but must appear in tandem with the tobacco monopoly. They should, moreover, appear as the reason for the latter, in order to help get it underway'.[107] Bismarck's overall strategy for solving Germany's and Prussia's political, economic and social problems, as he saw them, was nowhere more apparent than in the statement to the Prussian Cabinet on 22 August 1881:

> The proposed plans for accident and old-age insurance in the Empire, and for the state to share in the financial costs of schooling, poor relief and other public responsibilities hitherto devolved upon local authorities, as well as the creation of a comprehensive canal system in Prussia, cannot be carried out successfully unless there is the prospect of a rise in federal revenue. This can only be guaranteed by creating a tobacco monopoly or some similar measure, and if we combine the latter with the reforms which we intend to benefit the poorer classes in such a way that the tobacco revenue appears as a state revenue for the benefit of the worker and the poor — so that both seem mutually connected — the tasks we have set ourselves in both areas will have a greater chance of success.[108]

105. Bismarck, *Gesammelte Werke*, vol. 6c, p. 230.
106. Bourquin, '*Vie ouvrière' und Sozialpolitik*, p. 117–20. The regular contributions paid by the insured were invested in government bonds on which the state guaranteed an artificially high interest rate. Pensions were to be paid out from the funds thus accrued. While the later compulsory incorporation of entire occupational groups meant that the workers in state concerns, the railways and the mines enjoyed the benefits of a pension, there were very few self-insured parties, among whom workers formed only a minority.
107. Geheimes Staatsarchiv, Berlin-Dahlem, Rep. 90, vol. 1244.
108. Bismarck, *Gesammelte Werke*, vol. 6c, p. 222.

There can be no doubt then that Bismarck saw his social insurance reforms not only as a means of containing the threat from the socialists and solving concrete social problems. They were also intended to bolster his own shaky position in the German Parliament and at the same time solve the problem of pushing through his fiscal reforms aimed at strengthening Germany's economy and its constitutional monarchy. In fact, during the 1881 Reichstag elections, the prospect of old-age insurance did not make the acceptance of the tobacco monopoly any easier. Quite the reverse. The plan for the tobacco monopoly, which would have considerably added to the financial burden on the population at large and increased the power of the imperial government, resulted in the plans for social insurance being discredited.[109] The outcome of elections was a heavy defeat for the government. The parliamentary majority needed for the planned social reforms could not be found. In this difficult political situation, the royal message of 17 November 1881 was an attempt to win back the initiative. It tried to identify Germany's popular ageing monarch with the programme for social reforms, in order to promote its acceptance by the general public and put pressure on the political parties to support it.

The accident insurance law was finally passed in 1884 after two earlier bills had been defeated. In its final form it ran counter to the real desires of the government, especially in abandoning the idea of setting up an Imperial Insurance Board (*Reichsversicherungsanstalt*) to administer the insurance and introducing state supplements. The less controversial sickness insurance law of 1883, the significance of which was initially underestimated, only proposed the consolidation and development of existing institutions.[110] Because of the lack of statistics on which to base a realistic estimate of the costs involved and the difficulty of predicting its possible effects,[111] the government's

109. See Otto Quandt, *Die Anfänge der Bismarckschen Sozialgesetzgebung und die Haltung der Parteien (Das Unfallversicherungsgesetz, 1881–1884)*, Berlin 1938, pp. 73–85; Tennstedt, 'Vorgeschichte', *Zeitschrift für Sozialreform* 27, pp. 685–7.
110. Ute Frevert's *Krankheit als politisches Problem, 1770–1880: Soziale Unterschichten in Preussen zwischen medizinischer Polizei und staatlicher Sozialversicherung*, Göttingen 1984, and Sigrid Fröhlich's *Die Soziale Sicherung bei Zünften und Gesellenverbänden: Darstellung, Analyse, Vergleich*, Berlin 1976, both emphasise the continuity between the sickness insurance legislation of 1883 and older forms of deprivatisation and nationalisation of health services through state and municipal institutions and the voluntary insurance of journeymen and factory workers.
111. Government records concerning the age and disablement of workers, upon which the govenment's first draft bill was based, referred exclusively to railway officials, a section of railway workers and mine-workers in Germany and Austria. These figures cannot be taken as representative of the entire workforce. *See* criticisms of

proposed old-age and disablement insurance had to be postponed.[112]
Owing to lack of funds, it eventually took the form of a compulsory
insurance which was to be subsidised by the government. Its character
as an insurance, as opposed to the more traditional character of poor
relief, was given stronger emphasis by a law of 1889, which made
changes to the 'Principles' of 1887. The central government's intention
of paying a third share of contributions was replaced by a system
whereby the government paid a fixed state supplementary benefit of 50
marks per annum on each pension. The initial idea of limiting women's
contributions and pensions to two-thirds of men's was dropped and the
notion of a standard pension scrapped in favour of a system of
progressive contributions, calculated on the basis of four separate
categories of earnings (five after 1899 following a change in the law).[113]
It is interesting to note that even the Social Democrats' spokesman at
the time, obliged to take account of the interests of his party's strongest
basis of support among skilled workers, deliberately spoke in favour of
earnings-related pensions,[114] arguing that skilled workers had 'different
needs compared with so-called day-labourers'.

Germany's system of social insurance differed from the later British
system in several fundamental respects: in its progressive scale of

the absence of proper statistics on German workers by the Social Democratic
deputy, Grillenberger, in his Reichstag speech of 6 December 1888. Grillenberger
called for statistical information 'on the average lifespan of workers, alongside
studies on the various occupational diseases in the main branches of industry and
agriculture, and the probable incidence of disablement among these social groups'
(*Sten. Berichte des Reichstags*, VII, IV, vol. 1, p. 152).

112. Certainly, the Emperor's second message (2. *Kaiserliche Botschaft*) of 14 April 1883,
which urged the Reichstag to proceed with greater haste in introducing social
reforms, expressed the definite hope that 'further submissions concerning old age
and disablement might become law in the next parliamentary session' (Bismarck,
Gesammelte Werke, vol. 12, p. 401). No government initiative followed this pro-
nouncement, however.

113. *See* the law on disablement and old-age insurance of 22 June 1889 (*Reichs-Gesetzblatt*
13, pp. 97–144, esp. paragraphs 22–6, 96) and the disablement insurance law of
13 July 1899 (*Reichs-Gesetzblatt* 33, pp. 393–462, esp. paragraphs 20, 20a, 22, 25,
26a). Paragraph 16 of the draft bill on old-age and disablement insurance, sent to
the Reichstag after being passed by the Federal Council (*Sten. Berichte des Reichstags*,
VII, IV, 1888/89, vol. 4, vol. 1 of appendices, document, no. 10), proposed the
creation of five categories of locality, classified according to 'the amount earned
daily by adult male day-labourers, as laid down and normal for that locality'.
Contributions an pensions were to differ according to the worker's place of residence and not his income. The idea of wage categories was suggested by the
Reichstag commission (*Bericht der VI. Kommission . . .*, in, ibid., vol. of 2 appendices,
document no. 141, esp. pp. 911ff.).

114. Grillenberger's speech before the Reichstag on 6 December 1888, *Sten. Berichte des
Reichstags*, VII, IV, vol. 1, p. 156. Grillenberger believed that the better-paid
workers would also pay higher contributions in order to receive a pension which
was in keeping with the actual amount of their wage'.

old-age pension contributions and benefits, and in the extent to which it was borne by the insured party rather than the state. Yet these were precisely those elements which the government had never intended to be part of its social insurance system. They were the result of the Reichstag's opposition to any increase in the power of the imperial bureaucracy, and the government found itself forced to accept them after the failure of its plans to reform the tax system.

The fact that a large element of self-government became established in the management of Germany's insurance funds, thus providing a certain counterweight to the principle of compulsory insurance,[115] doubtless contributed to the effectiveness and growing popularity of the social insurance system. As a result of his Prussian noble origins and activities as a landowner and factory owner, Bismarck, throughout his entire life, remained sceptically aloof from the bureaucracy. This perhaps explains why he believed that a 'drop of democratic oil' was needed to lubricate Germany's social insurance: 'Here, as elsewhere, we have to make things palatable'.[116] Despite the employers' opposition to increased workers' participation, Germany's social insurance system managed to retain its elements of self-government. This was because Bismarck and the higher bureaucracy, who fully shared his views on this point, expected social insurance to bind the workers much closer to the new institutions created, and, hence, to the state itself.

The participation of insured workers in the management of Germany's social insurance system was made easier by reimbursing workers' representatives for loss of earnings while serving on bodies responsible for its administration. The workers' involvement in the system was also seen as an important factor in preventing fake insurance claims[117] and

---

115. *See* Michael Stolleis, 'Die Sozialversicherung Bismarcks: Politisch-institutionelle Bedingungen ihrer Entstehung', in Zacher (ed.), *Bedingungen*, pp. 387–411, esp. p. 406.

116. *See* his remarks to the leader of the Centre Party, Ludwig Windthorst, on 10 May 1884, who criticised him at a parliamentary social gathering on account of his proclaiming the 'right to work' and support for workers' committees in accident insurance, which would only 'increase divisions between employers and employees' and 'benefit the Social Democrats'. Alongside Adolph Wagner's report of this conversation (in Heinrich Ritter von Poschinger [ed.], *Fürst Bismarck und die Parlamentarier*, 2nd edn, 3 vols., Breslau 1894–96, vol. 1, pp. 259–63) a further detailed account also exists by Baden's ambassador in Berlin, Adolf Hermann Freiherr Marschall von Bieberstein on 11 May 1884 (Nachlass Schulz, 32, pp. 30–4).

117. *See* 'Begründung des Entwurfs eines Gesetzes betreffend die Krankenversicherung der Arbeiter', in *Sten. Berichte des Reichstags*, V, II, vol. 5 (Anlagen), no. 14, p. 139, which sets out the argument against large central organisations, and Brentano's 'Alters- und Invalidenversicherung', in *Jahrbücher für Nationalökonomie und Statistik*, Neue Folge, 16 (1888), pp. 35f.

helping keep down costs.

Worker's participation was, however, not simply the result of the government's deliberate policy of promoting the workers' integration into society and a link with older corporative traditions. It was essentially a logical consequence of the method finally adopted for financing the system after the government had failed to implement its original proposals for an accident and an old-age pension insurance financed mainly by the state's contributions. It was also a consequence of the apparently impossible task of trying to eliminate the workers' practical involvement in the various organisations which administered sickness insurance.

In the case of accident insurance, which was exclusively financed by the employers' occupational associations (*Berufsgenossenschaften*), the system of self-management meant that control over insurance lay mainly in the hands of the employers. Together with the Centre Party, they managed to prevent the acceptance of the government's original proposal to create separate workers' committees, charged with conferring with the executive boards of the associations.[118] They feared that corporate bodies representing the workers — earlier examples of which could be found in the journeymen's associations — would lead to even greater class divisions.[119] The place of these separate workers' committees was eventually taken by so-called workers' representatives. These men were not directly elected by the workforce but by its representatives who sat on the boards of the various organisations set up by sickness insurance funds and the miners' provident societies. The only proviso was that funds had to be registered in the same area as the employers' associations and employ at least ten persons from the firms which were members of the respective employers' occupational associations.[120] Whereas local authority sickness funds (*Gemeindekassen*) had no self-government and, therefore, no workers' representatives, the free benefit funds for the sick (*freie Hilfskassen*), which were exclusively financed and administered by the insured, were deliberately excluded from participating in the election of delegates, since they were regarded

118. Gustav Schmoller, *Die soziale Frage, Klassenbildung, Arbeiterfrage, Klassenkampf*, Munich and Leipzig 1918, p. 402; Quandt, *Anfänge*, p. 108 and Karl Diefenbach, 'Die sozialpolitischen Konzeptionen der Parteien und die Sozialgesetzgebung der 1880er Jahre in Deutschland (mit besonderer Berücksichtigung des Unfallversicherungsgesetzes)', MA thesis (MS), Munich 1980, pp. 46, 50, 52.
119. Kleeis, *Geschichte der sozialen Versicherung*, p. 126.
120. Only male fund members qualifying for insurance who had reached the age of majority and were employed in the firm of a member of the employer's occupational associations were eligible for election (para. 42 of the law, *Reichs-Gesetzblatt* 19, p. 88).

as having been infiltrated by the Social Democrats. The same rule discriminating against the free benefit funds was applied later to the election of workers' representatives in the running of disablement and old-age insurance. The workers' representatives in accident insurance had no say in initial decisions on levels of compensation to be paid out or in the administrative decisions of the employers' occupational associations. However, like the employers, they elected two members to the arbitration boards, which were chaired by a state official and which ruled on appeals against the amounts of pension awards. These members had to be consulted on the passage of legal safety regulations. Insured members were also represented at accident inquiries by a single authorised representative and, like the employers, could put forward two temporary appointees as members of the Imperial Insurance Office (Reichsversicherungsamt),[121] whose remit was to supervise the employers' associations and have the final say in appeals against rulings by the arbitration boards.

In the case of the independent local sickness insurance funds (Ortskrankenkassen), which compared with other sickness funds steadily grew in importance between 1885 and 1914,[122] insured workers' representatives were a dominant factor in keeping with their two-thirds share of contributions. Whereas the local authority sickness funds (Gemeindekrankenkassen) came under direct communal control and the sickness funds of individual firms, factories and guilds (Betriebs-, Fabriks- and Innungskrankenkassen) were effectively dominated by the employers, insured workers enjoyed complete control over those benefit funds which were exclusively financed through their own contributions.

Ignoring ten relatively small special funds, Germany's disablement and old-age insurance was organised on the basis of thirty-one regional insurance offices. Although these had representative bodies, made up equally from representatives of the employers and insured members, their management was from the outset dominated by a state-controlled bureaucracy.

121. Ibid., Section IV, 'Workers' Representation', paragraphs 41–5, p. 88f. See also the 'Regulation concerning the election of workers and their elected associated members [Beisitzer] of the court of arbitration as laid down in the accident insurance law of 6 July 1884 and the law extending cover of 28 May 1885', issued by the Reichs-Versicherungsamt on 26 September 1885 (Amtliche Nachrichten des Reichs-Versicherungsamts, 1885, pp. 244–47).

122. In 1885 they had 35.7 per cent and in 1914 62.2 per cent of all members of legally operating sickness funds (percentages calculated on the basis of membership figures at the end of these years in Karl Erich Born, Hansjoachim Henning and Manfred Schick (eds.), Quellensammlung zur Geschichte der deutschen Sozialpolitik 1867 bis 1914, Wiesbaden 1966, pp. 148f.).

The attitude of political and social forces towards workers' insurance

As has already been seen, a great variety of influences and factors lay behind the introduction of Germany's system of social insurance. One must be careful here not to exaggerate Bismarck's role in initiating and promoting his legislation. For example, he regarded his sickness insurance almost as a 'suppositious child'[123] and after his dismissal in 1890 disparagingly described the law on disablement and old age insurance as a 'changeling' foisted on him by 'Parliament and the civil servants'.[124] On the other hand, one should not underestimate his part either, as recent studies have done.

A crass example of this view is J. Tampke's article on 'Bismarck's Social Legislation: A Genuine Break-through?'. Tampke argues that there was nothing particularly new or specifically Bismarckian about Germany's social insurance laws. He sees these more as a continuation of the Prussian tradition, maintaining that in many ways they were anticipated by existing institutions, such as the miner's provident societies, individual firms' welfare arrangements and the proposals of the *Kathedersozialisten* and employers. Furthermore, he argues that the various forms of social insurance, whose importance he denies by, among other things, rightly pointing to its low level of benefits — in fact, the state's entire social policy — failed to prevent a deepening of social divisions in German society. According to this argument, Germany was possibly spared a violent social conflict only because of the outbreak of the First World War.[125] Tampke is certainly right in saying that the general term 'Bismarck's insurance legislation' is misleading, in that it underestimates the part played by other *personae* and influences in the framing and adoption of these laws. The term also identifies Bismarck too closely with the consequences of the legislation. It is worth noting, for instance, that the Chancellor made no mention of social insurance in his memoirs, *Erinnerung und Gedanke*. It is also true to say that the short-term effects of social insurance on the workers' situation and their relationship to the social and political order should not be exaggerated. Even so, his argument is wide of the mark.

124. Bismarck's address to the deputation from Sachsen-Anhalt on 21 April 1895, in Horst Kohl (ed.), *Reden und Ansprachen des Fürsten Bismarck: Historisch-kritische Gesamtausgabe in 14 Bänden*, vol 13 (1890–97), Stuttgart 1905: reprint edn, Aalen 1970, pp. 369–73, esp. p. 372.
125. Jürgen Tampke, 'Bismarck's Social Legislation: A Genuine Breakthrough?' in W. J. Mommsen (ed. in collaboration with Wolfgang Mock),*The Emergence of the Welfare State in Britain and Germany, 1850–1950*, London 1981, pp. 71–83.

Without Bismarck's power and energy, Germany's social insurance legislation would never have come into effect when it did. Its political aims were to complement the repressive anti-Socialist law and win over the worker's loyalty to the state. This, together with the fact that it was originally aimed at the country's industrial workers, (despite Bismarck's occasional pronouncements in favour of greatly extending its scope), all point directly back to the Chancellor. Not least, he directed his efforts towards making his legislation as comprehensive as possible. Apart from unemployment, the plight of widows and orphans[126] and the impoverishment caused by large families, which could only be avoided if burdens were somehow adjusted to individual family circumstances, his insurance laws covered all the fundamental material hazards a citizen might encounter in life. Furthermore, he emphasised the principle of compulsory insurance and, since he utterly rejected the idea of private insurance, strove to organise his on the basis of public law and subject to state supervision without any participation whatsoever by commercial interests.

Bismarck launched the idea of a general insurance law for the Empire (*Reichsversicherungsgesetz*) as early as 1879 in a published circular to the governments of the German federal states on 'Provisions for Regulating the Insurance System'. This gave rise to deep fears among interested parties and liberal circles that the private insurance system might be placed under state control, even though these fears were not actually justified by the wording of the circular. It proposed making 'all branches of life assurance, as well as insurance against accident, fire and agricultural damage (storm and livestock)' subject to new nationally applied regulations.[127] About a year later, Adolph Wagner, one of Germany's leading economists, Professor of Political Science (*Staatswissenschaften*) at Berlin University and co-founder of the Social Policy Association, published his article on 'The State and Insurance'. Thus it was Wagner who intellectually paved the way for Miquel's Prussian tax reforms of the early 1890s[128] which, mainly based on social criteria, introduced a progressive income tax. Now he argued in favour of transferring several important branches of insurance 'from private commercial undertakings to publicly run organisations', governed by

---

126. For ideas considered in these areas in the 1880s, *see* below, p. 88.
127. Bismarck's memorandum of 4 August 1879 on regulating the insurance system, published in no. 237 of the *Deutscher Reichs-Anzeiger und Königlich Preussischer Staats-Anzeiger vom Jahre 1879*, reprinted in *Zeitschrift für die gesammte Staatswissenschaft* 37 (1881), pp. 173–9.
128. *See* Hans Herzfeld, *Johannes von Miquel: Sein Anteil am Ausbau des Reiches bis zur Jahrhundertwende*, vol. 2, Detmold 1938, esp. pp. 212–20.

public law.[129] Wagner also proved to be Bismarck's effective mouthpiece on other occasions. At the latter's suggestion he became the first prominent supporter of the tobacco monopoly for the Empire, which he saw as 'a revenue for the have-nots', during the Reichstag elections of 1881.[130] He justified his initiative in the field of insurance by pointing to the already widespread existence of public control in the transport and communications sector as well as in municipal utilities. He believed that the desired change could be more easily effected on account of 'the proven all-round efficiency of our public administration, embodied above all in the moral and intellectual qualifications of our civil service'. 'In North America, Russia and probably England, too, circumstances are quite different in this respect. In France and Italy they are not so favourable. Only in German Austria are they not much less favourable than here. It is in the German states, therefore, that the best possible practical prospects exist for organising insurance in accordance with public welfare'.[131]

Bismarck, whose rejection of private commercial insurance was influenced by his own negative personal experiences as a landowner and factory owner,[132] not only excluded private insurers on principle from his social insurance. Between 1882 and 1885 he tried in vain to have the Prussian and imperial governments take over fire and storm damage insurance and to exercise at least strict control over livestock insurance and life assurance. Thus the idea of organising major parts of the insurance system in accordance with public welfare already had important antecedents. It was Bismarck himself, however, who, despite fierce opposition from all shades of liberal opinion, nearly caused even his plans regarding social insurance to fail at first, by sticking unconditionally to his principle of excluding private insurers.

Similarly, the way in which accident insurance was organised through the employers' occupational associations, following the failure of plans to administer the system directly through an Imperial Insurance Board, (*Reichsversicherungsanstalt*) was also in line with his own ideas. For example, he said to Theodor Lohmann on 5 October 1883 that:

---

129. Adolph Wagner, 'Der Staat und das Versicherungswesen, Principielle Erörterungen über die Frage der gemeinwirthschaftlichen Organisation dieses wirthschaftlichen Gebiets im Allgemeinen', in *Zeitschrift für die gesammte Staatswissenschaft* 37 (1881), pp. 102–72, esp. p. 106.
130. Tennstedt, 'Vorgeschichte', in *Zeitschrift für Sozialreform* 27 (1981), pp. 685f.
131. Wagner, *Staat und Versicherungswesen*, p. 132.
132. Vogel, *Arbeiterversicherung*, pp. 138f.; Otto Pflanze, '"Sammlungspolitik" 1875 –1886: Kritische Bemerkungen zu einem Modell', in idem (ed. in collaboration with Elisabeth Müller-Luckner), *Innenpolitische Probleme des Bismarck-Reiches*, Munich and Vienna 1983, p. 154–93, esp. pp. 169–73.

accident insurance was of secondary importance to him. The main thing at this stage was, as far as he was concerned, to arrive at a system of corporative associations, to be gradually established for all of Germany's productive classes. This would create the basis for a future representation of the people in place of or alongside the Reichstag and would be an important joint factor in shaping legislation, even if it meant ultimately staging a *coup d'état* to achieve this.[133]

Bismarck's hopes of outmanoeuvring the Reichstag by using the employers' occupational associations did not, however, materialise.

The subsequent development of the employers' associations was cut short by the fact that the original intention of modelling the new disablement and old-age insurance on their system of accident insurance was abandoned as a result of massive opposition from the powerful Central Association of German Industrialists (Centralverband Deutscher Industrieller — CVDI).[134] Instead, it was organised on the basis of regional insurance offices (*Landesversicherungsanstalten*). The CVDI looked upon the employers' occupational associations, created by the accident insurance law, and their newly founded federations as endangering its claim to the sole right of representing industry.

The CVDI's activities provide us with numerous examples of the considerable influence which certain employers' groups were able to exert on the shaping of social insurance.

Certainly, Bismarck's views coincided in many respects with those put forward by big business and heavy industry. Both these groups dominated the CVDI, helped to initiate the first draft of the accident insurance law and gave it their highly effective support. In contrast, the majority of small and medium-sized firms, which still lacked effective representation, and Germany's export industries, adopted a rather reserved attitude.[135] Thus, when the subject came up for discussion at a

133. Lohmann's letter to Wyneken of 5 October 1883, in Rothfels, *Lohmann*, pp. 63f.
134. *See* K. Oldenberg, 'Zur Alters- und Invaliditätsversicherung der Arbeiter', in *Schmollers Jahrbuch*, Neue Folge, 13 (1889), pp. 398–422, esp. pp. 405–10; Hans-Peter Ullmann, 'Industrielle Interessen und die Entstehung der deutschen Sozialversicherung, 1880–1889, in *Historische Zeitschrift* 229 (1979), pp. 574–610, esp. pp. 605–7. R. van der Borght, the Secretary of the Association of Mining Interests (*Verin für die berg- und hüttenmännischen Interessen*) in the district of Aix-la-Chapelle, favoured organising old-age and disablement insurance on an occupational basis: 'Zur Frage der Bewährung der berufsgenossenschaflichen Verwaltung', in *Schmollers Jahrbuch* 13 (1889), pp. 323–56. The article gives a good account of the work of the employers' occupational associations and their growth in the first few years following the accident insurance law.
135. For the views of employers and the influence of industry, *see* Ullmann, 'Industrielle Interessen', pp. 584–95; Vogel, *Arbeiterversicherung*, pp. 34–46; Monika Breger, *Die Haltung der industriellen Unternehmer zur staatlichen Sozialpolitik in den Jahren, 1878–1891*, Frankfurt 1982, pp. 83ff. Breger criticises Ullmann for taking Bismarck's intentions

meeting of the Prussian Cabinet on 28 August 1880, during which Bismarck first mentioned his plans for an accident insurance,[136] he referred to a memorandum of 30 April 1880[137] from the Bochum industrialist, Louis Baare. Rather than extend the scope of accident liability, as industry feared would happen, Baare thought that the idea of an accident insurance under state supervision and administered by the state 'merited serious consideration'. It was this memorandum which served as the basis for Theodor Lohmann's first draft of the accident insurance law. This, together with a rival draft, submitted by Baare after consultation with leading figures and representative organisations from Rhenish and Westphalian industry, in turn formed the basis for the government's proposed bill.[138] But there were other cases, too, where the employers' interests found a sympathetic spokesman in Bismarck; for example, when a major though unsuccessful effort was made to reduce the burdensome costs of accident insurance to the employers through government subsidies.[139] It could also be seen in the

and plans too much as his yardstick, and judging industry's attitude to social insurance in too negative a light. He is also criticised for not differentiating adequately between acceptance or rejection of specific aspects on the one hand and the employer's underlying attitude towards the state's social insurance on the other hand, and for not really doing justice to 'the complex discussion on social insurance, which, to some extent, ran across the lines of specific employer groupings or branches of industry' (pp. 223f.) when reviewing the motives of opponents and supporters of legislation. These criticisms seem somewhat exaggerated, since her own work, which mainly deals with the policy positions taken by various interest groups, essentially confirms Ullmann's conclusions. R. Baron's argument that the introduction of social insurance can be seen as a strategy by the employers to overcome 'a lack of competitiveness shown by national capital towards competitors in the world market' ('Weder Zuckerbrot noch Peitsche. Historische Konstitutions- bedingungen des Sozialstaats in Deutschland', in *Gesellschaft: Beiträge zur Marxschen Theorie* 12 [Frankfurt 1979], pp. 13–55, esp. p. 49) is not borne out by the sources and contradicts the findings of Ullmann and Breger that those branches of industry especially dependent on exports were negative or at least very reserved towards social insurance.

136. Minutes of Prussian State Ministry meeting on 28 August 1880, Geheimes Staats- archiv, Berlin-Dahlem, Rep. 90, vol. 1243.

137. Promemoria, betr. Versicherung der Arbeiter gegen Unfall und Beschädigung während der Arbeit beim Bergbau, bei der Industrie und sonstiger Gewerbetätigkeit sowie bei der Landwirtschaft.' An extensive summary of the content of this memorandum and Baare's record of his conversation with Bismarck about his memorandum on 18 September 1880 is published in Henry Axel Bueck, *Der Centralverband deutscher Industrieller, 1876–1901*, 3 vols., Berlin 1902–05, vol. 2, pp. 79–84.

138. *See* Ullmann, 'Industrielle Interessen', in *Historische Zeitschrift*, pp. 597f.; Rothfels, *Lohmann*, pp. 51–3; Vogel, Arbeiterversicherung, pp. 39–45; Wickenhagen, *Geschichte der gewerblichen Unfallversicherung*, pp. 32–34; Bueck, *Centralverband*, vol. 2, pp. 85–7. Text of the draft in nos. 37 and 38 of the magazine *Concordia* of 3 November 1880 and the *Annalen des Deutschen Reichs* 1880, pp. 69ff.

139. Baare proposed in his memorandum that employers, workers and local authorities

method of financing accident insurance, not by contributions and by creating a capital fund, but by the much cheaper method of apportioning actual annual costs to the members of the employers' occupational associations. This financial arrangement ran counter to all known insurance practice at the time. Other examples were the refusal to include occupational illnesses and the way in which the costs of medical treatment and upkeep of injured workers during the first thirteen weeks following an accident were shifted to sickness insurance which was two-thirds financed by the workers themselves.[140]

During these years the Chancellor tended to support the interests of the employers in other areas as well. For example, he blocked the further growth of factory inspection and protective labour legislation, which a majority of Reichstag deputies were prepared to support in the 1880s.[141] Thus, up until 1891, in contrast to Austria,[142] Germany remained at a level of development in this field which fell 'far behind the point already reached in 1847 by Britain's factory and trade union legislation' and 'state-sanctioned system of workers' self-help organisations'.[143] Behind Bismarck's obstructionist policy lay his constant efforts to preserve the competitiveness of the German economy at all costs. A further reason for rejecting any control by state officials over private industry was his belief that this would totally undermine the employers' authority. Among his motives for rejecting a policy aimed at providing workers' protection, we find him using astonishing arguments such as the suggestion that in restricting the workers' freedom to decide on his own employment and that of his wife and children, one was not only prejudicing his income but also curtailing his legal right as head of the family.[144]

---

should each pay a third share of the insurance premium. In Baare's draft for the law the employer's share was increased to a half and the local authority's and worker's shares each reduced to a quarter.

140. According to Bödiker's calculations in his 'Unfall-Statistik des Deutschen Reichs, 1881', in *Statistik des deutschen Reichs, Ergänzungsheft*, vol. 53, pp. 20f., the costs of accidents to the sickness insurance funds made up about 16.5 per cent of the entire costs of accidents, of which the workers had to finance 11 per cent through their average share of two-thirds of the contributions to the sickness funds.

141. Vogel, *Arbeiterversicherung*, pp. 135ff., 161ff., 168f.; Bismarck, *Gesammelte Werke*, vol. 15, Berlin 1932 pp. 489f. *See also* Rottenburg's letter written at Bismarck's request to the Secretary of State at the Imperial Office of the Interior, Karl Heinrich von Boetticher on 28 October 1885, which rejected the idea of making Sunday a compulsory day of rest, as moved for by the Centre Party leader, Windthorst, and seconded by the Free Conservative, Stumm: 'His Highness believes the main difficulty can be summed up in the question: how are the workers' lost wages to be made up?' (Nachlass Boetticher, Bundesarchiv Koblenz, no. 46).

142. *See* above, p. 11.

143. Rosenberg, *Grosse Depression und Bismarckzeit*, p. 213.

The delay in providing workers' protection must be seen as a victory for heavy industry, which was due solely to the fact that Bismarck shared its views. After the Reichstag had turned down the first accident insurance bill, the employers became increasingly critical of social insurance. At the same time, they still tried to bring their influence to bear by actively participating in the shaping of its terms. They tried to reduce the financial costs for industry and attempted to reverse the growth of the workers' influence within the self-managed insurance funds, although their efforts were largely unsuccessful. They looked for better ways of creating a disciplined workforce. In many cases their major demands were never realised. The sickness funds run by individual firms (*Betriebskrankenkassen*), which could easily be used as an instrument of control over the workers, were never made compulsory. In the case of the law on disablement and old-age insurance, the initially proposed government subsidy of a one-third share of contributions was intended to cover administrative costs as well, otherwise, the industrialists argued, the 'bureaucrats in charge' would become too 'well-disposed towards the workers' and would function 'too much in the interests of poor relief, whose costs were to be reduced'.[145] Again the employers' hopes were not realised. In view of the visibly increasing growth in opposition among industrialists to the terms of the laws, as determined by the majority of Reichstag deputies, but not to the idea of state social insurance, the subsequent statement by the CVDI's General Secretary, Henry Axel Bueck, that German industry was one of 'the most enthusiastic and effective of supporters' behind workers' insurance[146] must be seen as a later attempt to camouflage the employers' actual highly ambivalent attitude. In reality, industry widely shared Bismarck's view of social policy as a means of combating the socialists. Because of this, the industrialists began increasingly to turn away from social policy as soon as it became clear that their hopes of containing the growth of the Social Democrats and the trade union movement were not being realised.

The CVDI and the employers who supported Bismarck shared his hopes of solving the problems posed by the workers' autonomous organisations and their demands for political and social emancipation, by applying a policy of repression combined with paternalistic welfare measures. Important sections of the higher civil service, however, had their own ideas. Theodor Lohmann, who was initially Bismarck's

144. Bismarck, *Gesammelte Werke*, vol. 15, p. 489.
145. Oldenburg, 'Alters- und Invaliditätsversicherung', in *Schmollers Jahrbuch*, Neue Folge, 13 (1889), p. 407.
146. Bueck, *Centralverband*, vol. 2, p. 792.

closest advisor on social policy, was one of them. He played a vital part in framing Germany's sickness insurance law,[147] before he and Bismarck quarrelled on questions of fundamental principle in September 1883. Lohmann not only rejected the idea of an Imperial Insurance Board and supplementary government funding for accident insurance, but also the creation of compulsory employers' occupational associations and covering the costs of the scheme by apportioning actual annual costs to the members of these associations instead of creating a capital fund for the discharging of obligations. As a result of his disagreement with Bismarck, he was effectively excluded from any further participation in shaping the government's social policy during Bismarck's chancellorship.[148]

Lohmann favoured the idea of a 'conciliatory policy towards the workers',[149] based on Christian and humanitarian beliefs and having nothing in common with the ideas of *laissez-faire* liberalism. To some extent, he carried on the tradition of old Prussian conservatism, but, at the same time, in seeking to create really viable and functioning benefit societies, capable of their own initiatives in attempting to solve the social problem, he consciously leaned towards the English model of trade unions and Friendly Societies, which he had studied intensively. Such organisations would not come about as a result of compulsory measures but only by being indirectly encouraged by the state.[150] In particular, his ideas, which, in contrast to Bismarck's state socialism, stressed the notion of self-help, were meant to educate the workers towards an awareness of 'personal responsibility. . .and their own share of responsibility for the common good' via organisations they themselves had created.[151] Unlike Bismarck, therefore, Lohmann regarded it as absolutely essential that the workers should participate in the system through paying their own share of contributions. He tried to satisfy the workers' aspirations for equal rights, calling for greater freedom of combination, the creation of societies based on occupational membership to take on practical tasks, the setting up of workers' committees and workers' insurance funds, and, finally, a substantial increase in workers' protection and factory inspection.[152] After Bis-

---

147. Rothfels, *Lohmann*, pp. 54–6, 82.
148. Ibid., pp. 52–64.
149. Ibid., p. 38.
150. Ibid., pp. 63–7; Vogel, *Arbeiterversicherung*, pp. 92–101; Tennstedt, *Soziale Selbstverwaltung*, pp. 39f.
151. Rothfels, *Lohmann*, p. 45.
152. Lohmann was regarded as an expert in this field after the Prussian Minister of Trade commissioned him to publish a collection of factory laws from Germany, Alsace-Lorraine, Austria, Hungary, Switzerland, France, the Netherlands, Den-

marck's fall from power in 1890 he was to be instrumental in increasing the number of factory inspectors and extending their area of responsibility. Thus Lohmann anticipated several of the fundamental ideas on which the later welfare state with its participation of workers' organisations and idea of a 'social partnership' was based. On the other hand, one should not overlook the fact that his ideas were also ultimately aimed at strengthening Germany's existing monarchical state against pressures from below and containing the danger posed by the Social Democrats. Nor should one forget that, as can be seen from the low membership figures for independent benefit societies before the state's introduction of sickness insurance, a truly comprehensive system of social security taking in the vast majority of citizens and not just an élite of workers was simply not possible without some element of compulsion.[153]

Apart from Lohmann, three other senior members of the state bureaucracy played a significant part in shaping Germany's insurance laws. The first was Tonio Bödiker. In 1881 Bismarck appointed him to the Imperial Office of the Interior (Reichsamt des Innern), where he worked on commercial and insurance affairs before becoming the first president of the new Imperial Insurance Office from 1884 to 1897, a post in which he was able to wield considerable influence. The second was von Woedtke, who as full-time advisor at the Imperial Office of the Interior took charge of its social policy section between 1886 and 1901. It was he who was largely responsible for the draft of the disablement and old-age insurance law.[154] The third was Freiherr von Gamp, who was chief advisor to the Prussian Ministry of Trade, which Bismarck took direct charge of in the late summer of 1880. From December 1883 onwards, he was also attached to the Imperial Office of the Interior. On the level of heads of department, there was Karl

---

mark and Sweden in 1878: Die *Fabriken-Gesetzgebung der Staaten des europäischen Kontinents*, Berlin 1878. Britain's workers' protection measures, which Lohmann included in his comparative introduction, had already been published in German in 1876. He took the view that 'the steadily growing sense of community and interdependence of today's civilised peoples in the economic sphere and the great importance of factory legislation for the development of major branches of industry operating in the world market (...), meant that it might not be impossible to make the growth of factory legislation the subject of international agreements and also gradually develop international law in this field' (p. 7). *See also* his outright approval of extensive factory legislation.

153. For Lohmann's predominantly critical attitude towards the idea of compulsory insurance, *see* Rothfels, *Lohmann*, pp. 70–6.

154. He was also responsible for the quasi-official commentary on the law: Erich von Woedtke, *Das Reichsgesetz betr. Invaliditäts- und Altersversicherung vom 22. Juni 1889*, Berlin 1889.

Heinrich von Boetticher,[155] who, as Secretary of State in charge of the Imperial Office of the Interior played a major part in drafting the terms of the disablement and old-age insurance law and promoting its successful passage. Boetticher was also Bismarck's deputy as head of the Prussian Ministry of Trade. Less independent than Lohmann, these subordinates of Bismarck were able to influence the details of social insurance legislation to an extent which should not be underestimated. It would be wrong, however, to see in the German civil service, much influenced though it was by the ideas of the *Kathedersozialisten*, the 'actual vehicle for social insurance',[156] as Walter Vogel does in an account of the subject which ignores the importance of parliamentary discussions, while overestimating the decision-making within the executive.

The role of the Reichstag was, in fact, far more important for the final shape taken by Germany's social insurance legislation. Of all the country's political parties, it was mainly the Centre, in its role as both 'partner and opposition'[157] to Bismarck which exerted considerable influence on social insurance legislation. Up to the so-called 'Cartel' election of 1887, which led to a Reichstag majority of the two conservative parties and the National Liberals, its support proved indispensable in providing the government with a parliamentary majority. There was, however, no unity of views on social policy within the Centre Party itself. With the adoption of Galen's motion in March 1877, the Centre embarked on its first notable initiative towards improving workers' protection. This decision was made in the light of the Social Democrats' election successes in January 1877 and the challenge to official Centre candidates from Catholic Christian-Social candidates in Aix-la-Chapelle and Essen. Throughout the 1880s the main features of its social policy programme won the support of most Reichstag deputies.[158] It consistently and unanimously demanded a legal ban on Sunday work, together with either a ban or restrictions on the use of female and child labour. In 1882 it also called for the first time for

155. Vogel, *Arbeiterversicherung*, pp. 102–14.
156. Ibid., p. 117.
157. Heinrich Heffter, 'Bismarcks Sozialpolitik', in *Archiv für Sozialgeschichte* 3 (1963), pp. 141–56, esp. p. 152.
158. In addition to extending workers' protection, 'introducing industrial arbitration courts in which the workers' freely elected representatives would participate', Galen's motion also proposed revising the law on employer's liability, and a policy to benefit the artisans of the traditional middle class 'by limiting *laissez-faire*, regulating the relationship of apprentices and journeymen to master craftsmen' and 'encouraging corporative associations' (*Sten. Berichte des Reichstags*, III, I, vol. 3, document no. 74, p. 274).

statutary maximum working-hours for adult male workers. However, on the question of social insurance a number of differing views existed within the Party, the origins of which stemmed from conflicting ideas on the state's role in society. For example, Freiherr von Hertling, one of the Party's most prominent spokesmen on social policy, wanted the state to limit its activities to the legal sphere and joined the Centre Party's leader, Ludwig Windthorst, in sharply condemning state socialism in any form.[159] On the other hand, other important Centre politicians, like Franz Hitze, and even Freiherr von Franckenstein and Peter Reichensperger, argued that the state's responsibility for the spiritual and social welfare of its citizens should be recognised, at least in a subsidiary capacity to institutions like the family, the community, estates, guilds and other corporative bodies. Thus Reichensperger aroused Windthorst's anger when during the deliberations on disablement and old-age insurance he declared before the Reichstag on 4 April 1889 that the view of the state restricting itself entirely to the task of upholding the laws of the land and having no other function than 'taking care of the law' had been superseded. 'The state forms the organisational union of the people for the care of all physical and spiritual possessions; and this is what we intend to bring about'.[160]

There were not only differing ideas within the Party on the role of the state in society. There were also arguments about the extent to which the Centre should be identified with a corporative conception of the state, something Windhorst tended to view with some scepticism.

The Centre eventually had the final say in deciding the form taken by Germany's accident insurance law. It supported the principle of compulsory insurance, which the Left-liberals rejected, and denounced the idea of commercial insurance, while at the same time criticising government subvention and the planned setting up of an Imperial Insurance Board as products of a centralised bureaucracy. Bismarck compromised with the Party in abandoning the Board and creating employers' occupational associations to run the insurance.[161] The

159. For Windthorst's attitude to the Social Democrats and his views on social policy, *see* the important study by Margaret Lavinia Anderson, *Windthorst: A political Biography*, Oxford 1981, esp. pp. 207–12, 375–8.

160. *Sten. Berichte des Reichstags*, VII, IV, vol. 2, p. 1259. For Windthorst's reaction, *see* Anderson, *Windthorst*, p. 377. For the different views on the state within the Centre Party as it affected social policy, *see also* Karl Heidemann, *Bismarcks Sozialpolitik und die Zentrumspartei, 1881–1884*, Phil. diss., Göttingen 1929, Herford 1930, esp. pp. 25f., 71–5; Theo Wattler, *Sozialpolitik der Zentrumsfraktion zwischen 1887 un 1889 unter besonderer Berüksichtigung interner Auseinandersetzungen und Entwicklungsprozesse*, Phil. diss., Cologne 1978, esp. pp. 277–294.

161. Thus, in a conversation with Hertling on 7 April 1883 concerning the delay —

majority of the Centre Party, however, voted against the law on disablement and old-age insurance, since it was seen as a means of strengthening the power of the state *vis-à-vis* the workers. The main criticisms were directed against the government's proposed supplementary funding and the bureaucratic form of organisation adopted which ignored the Party's plea for the scheme to be administered by occupational associations. There was also criticism of the fact that the agricultural workers were to be included under the terms of the law. Despite such reservations, the law narrowly succeeded in being passed by the Reichstag, thanks to a minority of fifteen Centre deputies who voted for it.

Alongside the Centre Party, it was mainly the National Liberals who succeeded in having their views accepted on several important points. They initially wanted to see private insurance companies participating in the system. In the case of accident insurance they successfully opposed the setting up of an Imperial Insurance Board and government funding and were instrumental in bringing about a system of earnings-related contributions and pensions in disablement and old-age insurance.[162]

Bearing in mind that, apart from the creation of a new Civil Law Code, the social insurance laws were by far the most significant piece of legislation to be passed in the German Empire during the period from the late 1870s up to the First World War, one could say that, on balance, the Reichstag's influence on the emergence of Germany's social insurance system,[163] was probably greater than the contribution of the House of Commons to the expansion of Britain's state welfare

which Bismarck disapproved of — in the parliamentary debates on the second draft bill on accident insurance, the Chancellor mentioned that the draft providing for a corporative form of organisation of the insurance was framed 'directly to accommodate the Centre's wishes'. For a record of the conversation made immediately afterwards, *see* Georg von Hertling, *Erinnerungen aus meinem Leben*, 2 vols., Munich 1919/20, vol. 2, pp. 24–41, esp. p. 25.

162. For the attitude of the political parties on the individual problems raised by Germany's social welfare legislation, *see* Heidemann, *Bismarcks Sozialpolitik*; Quandt, *Anfänge*; Diefenbach, *Sozialpolitische Konzeptionen*; Wattler, *Sozialpolitik*; Rudi Müller, 'Die Stellung der liberalen Parteien im Deutschen Reichstag zu den Fragen der Arbeiterversicherung und des Arbeiterschutzes bis zum Ausgang des 19. Jahrhunderts', Phil. diss. (MS) Jena 1952. For the Social Democratic Party's position, *see* the studies by Wolff, Verhein and Benöhr cited below in notes 173 and 201.

163. On the Reichstag's considerable influence in shaping Germany's social insurance legislation, *see also* Hans-Peter Benöhr's study, 'Verfassungsfragen der Sozialversicherung nach den Reichstagsverhandlungen von 1881 bis 1889', in *Zeitschrift der Savigny-Stiftung für Rechtsgeschichte, Germ. Abteilung* 97 (1980), pp. 94–163, esp. pp. 99–108. Benöhr uses the Reichstag proceedings as his main source for an analysis of the legislative process and measurement of political power.

measures in the decade before 1914.

As Florian Tennstedt has recently and quite rightly pointed out, German historians have tended to pay more attention to the 'emancipatory political processes' of labour organisations, rather than 'the various problems of guaranteeing a regular level of subsistence'.[164] But, alongside strengthening their position *vis à vis* the employers, attempting to improve the level of social security was, in fact, always a main aim of the German workers' self-help organisations, which even took priority over the struggle for political emancipation. The journeymen's social welfare organisations, as distinct from those of the guilds, which embraced both masters and journeymen, could look back on a centuries-old tradition. Despite increasing state supervision, which attempted to limit their general representation of interests in the pre-1848 period to the care of individual cases of hardship, the journeymen's benefit funds gave their membership social cohesion, as did those of the factory workers at a later stage. These journeymen's organisations served as centres of communication and rallying points for political action, strikes and social protests. They, therefore, constituted the 'germ-cells' of the emergent German labour movement and its early forms of organisation.[165] Since they embraced a broader clientèle than the trade unions and the SPD, they served to make the workers familiar with the goals of the trade union and the socialist movement, while helping to recruit new members for them. At the same time, they transmitted their experience in creating common organisations, promoting collective interests and practising the principle of self-management, and, insofar as their welfare benefits offered members a certain degree of protection against complete impoverishment, they also contributed to the stability of the workers' political and trade union organisations.

During the 1850s period of reaction sickness benefit funds had emerged as the only legally permissible workers' and journeymen's organisations. It was thanks to their continuity in terms of personnel and ideals going back to the first nation-wide movement of skilled workers' associations during the 1848–49 Revolution that they were subsequently able to play a fundamental part in rebuilding the German trade union movement from about 1865 onwards.[166] It was they, above all, who, in the early days of the Social Democratic Party and the trade unions, recruited those skilled workers and journeymen who came to

164. Tennstedt, *Vom Proleten zum Industriearbeiter*, p. 16.
165. *See* Frevert, *Krankheit als politisches Problem*, p. 270.
166. Ibid., esp. pp. 314ff.

form their main support. In supporting the emergent labour movement, they were able to draw on pre-industrial traditions of organising
self-help on the basis of separate trades. In contrast, institutions
promoting social security among unskilled workers in industry or
trade, who had often been previously employed in the agricultural
sector, did not come about on any major scale until the sickness
insurance law of 1883 set up compulsory sickness funds (*Zwangskassen*).
These had the unintended long-term side-effect of breaking down the
very strong divisions which still existed within the independent benefit
funds betweek skilled and unskilled workers and workers of different
trades. In so doing, they helped strengthen the sense of class solidarity
among all workers and facilitated the recruitment of unskilled workers
for the Socialist Party and the trade unions.

Having still not evolved their own concept for a state welfare system,
the Social Democrats could hardly be in a position at first to influence
directly the concrete form taken by the insurance laws of the 1880s.
True, the appeal of 27 June 1848, signed by Stephan Born and others,
calling on all artisans' and workers' associations to convene a 'workers'
Parliament' in Berlin did say that 'state welfare for all destitute and
disabled workers would be among the topics debated'.[167] The Gotha
Programme of 1875 also contained the demand for an 'effective liability
law' and 'complete self-management for all workers' benefit and relief
funds'.[168] But the setting up of pension funds under state supervision
(*Altersversorgungskassen*) was rejected in 1868 at the fifth Congress of
Workers' Associations in Nuremberg, on the grounds that 'leaving the
management of a general pension fund to the employers would result in
the workers unconsciously acquiring a conservative interest in the
existing political order, in which they cannot place any confidence.
Trade unions were seen as the proper vehicles for such and similar
benefit funds.[169] The main thrust of the Social Democrats' demands for
social policy reforms was directed towards workers' protection. As
early as April 1877 they submitted a detailed draft bill to the Reichstag,
which later underwent major changes. Among other things, it envis-
aged a maximum working day of ten hours for male workers, a ban on
night and Sunday work with a few permitted exceptions, and far-
reaching safety regulations for women and juvenile workers.[170]

167. Kleeis, *Geschichte der sozialen Versicherung*, p. 55.
168. Text of programme in Susanne Miller and Karl Potthoff, *A History of German Social
     Democracy: From 1848 to the Present*, Leamington Spa, Heidelberg, New York 1986.
169. Wilhelm Schröder(ed.), *Handbuch der sozialdemokratischen Parteitage von 1863 bis 1909*,
     Munich 1910, p. 48.
170. *See* Max Schippel (ed.), *Sozialdemokratisches Reichstags-Handbuch: Ein Führer durch die*

The Social Democrats rejected the social insurance laws not only because of their obvious link with the repressive policy embodied in the anti-Socialist law but also because no provision was made for large sections of the population. Other grounds were the inadequacy of benefits, the insufficient degree of workers' participation in managing the funds and the limited role of the state. Unlike the Centre and the Liberals, the Social Democratic Party supported the idea of an Imperial Insurance Board for administering insurance and substantial government contributions to fund both accident and disablement insurance.[171] Many Social Democrats also feared that accumulated pension funds might be misused for purposes other than insurance.[172] They further criticised the fact that the independent benefit funds were excluded from participating in the management of both accident and disablement and old-age insurance and objected to the inclusion of elements designed to exercise social control over the workers.[173]

The Social Democrats launched a campaign against the use of receipt books, originally intended to act as proof of payment for the disablement and old-age insurance. The campaign eventually proved successful in that these books, which employers could easily have used as camouflaged work-records to blacklist 'undesirable' workers,[174] were replaced by a card-voucher system. Finally, with its criticism that the

---

Zeit- und Streitfragen der Reichsgesetzgebung, Berlin 1902, pp. 72ff.

171. The Erfurt programme finally called on 'the government to take over the running of the entire system of workers' insurance, but also to provide for a major degree of workers' participation in its administration' (Potthoff, *Sozialdemokratie*, p. 181).

172. Grillenberger feared that the huge sums of accrued funds would be used to benefit landowners by lowering mortgage interest rates (speech in Reichstag on 6 December 1888, in *Sten. Berichte des Reichstags*, VII, IV, vol. 1, p. 159).

173. On the Social Democrats' position, *see* Hertha Wolff, *Die Stellung der Sozialdemokratie zur deutschen Arbeiterversicherungsgesetzgebung von ihrer Entstehung bis zur Reichsversicherungsordnung*, Rechts- und staatswiss. diss., Freiburg 1933; Quandt, *Anfänge*; Diefenbach, *Sozialpolitische Konzeptionen*, esp. pp. 22–4, 34–6, 42f., 53–6, 64f., 75–8, 93–7, 107–11, and Hans-Peter Benöhr, 'Soziale Frage, Sozialversicherung und Sozialdemokratische Reichstagsfraktion (1881–1889)', in *Zeitschrift der Savigny-Stiftung für Rechtsgeschichte, Germ. Abteilung*, 98 (1981), pp. 95–156, esp. pp. 134–56.

174. The Reichstag received 3,287 petitions concerning the draft bill on disablement and old-age insurance. Of these, 2,142 objected to the proposed system of receipt books, while 1,004 supported the idea of independent funds (*see* the figures supplied by the Commission's reporter, Freiherr von Manteuffel, on 24 May 1889, *Sten. Berichte des Reichstags*, VII, IV, vol. 3, p. 1997). Social Democratic fears are revealed in Grillenberger's speech, in ibid., vol. 1, pp. 159f; August Bebel, 'Die Tätigkeit des Deutschen Reichstags von 1887–1889', in *Die Sozialdemokratie im Deutschen Reichstag, Tätigkeitsberichte und Wahlaufrufe in den Jahren 1871 bis 1893*, Berlin 1909, pp. 285–418, esp. pp.386–8. For the Social Democrats' attitude to the introduction of disablement and old-age-pensions insurance, *see also* Gudrun Hofmann, 'Die deutsche Sozialdemokratie und die Sozialreformen von 1889: Das Ringen der Sozialistischen Arbeiterpartei Deutschlands um die Verbesserung des Entwurfs eines

new law was a mere continuation of the old system of poor relief, rejected by the Party and industrial workers alike,[175] the costs of which would be partly shifted to the workers through their contribution payments, the Party's spokesmen could quote a whole variety of official government statements on the subject, as mentioned earlier.[176]

Despite its opposition, the Party was intensively involved in the Reichstag's detailed legislative work. The Social Democrats also, taking up a careless remark made by Bismarck in the Reichstag on 26 May 1884,[177] justifiably claimed that social reforms would never have come about at all had it not been for them.[178] This helps explain why the much-heard demand that the workers show their grateful appreciation of the state's welfare measures by giving up their political opposition and affirming their loyalty to the monarchy had so little effect.

Although intended to undermine the position of the Social Democrats and the socialist trade unions, the insurance laws of the 1880s had the opposite effect in that they helped strengthen the workers' organisations and improved their scope for agitation. Even before the anti-Socialist law was announced, many trade unions had tried to have their

---

Alters- und Invaliditätsversicherungsgesetzes', in *Zeitschrift für Geschichtswissenschaft* 30 (1982), pp. 511–23.

175. According to the 'manifesto of the Social Democratic parliamentary party for the first Reichstag election during the term of the anti-Socialist law (27 October 1881)', the government's proposed measures would simply result in a 'police and bureaucratic regulation of part of the system of poor relief' (text of manifesto in *Die Sozialdemokratie im Deutschen Reichstag*, pp. 187–217, esp. p. 201).

176. *See* above, pp. 41–48.

177. 'Social Democracy is what it is — always a continual, major sign and warning to the propertied classes that not everything is as it should be; that an attempt can be made to improve things, and in this respect, opposition is . . . indeed exceptionally useful. If there were no Social Democrats, and if so many people didn't fear them, the moderate advances we have made so far in terms of social reform would still not have materialised. (Shouts of 'hear! hear!' from the Social Democrat benches.) And in this respect, fear of Social Democracy in those who otherwise have no feelings, for their poor fellow-citizens, is a really useful thing. (Shouts of 'Bravo!' from the Social Democrats.) You see, on one point we do agree. (Laughter.)' [*Sten. Berichte des Reichstags*, VI, I, vol. 1, p. 25.]

178. *See* for example, Bebel's speech to the Party conference in St Gallen in 1887 (*Verhandlungen des Parteitags der deutschen Sozialdemokratie in St Gallen. Abgehalten vom 2. bis 6. Oktober 1887* Hottingen-Zurich 1888, p. 13) and Bebel's 'Die Tätigkeit des Deutschen Reichstags von 1887–1889', in *Die Sozialdemokratie im Deutschen Reichstag*, p. 285. Well before Bismarck's speech of 26 May 1884, Bebel had made a speech on 4 April 1881, which was much-praised by Marx and Engels, in which he argued that the official explanation for the first draft bill on accident insurance, which defended it as a positive measure to combat the Social Democrats, was proof that his party was the actual reason for the bill's existence (August Bebel, *Aus meinem Leben*, 3 vols., Berlin 1946, vol. 3, pp. 147f.; Werner Blumenberg (ed.), *August Bebels Briefwechsel mit Friedrich Engels*, The Hague 1965, Engel's letter to Bebel of 22 April 1881, pp. 109f.).

benefit funds officially registered. Following its introduction, however, the majority of benefit funds, like the SPD's party organisation and almost all the free trade unions, were immediately dissolved and the remainder placed under close state supervision.

Between 1879 and 1884, however, no fewer than twenty-seven central benefit funds (*Zentralkassen*) were set up, at first locally and later on a national basis. According to the Berlin Chief of Police, these central funds were 'almost all subject to Social Democratic influences', but could not be declared illegal under the terms of the anti-Socialist law, 'since it could not be proved that they were involved in political agitation according to the letter of the law'.[179] In preserving or setting up their own funds, the trade unions also took advantage of the fact that the authorities in the separate federal states applied different standards when enforcing the law. This explains why in the years before 1890 the city of Hamburg became the centre of the German trade union movement. From the outset, central benefit funds were able to operate there legally. The relatively liberal environment offered by the old free Hanseatic city induced more and more trade unions to make it the headquarters of their funds.[180]

Despite many misgivings, the independent benefit funds, of which the trade union central benefit funds were a variant, were finally allowed to operate as special sickness funds (*Ersatzkassen*) under the sickness insurance law of 1883. These funds allowed the Social Democrats to influence the workers via legally permitted organisations and in many ways acted as a substitute for their own outlawed party organisation. They were especially useful in providing a starting point for reconstructing the central associations of the free trade unions (*Zentralverbände*), a task already begun in the early 1880s.[181] The Social

179. Letter of 4 September 1886 from the Berlin Chief of Police, Freiherr von Richthofen to the Prussian Minister of the Interior, von Puttkamer, in Rudolf Knack and Wolfgang Schröder, 'Gewerkschaftliche Zentralverbände, freie Hilfskassen und die Arbeiterpresse unter dem Sozialistengesetz. Die Berichte des Berliner Polizeipräsidenten vom 4. September 1886 und 28. Mai 1888', in *Jahrbuch für Geschichte*, 22 (1981), pp. 351–481.

180. Stollberg, 'Die gewerkschaftlichen zentralisierten Hilfskassen', in *Zeitschrift für Sozialreform* 29 (1983), pp. 346f.

181. *See* Prussian Minister of the Interior's decree to the administrative districts of 27 November 1883, Hauptstaatsarchiv Düsseldorf, Regierung Düsseldorf 30430 I, folio 65; rough draft of the Düsseldorf administrative district's half-yearly report of 22 April 1884, to the Prussian Ministry of the Interior on the state of the Social Democratic movement, ibid., folio 119–24; report, dated 17 April 1884, concerning a gathering of carpenters attended by the police, Regierung Düsseldorf 8860, folio 48f. On government supervision of the *Hilfskassen*, *see also* Berlin Chief of Police, von Madai, to the Prussian Minister of the Interior, on 23 October, 1884, Staatsarchiv Münster, Oberpräsidium Münster 2693 I, folio 254f.

Democrats made a point of encouraging membership of these organisations rather than the compulsory funds. Thus, in 1884, August Bebel, Germany's most important Socialist leader during the pre-1914 period, wrote that the registered funds in conjunction with the trade unions were the only organisations 'which an ambitious and independently minded worker, seeking the maximum guarantee of his rights and freedom of movement, can and may — indeed, must — join'. The independence of the sickness funds was 'a question of survival' for the local and central trade union movement.[182]

Class-conscious socialist workers preferred to join the workers' own self-managed benefit funds on the grounds that they were independent working-class organisations operating in place of the Social Democratic Party and the free trade unions. But there was an additional factor. These funds often did not reimburse the costs of medical treatment but paid out higher sickness benefits instead.[183] As a result, they highly suited the needs of skilled male workers who were young, single and in good health. They tended to insure only 'good risk' applicants, demanding the production of health certificates and excluding on principle older workers and the chronically sick.[184] Despite their relatively low contribution payments and the absence of employers' contributions, which made workers joining these funds especially attractive to employers of small and medium-sized firms, they paid out relatively generous benefits. Because of their link with the Social Democrats and the socialist free trade unions, as well as their socially selective membership, these benefit funds came increasingly under attack from the authorities and the compulsory sickness funds. The workers' funds reduced the latter's potential scope for growth and also forced them to take on a disproportionate share of 'bad risks' as a result of the formers' strict selective vetting. After a strong upward surge in membership — the figure rose from about 60,000 at the end of 1880 to 875,000 at the end of 1885[185] — the funds lost some of their attraction for members following the introduction of new administrative measures and judicial decisions. Finally, in 1892, a change in the law forced the funds to

182. August Bebel, *Wie verhalten sich die Arbeiter gegenüber dem neuen Kranken-Versicherungsgesetz?*, Nuremberg 1884, pp. 14f.

183. In the case of the registered benefit funds (*eingeschriebene Hilfskassen*), the costs of sickness benefits amounted to 84.25 per cent of total costs in 1885 and 52.06 per cent in 1911. The corresponding figures for the local authority sickness funds (*Gemeindekrankenkassen*) were 30.08 per cent and 30.44 per cent (Tennstedt, *Soziale Selbstverwaltung*, pp. 37f.).

184. Stollberg, 'Die gewerkschaftsnahen zentralisierten Hilfskassen', in *Zeitschrift für Sozialreform* 29 (1983), pp. 351ff.

185. Schippel, *Reichstags-Handbuch*, p. 842.

follow the procedure of the local sickness funds in paying doctors' and chemists' fees directly, instead of leaving this to their members.[186] As a result, their share of the total membership of Germany's legally permitted sickness insurance funds dropped from over 20 per cent to less than 10 per cent between 1885 and 1895.[187]

While the workers' benefit funds were able to provide the Social Democrats and the trade unions with a substitute form of organisation, public discussion of the proposed social insurance laws and the form they should take gave the socialists plenty of opportunities to promote their cause. They were able to take full advantage of the situation by holding meetings, which originally had been virtually put a stop to by the anti-Socialist law. Thus, in a summary report on the state of the Social Democratic movement at the beginning of March 1884, the Berlin Chief of Police explained that since the end of July 1883, 'definitely more than 1,000 public meetings had been held in Germany', occasioned solely by the new sickness insurance law, 'at which Social Democrats either officiated as conveners or appeared as speakers'.[188]

During the period before 1890, when the anti-Socialist law was still in force, the Social Democratic Party emerged as Germany's strongest political party. Its share of the vote at the 1890 Reichstag elections climbed from 7.6 per cent in 1878 to 19.7 per cent in 1890. Although other factors obviously played a part, there can be no doubt that the party's dramatic growth, together with the more than fourfold increase in the membership of the free trade unions between 1878 and 1890,[189] was greatly helped by the determined use the socialists made of the propagandist opportunities provided by the insurance laws.

From the beginning of the 1890s the Social Democrats and the free trade unions successfully extended their influence over Germany's local sickness insurance funds, especially in the big cities.[190] After the lapse

186. Ritter, *Staat*, pp. 45f.

187. Schippel, *Reichstags-Handbuch*, pp. 843, 848f.

188. Text of report in Reinhard Höhn (ed.), *Die vaterlandslosen Gesellen: Der Sozialismus im Licht der Geheimberichte der preussischen Polizei, 1878–1914*, vol. 1 (1878–1890), Cologne and Opladen 1964, pp. 191–216, esp. p. 192.

189. *See* Gerhard A. Ritter and Klaus Tenfelde, 'Der Durchbruch der Freien Gewerkschaften Deutschlands zur Massenbewegung im letzten Viertel des 19. Jahrhunderts', in Ritter, *Arbeiterbewegung, Parteien und Parlamentarismus: Aufsätze zur deutschen Sozial- und Verfassungsgeschichte des 19. und 20. Jahrhunderts*, Göttingen 1976, pp. 55–101, esp. pp. 60–74.

190. *See* Tennstedt, *Soziale Selbstverwaltung*, pp. 52–66; idem, *Vom Proleten zum Industriearbeiter*, pp. 429–70; Schnorbus, *Arbeit*, pp. 116–122; Gerd Göckenjan, 'Verrechtlichung und Selbstverantwortlichkeit in der Krankenversorgung', in *Leviathan* 9 (1981), pp. 8–38, esp. pp. 24–7; Volker Eichler, 'Sozialistische Arbeiterbewegung

of the anti-Socialist law, these funds gradually developed into strong-holds of the socialist labour movement, even during the pre-1914 period. According to Florian Tennstedt, the free trade unions already controlled around 3,000 to 6,000 posts in these funds shortly after the turn of the century.[191] This was a considerably higher figure than the 678 full-time officials (2,867 in 1914) employed directly by the free trade union associations.[192] The sickness insurance funds not only gave workers an opportunity for social advancement but also made it possible to provide for workers, who had been punished on account of their political or trade union activities, free of cost to the organisation.

Of even greater importance was the experience of self-administration

---

in Frankfurt am Main, 1878–1895', Phil. diss. (MS), Frankfurt am Main 1980, pp. 340–4. Participation in the election of insured workers' representatives in the local sickness insurance funds (*Ortskrankenkassen*) was extremely low. According to a survey based on a questionnaire by Friedrich Kleeis which covered sixty-five of the larger local sickness insurance funds with 1,359,503 members (832,261 men and 527,242 women), ('Statistisches über die innere Organisation der Orts-Krankenkassen', in *Die Arbeiter-Versorgung, Zentral-Organ für das gesamte Kranken-, Unfall-, Invaliden- und Hinterbliebenen-Versicherungswesens im Deutschen Reiche. Organ der Ortskrankenkassen im Deutschen Reiche* 29 (1912), pp. 293–5), only 15.5 per cent of male members and 3.5 per cent of female members exercised their vote. A smaller sample which included only one-sixth of the total number of members covered by the questionnaire, put the proportion of those entitled to vote (i.e. who were over the age of majority) at 75 per cent of insured male members and 64 per cent of insured female members.

After the new Imperial Insurance Code of 1911 had introduced proportional representation, thereby increasing the possibility of the free trade unions' rivals winning more seats, a further survey carried out by Kleeis on eighty-two of the larger local sickness insurance funds comprising 2,166,192 members ('Statistisches über die Neuwahl der Krankenkassenorgane', in *Die Arbeiter-Versorgung* 31 (1914), pp. 277–81) showed an increase in participation. Now 31.4 per cent of members cast their vote (only 14.4 per cent in the case of female members). This brought the figure for electoral participation among those entitled to vote (based on a sample of only a quarter of members covered by the questionnaire) to 43.6 per cent of insured male members (24 per cent of female members). In an article entitled 'Hab acht auf die Krankenkassenwahlen!', the Chairman of Germany's Free Trades Union Council, Carl Legien, pointedly referred to the sickness insurance fund elections in 1913 as an event which deserved to have 'no less attention paid to it' than 'any other political election' (*Correspondenzblatt der Generalkommission der Gewerkschaften Deutschlands* 23, 16 August, 1913, pp. 497f.). On elections to the governing bodies of the sickness funds before 1914, *see also* Tennstedt, *Soziale Selbstverwaltung* pp. 64–66; Lothar Feige, *Sozialpolitische Analyse der Organisation von Interessen in der gesetzlichen Krankenversicherung: Von den Anfängen der sozialen Sicherung bis zur Notgesetzgebung 1932 in Deutschland*, Wirtschafts- und sozialwiss. diss., Cologne 1980, pp. 52–65; 'Wahlen zu den sozialpolitischen Körperschaften im Jahr 1912', in *Statistische Beilage des Correspondenz-Blatt*, 6 December 1913, pp. 249–60.

191. Tennstedt, 'Sozialgeschichte der Sozialpolitik', in Blohmke (ed.), *Handbuch*, p. 234.
192. Klaus Schönhoven, *Expansion und Konzentration: Studien zur Entwicklung der Freien Gewerkschaften im Wilhelminischen Deutschland 1890 bis 1914*, Stuttgart 1980, pp. 229f.

which workers were able to gain as a result of their participating in the running of the insurance system. At the Trade Union Congress of 1902, the figure for workers' representatives in the various branches of social insurance was given as 118,255. That of delegates to the sickness funds was put at around 500,000.[193] The significance of this level of practical involvement in breaking down the workers' social isolation, defusing class tensions and furthering reformist tendencies within the workers' own organisations can scarcely be exaggerated, working as they did within the insurance system in close cooperation with members of other social classes. Although there was still a long way to go, the workers' integration into the social and political order was well underway by 1914. This process did not take place, as Bismarck had wished, by bringing about the workers' alienation from their own organisations. In fact, it came about precisely through their own organisations.

Germany's social insurance also proved significant for the insured in a socially educational sense, in that it strengthened their collective consciousness as workers.[194] Also, like universal suffrage, it helped along the process of making the workers identify with the values of German society.[195] By reducing their direct dependence on the em-

---

193. Reports by Simanowski of Berlin on 'Elections and Organisation of Representatives in Social Welfare Legislation' at the 4th German Trades Union Conference of 1902:

> Every year we have elections, the number of representatives is by no means inconsiderable. This fact alone suggests that the trade unions cannot take on these elections as well. We have the Reichsversicherungsamt with its 106 representatives, eight *Landesversicherungsämter* with 48, thirty-one administrative boards of *Landesversicherungsanstalten* with 30, and thirty-one committees with 305 representatives. There are a further 5,363 associate committee members in the lower administration. To these must be added 123 arbitration courts, eighty-nine of which with 3,329 associate members deal with workers' insurance, twenty-five arbitration courts for the railways and steamer traffic, nine arbitration courts of miners' provident societies, a further sixty-five employers' occupational associations to deliberate on accident cases with 9,064 representatives and 22,000 sickness funds with 100,000 workers' representatives, altogether a total of 118,255 persons. Over and above this, there are about 500,000 delegates of sickness funds. This forms the basis of all elections and is the vital factor . . . As regards the labour movement, we have to take three factors into account: firstly, the political party, whose task is, so to speak, to cater to the workers' spiritual well-being. Secondly, the trade unions, whose task is to cater to the workers' physical well-being, inasmuch as they are the guarantee of bread and nourishment for healthy workers. And thirdly, we have to work in the direction of extending the scope of social policy legislation and wrest what can be wrested for the workers. Otherwise what good is the best social legislation to us? The workers so far have failed to take advantage of all this legislation; the trade unions must do more for insured workers than they have done up until now'. [Protokoll der Verhandlungen des vierten Kongresses der Gewerkschaften Deutschlands . . ., 1902, pp. 146f.]

Simanowski's suggestion that a separate organisation of workers' representatives in social insurance should be created, to operate along trade union lines, was, however, rejected by the Conference (ibid., p. 165).

194. This completely supports the official account by Lass and Zahn, *Einrichtung*, p. 217.
195. *See* Heide Gerstenberger, 'Von der Armenpflege zur Sozialpolitik, oder: Plädoyer

ployers, relaxing the strict social control associated with poor relief, improving their legal position and facilitating greater geographical mobility, it also contributed to their gradual emancipation. The workers were bound to experience their partial liberation from certain social risks as an increase in real freedom, as well as a step forward on the way towards eliminating social inequality. At the same time, it is also true that the insurance laws, like the independent workers' or journeymen's funds before them, also contained elements designed to create a disciplined workforce. For instance, insured members were obliged to find steady work if they were to be at all able to pay regular contributions, and the extent to which they led a healthy life was monitored in order to save the funds, as collective enterprises, any unnecessary costs.

Between 1891 and 1893, mainly as a result of the economic crisis of the early 1890s, the figure for free-trade-union membership plunged by about a quarter.[196] Against this background, August Bebel made a speech at the 1893 Social Democratic Party Conference in Cologne, in which he predicted that Germany's trade unions would be weakened on account of the state's new social activities:

> In Germany, social policy, especially insurance legislation, has removed this branch of social activity from the unions, thus severing a vital cord; one which has been instrumental in helping the unions flourish, as can be seen in the case of England or the German union of printers. Other important areas of activity which are among the main tasks of the trade unions have been removed by legislation in the field of commercial law . . . ; every new extension of state power is narrowing down the sphere of union activity even further.[197]

Yet Bebel's pessimism was not borne out. In reality the level of the trade unions' own insurance provisions, designed to strengthen members' solidarity and reduce the high rate of fluctuating membership,

---

für eine materialistische Fragestellung', in *Leviathan* 9 (1981), pp. 39–61, esp. p. 43. However, Gerstenberger sees this integrative process which 'made good workers out of proletarians' (p. 43) in negative terms as an accommodation to the existing social and political order. The same position is taken by Göckenjan, 'Verrechtlichung und Selbstverantwortlichkeit in der Krankenversicherung', in *Leviathan* 9 (1981), pp. 8–38.

196. *See* Ritter and Tennfelde, 'Durchbruch', in Ritter *Arbeiterbewegung*, table opp. p. 96. The trade unions experienced an upward surge in membership with the end of the economic crisis in 1894.

197. *Protokoll der Verhandlungen des Parteitags der Sozialdemokratischen Partei Deutschlands*, Cologne 22–28 October 1893, p. 201. Bebel's remarks followed disagreement between the Party and the Trades Union Council concerning their relationship to one another.

began to improve from the turn of the century onwards. Figures from before the First World War show that over 60 per cent of the total expenditure of the socialist free trade unions and the liberal Hirsch-Duncker unions and 40 per cent of the Christian trade unions was paid in benefits to members.[198] Alongside unemployment insurance, which Germany's trade unions virtually monopolised before 1914, the benefits paid out by trade union sickness funds added quite considerably to those made under the state's insurance system. In 1913 they accounted for almost a fifth of all benefits paid out by the sickness insurance funds operating under the 1883 law.[199]

In the controversial internal party discussions of the 1880s the insurance laws had played an important part. A majority of Social Democratic Party members at that time had rejected them as a form of state socialism.[200] However, the beneficial results of the new system of social security for the individual worker, together with increased benefits, gradually gave rise to a more positive view of social insurance among Germany's Social Democrats.[201] This new attitude, which came

198. Klaus Schönhoven, 'Selbsthilfe als Form der Solidarität: Das gewerkschaftliche Unterstützungswesen im Deutschen Kaiserreich bis 1914', in *Archiv für Sozialgeschichte* 20, 1980, pp. 147–93, esp. pp. 157f. Of the expenditure on assistance about one-third from the free trade-unions, approx. 40 per cent from the Christian trade unions and nearly a quarter from the Hirsch-Duncker unions was paid out striking and disciplined workers.

199. The free trade unions paid out on average 5.43 marks per annum on each member in cases of sickness. The sickness benefit funds set up under the sickness insurance law paid out 28.80 marks (i.e. 76.1 per cent of their total expenditure) on medical and sickness benefits (*see* Schönhoven, 'Selbsthilfe', p. 180; Born *et al.* [eds.], *Quellensammlung*, p. 149).

200. *See* Vernon L. Lidtke, 'German Social Democracy and German State Socialism, 1876–1884', in *International Review of Social History* 9 (1964), pp. 202–25; idem, *The Outlawed Party: Social Democracy in Germany, 1878–1890*, Princeton 1966, pp. 158ff.

201. *See* the resolution on social insurance put forward by Hermann Molkenbuhr at the Social Democratic Party Conference of 1902 (*Protokoll über die Verhandlungen des Parteitages* . . ., Munich 1902, Berlin 1902, p. 245). On the Social Democratic Party's changing attitudes towards social insurance at the turn of the century, *see also* Wolff, *Stellung*, esp. pp. 20ff.; Heinrich Verhein, *Die Stellung der Sozialdemokratie zur deutschen Krankenversicherungsgesetzgebung und ihr Einfluss auf dieselbe*, Phil. diss., Halle-Wittenberg 1914, Halle 1916, esp. pp. 32ff.; for the way in which workers' insurance legislation influenced the development of the Social Democratic Party's policy on questions of health, *see* Alfons Labisch, 'Die gesundheitspolitischen Vorstellungen der deutschen Sozialdemokratie von ihrer Gründung bis zur Parteispaltung (1863–1917)', in *Archiv für Sozialgeschichte* 16 (1976), pp. 324–70, esp. pp. 352–4, 362f. Paul Kampffmeyer's statement in the *Sozialistische Monatshefte* of 1902 is typical of the change in attitude, as well as the new view of social reform as a means of strengthening the workers' organisations:

Germany's workers' insurance signifies an actual improvement in the workers' economic position of 1 1/2 billion Marks . . . Our . . . argument . . . has shown that Germany's workers' insurance has without doubt greatly improved the physical strength of Germany's

to prevail after the turn of the century, could be seen when, in 1899, it was proposed that the old-age pension insurance law be reformed. For the first time ever, the Social Democrats in the Reichstag voted in favour of a government social policy proposal. This shows that, on the whole, their tendency to condemn new government measures outright gave way to a new attitude. Although criticism of details in the laws had already been voiced in the 1880s, they were now connected with the development of concrete ideas for expanding or modifying the social insurance system and suggestions for their practical application.[202] This change of vision came about partly as a result of the work of the workers' secretariats (*Arbeitersekretariate*), legal advice bureaux,[203] set up after the mid-1890s by the free trade unions, Hirsch-Duncker and Christian unions and the local and state authorities. The workers' secretariats represented citizens seeking advice, especially those with claims against social insurance institutions, right up to the level of Imperial Insurance Office and played an important role in showing the workers how to make full use of their rights under the system.

---

working class. This improvement has, however, by no means weakened the working class' willingness to fight for its rights. Rather, it has increased this willingness considerably. Indeed, we Social Democrats see this improvement as a necessary prerequisite in liberating the working class from the capitalist wage-system. It is for this reason that we, too, are developing such great enthusiasm for the growth of workman's protection. ['Die Arbeiterversicherung und die Sozialdemokratie', in *Sozialistische Monatshefte* 6 (1902), pp. 685–93, esp. p. 687].

202. For the detailed criticisms, *see* Verhein, *Stellung*, pp. 37ff., and esp. the annual reports of the workers' secretariats. Although these reports have been more or less ignored up until now, they provide an excellent source of information on social conditions and the actual work of the social insurance institutions created by Germany's welfare legislation. They also provide insights into the work of other social institutions and the bureaucracies of state and local government in the area of social affairs. On the Social Democratic Party's reform plans, cf. alongside the 1902 Party Conference resolution (see previous note) and the detailed resolution on the Office of the Interior's proposed bill for an Imperial Insurance Code at the 1909 Party Conference (*Protokoll über die Verhandlungen des Parteitages.* . ., Leipzig 1909, Berlin 1909, pp. 221–24, supplemented by motion no. 282, p. 225), esp. Tennstedt, *Vom Proleten zum Industriearbeiter*, pp. 506–33 and Friedrich Kleeis, *Der Aus- und Umbau der Arbeiter-Versicherung vom Standpunkt der Versicherten*, Berlin 1907; idem, *Die Sozialpolitik der Sozialdemokratie*, Halle 1911.

203. For literature on the workers' secretariats, *see* Ritter, Staat, pp. 130f., and Karl Boehmer, *Die Arbeitersekretariate in Bayern mit besonderer Berücksichtigung des Nürnberger*, Nuremberg 1915; Paul Kampffmeyer, 'Ein Wort über die deutschen Arbeitersekretariate', in *Archiv für soziale Gesetzgebung und Statistik* 16 (1901), pp. 393–412; Johannes Timm, 'Die Bedeutung und die Aufgaben der Arbeitersecretariate bei der Ausführung der Versicherungsgesetze', in *Sozialistische Monatshefte* 6 (1902), pp. 693–9. The *Statistische Beilage des . Correspondenz-Blatt*, 14 November 1914, pp. 202–40, gives an overview of the work of the workers' secretariats and information bureaux in Germany in 1913.

Social policy and social insurance, 1890–1914

Following Bismarck's dismissal in 1890, the social policy of Germany's imperial government, federal states and local authorities concentrated on several areas. These included improving workers' protection and factory inspection, setting up industrial courts to rule in disputes between individual employees and their employers, encouraging the settling of disputes between trade unions and employers by arbitration, establishing optional workers' committees (later made obligatory in the mining industry) and taking the first steps towards regulating the labour market by a system of local labour exchanges.[204] Also, the gradual spread of the system of collective bargaining between employers and employees, which because of opposition from important groups of employers remained limited before 1918,[205] was a development which met with the approval of the authorities.

However, the intended effects of these social policy measures and first steps towards rationalising conflicts of interest between employers and employees remained limited. The political and trade union loyalties of the workers and the conduct of their organisations were not basically changed. This was partly due to the employers' growing opposition to extending the scope of social legislation and their refusal to recognise labour organisations. At any rate, the far-reaching plans of the Prussian Trade Minister, Berlepsch, which ultimately aimed at the workers' future political emancipation, did not become government policy. Following the lapse of the anti-Socialist law on 30 September 1890, the policy of repression against socialist labour organisations was not really ended. Although new attempts to pass repressive legislation failed, strict law enforcement by the police, the judiciary and the bureaucracy partly made up for it.[206] Neither the introduction of a statutory working-day for male workers, nor the creation of 'Chambers

204. *See* Ritter, *Staat*, pp. 56–62.
205. For the position regarding negotiated wage settlements in the various branches of German industry before the First World War, *see* Kaiserliches Statistisches Amt, Abteilung für Arbeiterstatistik, *Die Tarifverträge im Deutschen Reiche am Ende des Jahres 1914*, 12. *Sonderheft zum Reichs-Arbeitsblatte*, Berlin 1916, esp. pp. 14*f.
206. *See* Alex Hall, 'By Other Means: The Legal Struggle Against the SPD in Wilhelmine Germany, 1890–1900', in *Historical Journal* 17 (1974), pp. 365–86; Klaus Saul, 'Der Staat und die "Mächte des Umsturzes": Ein Beitrag zu den Methoden antisozialistischer Repression und Agitation vom Scheitern des Sozialistengesetzes biz zur Jahrhundertwende', in *Archiv für Sozialgeschichte* 12 (1972), pp. 293–350. For the period after the turn of the century, *see* idem, *Staat, Industrie, Arbeiterbewegung im Kaiserreich: Zur Innen- und Aussenpolitik des Wilhelminischen Deutschland, 1903–1914*, Düsseldorf 1974. (Although the term '*Aussenpolitik*' appears in the title of this book, from the point of view of its content '*Sozialpolitik*' would be more apt.)

of Labour' (*Arbeitskammern*), already proposed by William II in his social policy pronouncements of 4 February 1890, ever materialised.[207]

From the middle of the 1890s onwards, one can generally detect a growing polarisation of positions on social policy issues. Influential groups among the employers, who were largely responsible for Berlepsch's dismissal in 1896, not only criticised the burden which the costs of social policy placed on German industry,[208] thus endangering its competitiveness *vis-à-vis* foreign rivals; they also questioned the basic premises of Germany's social legislation. They argued, for example, that it was not producing a more contented workforce, but simply increasing the workers' expectations even further. Instead of weakening the socialist labour organisations, social insurance laws had, as evidenced by the Social Democrats' hold over the local sickness insurance funds,[209] merely provided them with new footholds of power and the chance to collect material on which to base further demands. In 1912 Ludwig Bernhard's book, entitled *The Undesirable Consequences of Germany's Social Policy*, which because of its particularly radical views received considerable attention, even argued that the accident insurance law, in particular, had in many cases led to prolonged convalescences and depraved the workers by virtually provoking the faking of illnesses, 'pension hysteria' and accident neuroses.[210]

In contrast, trade unions representing all shades of opinion joined

207. *See* Born, *Staat*, pp. 191f., 225ff.; Rassow and Born, *Akten*, pp. 344–411.

208. According to a contemporary estimate by the factory manager Greißl, 'Wirtschaftliche Untersuchungen über die Belastung der deutschen Industrie durch die Arbeiter-Versicherungs- und Schutzgesetzgebung', in *Schmollers Jahrbuch*, Neue Folge, 23 (1899), pp. 855–912, the highest possible costs to employers, graded according to the highest category of risk in accident insurance, amounted to 5.5 per cent of their wage bill (pp. 861–5). Neither the development of industry nor the export trade was, in his opinion, affected by this or by workers' protection measures.

209. A typical example of this contemporary criticism of the apparent misuse of sickness insurance by Social Democrats is Wilhelm Möller's book, *Die Herrschaft der Sozialdemokratie in der deutschen Krankenversicherung*, Berlin 1910, published by the Reichsverband gegen die Sozialdemokratie.

210. Ludwig Bernhard, *Unerwünschte Folgen der deutschen Sozialpolitik*, Berlin 1912, esp. pp. 47ff. For Bernhard's criticism of 'the party-political misuse of social policy arrangements' *see* pp. 93ff. For counter-criticisms of his argument, *see* esp. the book by the Centre's leading spokesman on social policy, Franz Hitze, *Zur Würdigung der deutschen Arbeiter-Sozialpolitik. Kritik der Bernhardschen Schrift: Unerwünschte Folgen der deutschen Sozialpolitik*, Mönchen-Gladbach 1913. Hitze concluded that 'the costs of social policy' had not proved to be 'oppressive'. Rather, industry had managed to take on considerable increases in wages over and above its contributions and had still made handsome profits' (p. 119). A survey conducted by the Central Association of Germany's local sickness insurance funds (Zentralverband der Ortskrankenkassen im Deutschen Reich), which questioned employers' representatives on the governing boards of local sickness funds, revealed that the accusation concerning

with middle-class social reformers from the Centre Party, National Liberals, Progressive Liberals (Freisinnige Vereinigung), the Progressive People's Party (Fortschrittliche Volkspartei), comprising left-wing liberal groups united in 1910, and the relatively influential members of the Society for Social Reform of 1901,[211] in calling for an end to repressive legislation in favour of greatly extending the scope of social welfare policy by the state as well as the workers' active participation in it. The workers were increasingly viewed not merely as the passive object of welfare provisions but as the active subject of social policy. Official government policy wavered between these two positions, but still held on to the hope that the Social Democrats could be contained by a combination of social legislation and repression.

After the turn of the century, Germany's social insurance system entered a period of expansion. Sickness insurance benefits were increased and coverage extended to new social groups. In 1885, including the members of the miners' provident societies, barely a quarter of employed persons and slightly over 40 per cent of wage-earners enjoyed the benefits of sickness insurance. By 1914 this figure had risen to take in almost all wage-earners, considerable numbers of salaried white-collar workers and over half the entire workforce. By 1913 Germany's welfare provisions, which the insurance funds gradually extended to members' dependants, may well have covered some 24 million citizens, or approximately 36 per cent of the population; that is, even before cover was extended to all agricultural employees, domestic servants, casual and itinerant workers and the domestic industry on 1 January 1914.[212] The general improvement in the level of benefits can also be seen in the considerable per capita rise in payments for medical charges from 11.05 marks in 1885 to 28.49 marks in 1914.[213]

During the late 1880s, accident insurance also was extended to take in new groups. In 1886, if one includes the miners' provident societies,

---

the misuse of sickness insurance for party-political ends was almost unanimously considered unfounded (Kleeis, *Aus- und Umbau*, pp. 51f.).

211. *See* Ursula Ratz, *Sozialreform und Arbeiterschaft: Die 'Gesellschaft für Soziale Reform' und die sozialdemokratische Arbeiterbewegung von der Jahrhundertwende bis zum Ausbruch des Ersten Weltkrieges*, Berlin 1980; Rüdiger vom Bruch, 'Bürgerliche Sozialreform und Gewerkschaften im späteren Kaiserreich: Die Gesellschaft für Soziale Reform (GSR), 1901–1914', in *Internationale Wissenschaftliche Korrespondenz zur Geschichte der deutschen Arbeiterbewegung* 15, 1979, pp. 581–610.

212. I am accepting Tennstedt's estimate ('Sozialgeschichte der Sozialversicherung', in Blohmke (ed.), *Handbuch*, p. 403) of 10 million dependants who, in addition to 14 million insured workers, also received medical benefits in kind. By 1885 the proportion of the population receiving medical benefits may well have been only a little over the 10 per cent proportion of insured persons.

213. *See* Table 1, p. 187.

it covered approximately a third of all wage-earners. By the end of the decade, however, accident insurance had already been sufficiently extended to cover virtually all Germany's wage-earners, most of its white-collar workers and a good many owners of small businesses. In addition, accident insurance benefits increased at a faster rate than the number of persons insured.

Disablement and old-age pension insurance covered virtually all wage-earners, domestics, junior white-collar workers and some owners of small businesses.[214] The law on disablement and old-age insurance was relatively unpopular at first. It was mockingly dubbed the 'sticky law' (*Klebegesetz*) since it involved workers having to stick contribution stamps on their payment receipt-cards. In Bavaria alone, a petition seeking to abolish the law collected 245,745 signatures by 1894,[215] with the result that detailed plans for its reform were soon laid before the Reichstag. The conditions which had to be met in order to qualify for a pension were complicated and difficult to understand. Pension awards were still relatively small. No provision was made for part-pensions in the case of the partial disablement, and the long payment period of five years' contributions for a disablement pension and thirty years for an old-age pension (though not immediately applied) also did little to enhance the law's general popularity. Thus W. Kulemann's proposal

214. According to the law, insurance cover was extended to all wage-earners. But, during the initial period of the law's application, this could not be enforced for so-called casual workers who constantly changed employers; for example, day-labourers, dressmakers, seamstresses, laundresses (Dr Althoff, 'Erinnerungen aus den Anfängen der Invalidenversicherung', in *Zentralblatt für Reichsversicherung und Reichsversorgung* 11 (1940), pp. 181–4, 214–18, esp. p. 183). The law's provision (para. 2) that a Federal Council decree could extend insurance liability to take in small entrepreneurs with no employees or a single wage-earner and the workforce of the cottage industry resulted in the partial incorporation of small businesses, as happened in the case of the tobacco and textile industries.

215. See W. Kulemann, 'Die Reform unserer Sozialversicherung', in *Schmollers Jahrbuch*, Neue Folge, 18 (1894), pp. 853–919, 1117–79, esp. pp. 856ff. The overwhelmingly critical reaction to the Federal Council's decree of 1894 was typical. The decree extended a law engendered by conditions of the organisation of modern production especially in factories to independent handloom weavers, still subject to proto-industrial conditions. Applying the law gave rise to specific problems owing to the nature of family work, the weavers' pronounced conditions of distress and their frequent practice of working for several retailers, which made fixing the employers' share of contributions difficult. See Jean H. Quataert, 'Workers' Reaction to Social Insurance: The Case of Homeweavers in the Saxon Oberlausitz in the later Nineteenth Century', in *Internationale Wissenschaftliche Korrespondenz zur Geschichte der deutschen Arbeiterbewegung* 20, 1984, pp. 17–35. Social historians have up until now ignored sources dealing with the problems of applying social insurance. As Quataert's article demonstrates, their study would, however, be rewarded with deeper insights, not only into the true social conditions which prevailed, but the life-style and mentality of those sections of the population affected by social insurance.

to change the terms of the law to something resembling Bismarck's idea of a general state insurance covering all persons in need was widely discussed.[216] Other proposals he made included dropping the idea of a strict correlation between the levels of contributions and benefits and extending cover to the owners of small businesses.

The number of old-age pensioners was initially greater than the number of those in receipt of a disablement pension. This was because the former figure included anyone over the age of seventy who had been employed in an occupation covered by the law in the three years prior to its taking effect. However, this figure dropped from just one quarter of a million in 1897 to under 100,000 in 1914. In the same period the number of disablement pensions rose from just a quarter million to over 1.1 million. Of the disablement pensions approved in 1913, 35.1 per cent were awarded to people under the age of fifty-five and a further 51.4 per cent to those between the ages of fifty-five and sixty-nine. This meant that the majority of Germany's retired workers enjoyed a pension before reaching the age of seventy.[217]

As a consequence of this, pension insurance gradually came to be accepted as an advance over traditional provisions for the old and disabled under the existing system of poor relief. The fact that initial problems in applying the law were soon overcome and that it proved possible to increase benefits for medical care from 1.8 million marks in 1897 to 26.1 million in 1913,[218] was another major factor behind its growing acceptance. At the same time, critics of the system continued to point to the low level of disablement pension awards, which were only paid out once the insured was deemed incapable of producing less than a third of a healthy worker's output. Other criticisms concentrated on the practice of depressing pension amounts by applying the law rigorously when determining disablement awards. Despite the growing proportion of higher wage-earners included in the scheme,[219] the average yearly pension went up by relatively little between 1891 and 1914, from 123 to 168 marks for old-age pensions and from 113 to 201 marks for disablement pensions.[220] The total pension for a worker

216. Kulemann, 'Reform', esp. pp. 861ff., 1117ff.
217. *Amtliche Nachrichten des Reichs-Versicherungsamts* 31 (1915), p. 161.
218. Tennstedt, *Sozialgeschichte der Sozialversicherung*, p. 457.
219. In 1891, 25.3 per cent of received weekly contributions were paid in by workers in the lowest earnings category (i.e. category I) and 14.6 per cent by those in the highest (i.e. categoy IV). In 1913 the proportion of weekly contributions in category I dropped to 7.8 per cent, as against a rise to 16.4 per cent in category IV and 29.2 per cent in category V, as newly created by the law of 1899 (*Amtliche Nachrichten des Reichs-Versicherungsamts* 31 (1915), p. 155).
220. *See* Table 3, p. 191. After contributions and pensions had been increased and the

employed in industry, commerce or transport only amounted to a sixth
of his average yearly earnings[221] and fell well below the minimum
necessary for an individual or family to survive on, even in the countryside, where the cost of living was cheaper.

The continuing failure to exploit the new opportunities presented by
a state social insurance policy was most clearly seen in the way that the
introduction of welfare provisions for working men's widows was
delayed for decades. If a husband died as a result of an industrial
injury, his widow received an accident pension amounting to 20 per
cent of the deceased's yearly earnings. But, under the provisions of
disablement and old-age insurance, widows and orphans were only
entitled to the amount of contributions paid in by the insured husband
and then only on condition that the deceased had not drawn a pension
before his death.

Bismarck referred to the introduction of a widows' and orphans'
pension in a letter he wrote as early as 5 August 1879.[222] When the
basic terms of disablement and old-age insurance were discussed in
1887, this form of insurance was regarded as 'desirable' but held back
until the application of the disablement and old-age insurance law had
allowed sufficient time to see 'whether industry could shoulder the
substantial extra costs involved in providing for widows and orphans'.[223]
Thereafter, the introduction of this form of pension was repeatedly
delayed as a result of reservations concerning the additional financial
burden it would place on the imperial government and the federal states
which were obliged to contribute to the Reich's finances.

In 1907, there were almost 2.5 million widows in Germany; that is,
almost three times the number of widowers. Their social situation was
generally very miserable. This can be seen in the high rate of employment among this group: in 1907, 52.6 per cent of widows and
divorcees below the age of seventy (or 47 per cent, if the number of
those working in family enterprises is excluded) had some form of
employment. In contrast, the corresponding figures for married women
in the same age group were only 26.4 and 8.7 per cent, respectively.[224]

---

law of 1899 had introduced a new category V, annual old-age pensions amounted to
between 110.40 and 230 marks, depending on the earnings category, and disablement between 116.40 and 450 marks, depending on earnings category and number
of weekly contributions.

221. Ritter, *Staat*, p. 52.
222. Geheimes Staatsarchiv, Berlin-Dahlem, Rep. 90, vol. 1263.
223. 'Denkschrift betreff. Alters- und Invalidenversicherung' of 6 July 1887, ibid.
224. Calculations based on figures from the occupational census of 1907, *Statistik des
Deutschen Reichs*, vol. 211, pp. 18–21, 44. The employment figures for women do not
include separate figures for divorcees. Divorcees, however, accounted for less than 4

The mortality rate among widows and divorcees was 27.7 per cent higher than that for married women. Widows were also demonstrably more involved in crimes against property and their rate of suicide was twice that of married women.[225]

The decisive impetus behind the introduction of an insurance for bereaved dependants was provided by the new protective tariff legislation of 1902. As a result of a Centre Party initiative, the new measures included the stipulation that the extra revenue from specific duties on agricultural produce, the costs of which fell mainly on the less well-off, should be channelled into a fund to help cover the costs of an insurance for bereaved dependants, which the government planned to introduce until 1 January 1910.[226] This would make it possible to introduce a widows' and orphans' insurance, which would relieve the burden on poor relief, reduce the extent to which a widow was tied to her place of residence and supplement the protective legislation which restricted the use of female labour. In fact, this insurance was not introduced until the Imperial Insurance Code took effect after 1 January 1912. In order to keep costs down, 'disabled' widows were allowed to claim benefits only if they themselves were not in receipt of a pension and if their insured husband had died after the 1 January 1912 having qualified by having made at least five years' contributions for a disablement pension.[227] The pension award amounted to three-tenths of the deceased's entitlement based on paid-in contributions, an amount which was increased annually by a government supplement of 50 marks. The orphans' allowance for children under the age of fifteen was even smaller. Like the widows' pension, it was far from adequate to cover even the bare necessities of existence.[228] It consisted of a government supplement of 25 marks for each child together with 15 per cent of the pension entitlement (based on the paid-in contributions) for the first child and 2.5 per cent for each subsequent child. The average

---

per cent of widows.

225. *See* Wolfgang Dreher, *Die Entwicklung der Arbeiterwitwen-Versicherung in Deutschland nach z. T. unveröffentlichten Quellen*, Berlin 1978, p. 39.

226. Ibid., pp. 32–57.

227. On the death of an insured husband, widows entitled to their own pension received a lump sum amounting to one year's widows' pension. In addition, an orphan's endowment amounting to eight times the monthly orphan's pension was paid out on the child reaching its fifteenth birthday. The widow's lump sum, of which 8,081 were paid out in 1913, amounted on average to 76.45 marks. The orphan's endowment, of which there were only 459 in 1913, amounted on average to 22.24 marks (*Amtliche Nachrichten des Reichs-Versicherungsamts* 31 [1915], p. 163).

228. *Amtliche Nachrichten des Reichs-Versicherungsamtes* 31 (1915), pp. 161f.

award under the bereaved dependants' insurance, approved in 1913, for widows or widowers deemed incapable of work and in need, where the wife had provided the greater share of the family income before her death, was 78 marks. The average allowance for orphans, which usually had to provide for several children in a family, was 80 marks.

The Imperial Insurance Code nevertheless provided increased allowances for the first time for pensioners with children under the age of fifteen and improved the workers' right of appeal in settling the amounts of accident pensions. It abolished the less viable local authority sickness funds in favour of the local sickness funds and increased maternity allowances. As has already been shown, it also established a legal basis for the care of bereaved dependants, whereby material benefits could be subject to later increases.

Alongside these improvements and the growth in the number of persons insured, especially in the case of sickness insurance, there were,. however, certain regulations designed to counteract the influence exerted by the Social Democrats and the socialist free trade unions on the local sickness funds. As the State Secretary of the Interior, Bethmann Hollweg, put it on 15 October 1908 in a confidential memorandum to the federal governments, he laid great store on efforts 'to strip the Social Democrats of their power in determining the staffing of official paid posts in the funds'.[229] After the Reichstag's opposition had led to the failure of the government's original plans for employers to pay an equal share of contributions alongside the workers and thus involve the former more in managing the funds, the Imperial Insurance Code eventually laid down, in terms clearly directed against the socialist labour organisations, that certain decisions required unanimity between the separately cast votes of the majority of employers' representatives and those of the insured.[230] This condition applied in the case of electing a chairman and in the hiring and firing of fund officials. If there was no unanimous choice of chairman, the position was forcibly filled by appointment from above. In addition, the election of representatives to the management committee had to take place in accordance with the principle of proportional representation. This was done to increase the potential representation of non-socialist workers' organisations. The Code also laid down rules on the minimum number of members a fund was allowed to have. This regulation and the winding up of the local authority funds resulted in a large drop in the number of funds from

229. Text of letter in Rassow and Born, *Akten*, pp. 424–6.
230. In 1919 the rules governing separate voting by employers' and the insured's representatives in certain cases were abolished.

21,342 in 1913 to 9,854 in the following year. At the same time, the average number of members per branch rose from 636 to 1,584.[231] The general assemblies, in which each member had been allowed to vote on management issues, and which wielded considerable influence on the running of small funds, were abolished. Case rules were also laid down, limiting the right of the funds to determine the extent of members' contributions and compensations. Furthermore, central government and local authority supervision over the funds was increased.

As well as improving the efficiency of the funds and expanding their membership, the reorganisation of sickness insuance under the new law of 1911 had several important aims. These included strengthening the employers' influence, containing the power of the socialist labour organisations, increasing legal control over the insurance system and limiting the rights of insured workers' to self-manage their funds in favour of control by the state and local authorities. The influence of these authorities was strengthened by the creation of superior insurance offices (*Oberversicherungsämter*) in each government district and local insurance offices (*Versicherungsämter*) in each local government district (*Landkreis*) and big city. These were to act as a basis for the central Imperial Insurance Office (Reichsversicherungsamt).

Political motives also played a crucial part in the introduction of a disablement and old-age pension and bereaved dependants' insurance for white-collar workers in December 1911. What occasioned this new insurance law was the spectacularly large growth in the number of white-collar workers employed in administrative and technical posts. According to the official occupational census, the number of white-collar workers in agriculture, industry, trade and transport rose from 307,000 in 1882 to 1,291,000 in 1907; that is, a more than fourfold increase. In contrast, the number of industrial workers in these sectors increased in the same period only from 10.7 to 17.8 million; that is, by about two-thirds. In fact, in accordance with modern practice, we should add to the figures for white-collar workers around 166,000 shop assistants for 1882 and 406,000 for 1907, who were included in the survey under the heading 'workers'.[232] In 1907 an additional 297,000 white-collar workers were included in the category of public servants and the liberal professions (excluding the armed forces). There were a number of reasons for this overproportional increase in the number of white-collar employees. They included the growth of large-scale industrial concerns, the appearance of new branches of industry with

231. Feige, *Sozialpolitische Analyse*, p. 50.
232. *See* Hohorst, et al., *Sozialgeschichtliches Arbeitsbuch* II, pp. 59, 66–8.

complicated production methods (i.e. a high demand for scientists and technicians) and the extremely rapid expansion of the service sector.

By the late 1890s, Germany's white-collar workers were no longer exclusively entrusted with management tasks. In many respects, their social situation, like that of the workers, had become precarious.[233] In a speech to a Christian-Social conference in 1897 Schmoller described them as the 'nucleus of the newly emerging middle class',[234] and from the 1890s onwards, the appearance of a powerful white-collar movement in Germany signalled their growing political importance.[235] This movement led to the creation of white-collar associations which were heavily orientated towards pursuing ideological ends. They concentrated, for example, on fostering members' awareness of their separate status as white-collar workers and established a strict distance between them and the general wage-earning population. From the turn of the century onwards, they aimed at achieving a separate state pension and bereaved dependant's insurance for white-collar employees. This policy was coordinated by a committee formed on 1 December 1901, which was a forerunner of the main committee founded on 1 March 1903 comprising twenty-four affiliated white-collar organisations. Representing over 700,000 white-collar workers at one point, this committee largely moulded the policy of the white-collar movement.[236]

The white-collar movement proved very effective in influencing public opinion. A growing awareness of the significant voting potential of white-collar workers meant that it won increasing support from within the Reichstag and eventually within the government itself. As had previously been the case in its support of demands by the 'old' middle class of artisans and small shopkeepers, the government hoped to use this movement to erect a barrier to halt the continuing advance of the Social Democrats. However, it was not until December 1911,

---

233. For white-collar workers' changing functions and their social position, *see* Jürgen Kocka's excellent case study, *Unternehmensverwaltung und Angestelltenschaft am Beispiel Siemens 1847–1914: Zum Verhältnis von Kapitalismus und Bürokratie in der deutschen Industrialisierung*, Stuttgart 1969. Kocka states the problem in terms of the evolution of bureaucracy.

234. Gustav Schmoller, 'Was verstehen wir unter dem Mittelstande? Hat er im 19. Jahrhundert zu- oder abgenommen?', in *Die Verhandlungen des achten Evangelisch-sozialen Kongresses . . . 1897*, Göttingen 1897, pp. 132–61, esp. 154.

235. For the growth in the membership figures of the larger white-collar associations, *see* Hohorst *et al.*, *Sozialgeschichtliches Arbeitsbuch* II, pp. 138–40.

236. An analysis of the establishment of Germany's white-collar insurance against the background of the white-collar movement and public discussion of the political and social status of white-collar workers remains an important desideratum for future research. But *see* Emil Lederer, 'Die Pensionversicherung der Angestellten', in *Archiv für Sozialwissenschaft und Sozialpolitik* 33 (1911), pp. 780–841.

following statistical surveys on the economic situation and existing welfare provisions for old and disabled white-collar workers in individual firms,[237] that a white-collar insurance law was unanimously approved by the Reichstag. This was partly modelled on the law of December 1906 which introduced white-collar workers' insurance in Austria. Germany's law was hastily pushed through a few weeks in advance of the Reichstag elections of January 1912, in which the idea of winning over the middle class figured prominently in the election campaign of the parties.[238]

On the strength of its legal definition of the term 'white-collar worker' (*Angestellter*) in enumerating the categories of employees covered,[239] the law was to have lasting significance.[240] In the following decades, a white-collar worker came to be defined as anyone who qualified for insurance under the terms of this law. At the same time, it led to the setting up of a separate Imperial Insurance Board (Reichsversicherungsanstalt) for white-collar workers, which administered this law directly and independently of existing social insurance provisions. Some 1.4 million white-collar workers in private employment

237. Kleeis, *Geschichte*, pp. 148–51.
238. *See* Walter Kaskel, 'Gründe und Gegengründe einer Sonderversicherung der Angestellten', in *Zeitschrift für die gesamte Versicherungswissenschaft* 17 (1917), pp. 538–46, esp. p. 543; Jürgen Bertram, *Die Wahlen zum Deutschen Reichstag vom Jahre 1912: Parteien und Verbände in der Innenpolitik des Wilhelminischen Reiches*, Düsseldorf 1964, esp. pp. 167–73.
239. Versicherungsgesetz für Angestellte vom 20. 12. 1911, in *Reichs-Gesetzblatt* 1911, pp. 989–1061. According to paragraph 1 of the law, the following categories of occupation qualified for white-collar insurance:

1. Salaried employees in management positions, where this activity constitutes their main employment.
2. Management officials, foremen and other employees in a similarly promoted or senior position, regardless of qualifications; office workers, insofar as they are not employed on menial or simply routine duties. . . .
3. Commercial clerks and chemists' assistants.
4. Stage crews and orchestral players, regardless of the artistic value of their contribution.
5. Teaching and educational staff.
6. Certain members of ships' crews.

The annual earned income of employees liable for insurance contributions was not allowed to exceed 5,000 marks per annum. For further details on the definition of 'white-collar' workers, *see* Jürgen Kocka, *Die Angestellten in der deutschen Geschichte 1850–1980: Vom Privatbeamten zum angestellten Arbeitnehmer*, Göttingen 1981, pp. 116–41.
240. On the use of the term 'white-collar worker' in social and labour legislation, *see* G. Schelp, 'Das Angestelltenproblem in der Gesetzgebung', in Hans Bayer (ed.), *Der Angestellte zwischen Arbeiterschaft und Management*, Berlin 1961, pp. 187–202. On the division between 'white-collar' and 'blue-collar' workers by the white-collar insurance law of 1911, its official justification and real motives, *see also* Kocka, *Unternehmensverwaltung*, pp. 518., 540–4.

with a yearly income of below 5,000 marks qualified for cover under the terms of the new law. Of these, however, some two-thirds with an income below 2,000 marks were, in addition, still covered by the existing state pension scheme. The benefits of white-collar insurance were much more generous than those of the workers' disablement and old-age insurance. The white-collar employee qualified for an old-age pension at the age of sixty-five rather than seventy. Disablement was defined as the inability to perform half the previous work effort, whereas workers were awarded a disablement pension only when their capacity for work had been reduced by two-thirds. In making this calculation the law distinguished between, in the case of the salaried employee, the inability to follow his chosen profession (*Berufsunfähigkeit*), and, in the workers' case, the inability to pursue gainful employment (*Erwerbsunfähigkeit*). This was a crucial qualitative distinction in that assessment of the latter took into account, even for skilled workers, the entire labour market (including low-paid and unattractive jobs), whereas the former was judged only in relation to types of employment which would not incur loss of social prestige for the individual concerned. This qualitative distinction was further emphasised by the rulings of the Imperial Insurance Office.[241] In addition, all widows of white-collar workers and their orphans under the age of eighteen were entitled to benefits and not just 'disabled' widows and orphans under the age of fifteen, as was the case in workers' insurance. Moreover, the fact that the pension award was calculated on the basis of previous salaries showed that the law was guided by the consideration of maintaining, at least in part, the dependants' accustomed standard of living.

Minimum retirement pay, paid out after 120 monthly contributions, amounted to 20 per cent of the individual's salary. This rose by 1 per cent for each further year of contributions until it reached a ceiling of 50 per cent of salary after forty years' contributions. Widows received 40 per cent, orphans 13 per cent and single-parent children 8 per cent of the deceased's retirement pay. The orphans' pension was only reduced after the eighth child. It was argued that the more generous provisions for widows and orphans under white-collar insurance, compared with workers' disablement insurance, was justified because 'their lack of professional training' meant that white-collar widows 'find it difficult in many cases to find suitable employment following the death of their husband, or are less able than workers' widows to adapt to any available type of employment. Over and above this, the higher costs of

241. *See* Florian Tennstedt, *Berufsunfähigkeit im Sozialrecht: Ein soziologischer Beitrag zur Entwicklung der Berufsunfähigkeitsrenten in Deutschland*, Frankfurt 1972, esp. pp. 25–62.

educating and bringing up their children make their situation of hardship even worse than that of the workers'.[242] Certainly, these more generous benefits involved the payment of considerably higher contributions. Amounting to around 7 to 8 per cent of salary and shared equally by employer and employee (no government supplement being granted), they were about 4 times greater than contributions for workers' insurance.

To some extent, white-collar insurance achieved its political aim of promoting the status consciousness of white-collar workers *vis-à-vis* other workers, even though the former by no means constituted an homogenous group. It was also relatively successful in preventing them being politically organised by the Social Democrats or unionised by socialist labour organisations, at least up to the end of the Weimar Republic.[243]

The auxiliary service law of 1916 (*Hilfsdienstgesetz*), which set up special white-collar workers' committees alongside the blue-collar workers' committees in large firms, showed that the originally artificially created term '*Angestellter*' was already beginning to be applied in other areas of civil and labour law outside of insurance. But it was not until the creation of the welfare state during Weimar, when the government began to intervene in economic and social affairs on a far greater scale than the old governments of the Empire had done, that the development of white-collar workers as a quite distinct and separate group from the rest of the workforce reached its peak. Despite opposition from the Independent Socialists (USPD), the privileged position of white-collar workers in industry established by the law of 1916 was confirmed by the 1920 law on workers' committees (*Betriebsräte-gesetz*). This law provided for separate committees for white-collar workers. The regulations of 1923 governing the arbitration of labour disputes provided for the possibility of setting up special boards for white-collar workers, which were later made compulsory by the law of 1926 on industrial courts (*Arbeitsgerichtsgesetz*). Laws on statutory working hours also made a distinction between white-collar and industrial workers. Despite bitter opposition from the Social Democratic Party, the law of 1927 on unemployment insurance and labour exchanges made special provisions for white-collar workers. Thus it recognised the white-collar workers' independent labour exchanges which, it was

242. Tennstedt, 'Sozialgeschichte der Sozialversicherung', in Blohmke (ed.), *Handbuch*, p. 452.
243. For the social and political attitudes of white-collar workers in the period since the First World War, *see* Jürgen Kocka, *Facing Total War: German Society 1914–1918*, Leamington Spa 1984, pp. 77–98; idem, *Die Angestellten*, pp. 142–229.

hoped, could be used to regulate the labour market on a quasi-corporate basis after the model of the craftsmen's guilds. Besides this, special departments were set up in Germany's state labour exchanges whose job was to cater for the separate needs of white-collar workers. Although white-collar workers failed to achieve their demand for a separate unemployment benefit fund, which would have made it more difficult to adjust between the high risk of unemployment among workers and the lower risk among white-collar workers — thus increasing the cost of the workers' unemployment insurance — they nevertheless managed to hold on to their privileged position as regards pension benefits. In the case of sickness insurance also, a growing number of white-collar workers were covered by separate special funds, which offered more generous benefits than the general local sickness insurance funds. The 1926 law governing termination of contract (*Kündigungsfristgesetz*) extended the period of notice a private employer had to give his white-collar workers up to six months in cases where the employee had been with the firm for a long time. This gave white-collar staff considerably greater job security than the average worker. The emergency decrees (*Notverordnungen*) of 1 December 1930 and 5 June 1931 extended a further legal privilege to white-collar workers which industrial workers were denied, namely their right to receive full payment of salary for six weeks following illness — a measure which greatly reduced the financial burden on their sickness funds.[244]

The interaction between 'the early appearance of an interventionist state welfare policy, the steps taken by white-collar workers to organise themselves and the general trend towards separate legal treatment for blue-collar and white-collar workers' was a marked feature of German social policy before the First World War and continued to exist to an even greater extent in the Weimar Republic. Thus Germany's state welfare legislation lent 'increasing material substance' to the distinction drawn between blue-collar and white-collar workers.[245]

During the National Socialist period, the government's chief priority of rearmament worked in the opposite direction of previous developments in that it tended to close the gap which existed between blue-collar and white-collar workers. This was a result of the regime's desire to integrate the workers into the system, which involved promoting the

---

244. *See* Michael Prinz, 'Vom "neuen Mittelstand" zum Volksgenossen: Ausprägung und Entwicklung der Kragenlinie in der deutschen Sozialstruktur 1890–1945', Phil. diss. (MS), Bielefeld 1983, pp. 121–45, 620–6. This study is due to appear in 1986 in the series 'Studien zur Zeitgeschichte' published by the Institut für Zeitgeschichte in Munich.

245. Ibid., p. 143.

ideology of a unified people's community (*Volksgemeinschaft*) to be equally applied in firms (*Betriebsgemeinschaft*). This tendency to level down the differences between blue-collar and white-collar workers was especially fostered by the National Socialist 'factory-cells' organisation (Betriebszellenorganisation — NSBO) and the German Labour Front (DAF), though it was opposed both by the employers and the state officials in the Imperial Ministry of Labour. It was put into practice, for example, by the Labour Regulation Law (*Arbeitsordnungsgesetz*) of January 1934, which created councils (*Vertrauensräte*) comprising both white-collar and factory-floor workers in individual firms. These councils often pressed for an end to the separate treatment of different groups of employees within a firm.[246] It was also demonstrated by the German Labour Front organisation, which, following the elimination of the trade unions and white-collar associations, took in blue-collar and white-collar workers (as well as employers), and by the complete collapse of the white-collar idea of separate corporative status. It was again in evidence in the controversial plan to create a 'German people's welfare system' put forward in the autumn of 1940 by the DAF leader, Robert Ley. Besides the creation of a general health service, the plan proposed abolishing the privileged status of white-collar workers in pension insurance in favour of a scheme of welfare provisions for all of Germany's senior citizens, modelled on civil service pensions and financed from tax revenue.[247] These plans for welfare provisions to cover all citizens, propagated by the German Labour Front with express reference to Bismarck's original schemes, encountered massive opposition from the officials in the Imperial Ministry of Labour, the employers and the medical profession. As a result of this opposition, as well as lack of finance, they were shelved until the post-war period. Though one can only speculate as to whether these ideas would have really been put into effect in the event of a victory for the National Socialists, there are some striking parallels between the scheme and Beveridge's plan in Britain during the same period. One major difference, however, was that Ley's proposal of a German people's welfare system, unlike Beveridge's proposals, aimed at strengthening the state's control over its citizens. The changes actually brought about were, in the end, of a rather limited character and amounted mainly to extend-

246. Ibid., pp. 432ff.
247. Cf. alongside Teppe, 'Zur Sozialpolitik des Dritten Reiches', in *Archiv für Sozialgeschichte* 17 (1977), esp. pp. 244–8, the recent post-doctoral thesis by Marie-Luise Recker, 'Staatliche Sozialpolitik im Deutschen Reich während des Zweiten Weltkrieges' (MS), Münster 1983, pp. 230–72, appended vol. pp. 91–105, now published as *Nationalsozialistische Sozialpolitik im Zweiten Weltkrieg*, Munich 1985.

ing to all employees some of the privileges originally granted only to white-collar workers in the welfare schemes of individual firms.

The widespread distaste felt for Ley's plans in the post-war period was one of the reasons why the Allied plan for a complete reform of Germany's social insurance system and the introduction of a unified insurance covering all kinds of risks and groups of employees failed to be implemented, except in East Germany. Germany's social insurance system remained split into different organisations for different risks and groups of employees. It remained characterised by its highly differentiated scale of contributions and related benefits.

The important long-term significance of white-collar workers' insurance, along with their privileged treatment in other areas of social and labour legislation, could be seen in the way that regulations governing white-collar workers became the model for all future attempts at improving the position of Germany's workers. It seems to me, therefore, that the emphasis which some German historians have placed on the pre-industrial elements and social values contained in the ideology and demands of the white-collar movement might well be somewhat exaggerated.[248] It was indeed the desire to emulate the civil servant which determined their plans to create a separate white-collar insurance after the turn of the century. This, as well as their conscious collective effort to avoid sinking into the proletariat and their resistance to an uninhibited capitalism free from state interference appear, however, to be less the expression of pre-industrial attitudes and values than an outlook which is characteristically found in the modern interventionist welfare state. Germany's white-collar workers thus became pacemakers in the field of social and labour legislation, to be followed initially by public service workers and later by all employees. This was especially the case in social insurance, where the equal treatment of Germany's workers was achieved on a major scale only after the sweeping pension reforms of 1957.[249]

The great gap in Germany's system of social security before 1914 was its lack of any adequate provision against the effects of unemployment. Only after the serious economic crisis from 1873 onwards was it gradually recognised that alongside traditional seasonal unemploy-

---

248. Although they have played a great part in enriching historical scholarship in this field since the late 1960s, I find myself in disagreement here with the otherwise excellent studies by Jürgen Kocka on Germany's white-collar workers, as well as the generally very valuable work of his student, Michael Prinz.
249. *See* Hans Günter Hockerts' important study, *Sozialpolitische Entscheidungen im Nachkriegsdeutschland. Alliierte und deutsche Sozialversicherungspolitik 1945 bis 1957*, Stuttgart 1980.

ment (e.g. in the construction, brick manufacturing and clothing industries, inland waterways, agriculture and casual work — as in the case of dockers and day-labourers), there was another type of unemployment which resulted from the effects of the economic cycle and could not be attributed to any lack of willingness to work on the part of the individual.

The measures taken against unemployment by Germany's central government, federal governments and local authorities met with little success prior to 1914. In a speech made on 2 April 1881 Bismarck spoke out in favour of a massive work-creation programme to be initiated by the state in special emergencies such as the collapse of large-scale enterprises: 'We just couldn't let twenty thousand or several hundred thousand workers go to the dogs or starve to death. We'd really have to resort to state socialism and find work for these people, as, indeed, we always do in cases of emergency. . . . When such cases occur, we occasion the construction of railways, whose profitability is doubtful. We initiate land improvement schemes, which we'd normally leave to others to take upon themselves'.[250] In actual fact, the various relief works instigated by the local authorities, particularly during the depression years of 1876–77, 1891–94, 1901–02 and 1907–08, had only a marginal effect on the labour market, as did the increased investment programmes of the federal governments during periods of economic stagnation.[251] Indeed, one could say that before 1914, Germany's central government, federal states and local authorities had no effective policy to combat the effects of fluctuations in the economic cycle.

In contrast, from the end of the nineteenth century onwards, an important instrument for monitoring and controlling unemployment was created in the shape of municipal labour exchanges. These developed on a major scale in the towns, particularly the big cities, where they were often controlled by commissions[252] composed equally

250. Bismarck, *Gesammelte Werke*, vol. 12, p. 246.
251. See Frank Niess, *Geschichte der Arbeitslosigkeit. Ökonomische Ursachen und politische Kampfe: ein Kapitel deutscher Sozialgeschichte*, Cologne 1979, pp. 211–14; *Soziale Praxis* 5 (1895/96), pp. 584–9; and 11 (1901/02), pp. 66f., 118f., Paul Meyer, *Die Notstandsarbeiten und ihre Probleme: Ein Beitrag zur Frage der Bekämpfung der Arbeitslosigkeit*, Jena 1914, esp. pp. 15–21; Ernst Bernhard (ed.), *Die Vergebung der öffentlichen Arbeiten in Deutschland im Kampf gegen die Arbeitslosigkeit: Eine Erhebung der deutschen Gesellschaft zur Bekämpfung der Arbeitslosigkeit*, Berlin 1913, esp. p. 22; Kaiserlich Statistisches Amt. Abteilung für Arbeiterstatistik, 'Die Regelung der Notstandsarbeiten in deutschen Städten', in *Beiträge zur Arbeiterstatistik*, no. 2, Berlin 1905; *Statistisches Jahrbuch der Deutschen Städte* 5 (1896), p. 261.
252. See Paul Francke, *Zur Geschichte des öffentlichen Arbeitsnachweises in Deutschland*, Phil. diss., Halle-Wittenberg, Halle 1913.

of employers' and workers' representatives. From the end of the nineteenth century onwards, the Federation of German Labour Exchanges
(*Verband deutscher Arbeitsnachweise*) together with the trade unions,
middle-class social reformers and the German People's Party (*Deutsche
Volkspartei*) became one of the main forces behind the movement to
establish compulsory unemployment insurance. At its party conferences of 1896 and 1899 the DVP put forward an 'outline for an imperial
law for local authority unemployment insurance'.[253]

One of the problems with which this movement had to cope was the
unsatisfactory availability of statistics on unemployment in Germany.
A survey based on the occupational census of 14 June 1895 and the
general census of 2 December 1895 provided the only survey of Germany's national unemployment figures at this time.[254] However, this
was unreliable on account of its serious methodological deficiencies.
Apart from these sources of information, there were some figures on the
number of job vacancies in relation to the number of people seeking
employment, but these only existed for some local authority labour
exchanges.[255] Those trade unions which paid unemployment benefits
to their members also kept records on their unemployed members.[256]
However, the official trade union figures, collected and published by
the Imperial Statistical Office's Section for Workers' Statistics (*Abteilung für Arbeiterstatistik im Kaiserlichen Statistischen Amt*), set up in

253. These proposed that communities of over 10,000 inhabitants be empowered to
     provide insurance against unemployment and charge employers and employees
     compulsory contributions (Kleeis, *Geschichte*, pp. 179f.).
254. Published in *Vierteljahreshefte zur Statistik des Deutschen Reichs, Ergänzung zum 4. Hefte*,
     Berlin 1896. A comparatively detailed summary of these statistics with some
     additional analysis is contained in the published results of the occupational census
     of 14 June 1895, in *Statistik des Deutschen Reichs*, Neue Folge, 111, pp. 245–61,
     339–41. On the inadequacies of the census, *see* Georg Schanz, 'Die neuen Statisti-
     schen Erhebungen über Arbeitslosigkeit in Deutschland', in *Archiv für Soziale
     Gesetzgebung und Statistik* 10 (1897), pp. 325–78, esp. pp. 327–34. The unemploy-
     ment figures for 14 June 1895 were given as 1.85 per cent of the total workforce, or
     1.11 per cent excluding sick workers. These figures were based on a census of 16.1
     million employees and took no account of the self-employed. The figure for 2
     December 1895 was calculated at 4.73 per cent of the total workforce or 3.4 per cent
     excluding sick workers.
255. *See* Ignaz Jastrow's study which analyses the reports of thirty-eight of the larger
     municipal labour exchanges for the period January 1896 to December 1901,
     *Sozialpolitik und Verwaltungswissenschaft. Aufsätze und Abhandlungen, vol. I: Arbeitsmarkt
     und Arbeitsnachweise, Gewerbegerichte und Einigungsämter*, Berlin 1902, p. 91.
256. Statistical summary up to and including December 1914, in Wladimir Woytinsky,
     *Der deutsche Arbeitsmarkt: Ergebnisse der gewerkschaftlichen Arbeitslosenstatistik 1919 bis
     1929*, 2 vol., vol. 1, p. 102. According to Woytinsky's figures, the average annual
     unemployment figure for the period 1904 to 1913 lay somewhere between 1.1 per
     cent in 1906 and 2.9 per cent in 1908 and 1913.

1902, applied only to a small section of the workforce[257] and were certainly not representative. As a result of their lack of union organisation, workers in the agricultural sector and domestic industries were, like casual workers, hardly incorporated, if at all. The same was true of workers whose opportunities for work were subject to fluctuations in the economic cycle, such as those in the clothing or construction industries, in which unions long held back from introducing unemployment benefit because of their members' high seasonal unemployment during the winter months.[258] The figures also failed to reflect the numbers of unskilled workers and women who were as yet hardly represented in the unions.

The unsatisfactory state of statistics on the subject resulted, therefore, in considerable uncertainty about the true extent of unemployment and, hence, the actual costs an unemployment insurance would involve. The system for helping workers find employment remained at a rudimentary stage of development, and there were widespread fears that the work-shy would take advantage of unemployment benefits. Employers expected unemployment insurance to strengthen the trade unions' position in the labour market and, hence, resisted it in any form. In addition, different opinions existed on the appropriate form such an insurance should take and how it should be organised, whether through central government, the federal governments, local authorities or existing social insurance institutions. On top of this, the proposals encountered reservations on the part of the imperial government, which, to some extent, can be accounted for in terms of its anti-trade-union sentiments.[259] On account of a Reichstag initiative, which had asked Chancellor Bülow to set up a committee of experts to study existing arrangements for unemployment insurance and submit suggestions concerning how such an insurance should be developed, the Workers' Statistical Section was commissioned to compile a report on the extent of unemployment insurance. In 1906 the Imperial Statistical

257. The number of insured trade union members climbed from 213,962 on 30 June 1903 to 2,161,470 in late 1912, but even at the later date included less than one in seven of the 15.4 million wage-earners covered by the 1907 census.
258. The Association of Building Workers (Bauarbeiterverband), founded in 1910 through the amalgamation of skilled bricklayers and unskilled construction workers' association only paid unemployment benefits from 1914 onwards (*see* Karl-Gustav Werner, *Organisation und Politik der Gewerkschaften und Arbeitgeberverbände in der deutschen Bauwirtschaft*, Berlin 1968, pp. 90f.). During the severe winter of 1908/09 unemployment reached a level of 60 per cent among members of the bricklayers' association and approx. 44 per cent among members of the building workers' association during the winter of 1911/12 (Woytinsky, *Arbeitsmarkt*, vol. 1, pp. 115–17, vol. 2, Table 44).
259. *Sten. Berichte des Reichstags*, XIII, I, vol. 291, pp. 6213, 6218.

Office published a three-volume report on *Existing Insurance Arrangements in the German Empire and Abroad for Dealing with the Effects of Unemployment*, but concluded that the question of compulsory insurance was as yet not ripe for a solution. On 5 December 1913 Clemens von Delbrück, the State Secretary of the Interior, informed the Reichstag that the demand for unemployment insurance had to be seen as 'precipitate', given 'the present economic climate'. He especially doubted whether this kind of insurance could be properly financed and believed that the consequences of a 'universal, compulsory unemployment insurance' could not be calculated in view of the lack of sufficient unemployment statistics. The result of these various efforts to resist state unemployment insurance and its many associated problems was that, in contrast to Great Britain where it was introduced in 1911 for specific areas of employment, there was no legal provision for unemployment benefits in Germany prior to 1914. If we ignore the occasional experiments made in several towns and some individual firms, unemployment insurance in Germany remained almost exclusively confined to the trade unions. Because of fears concerning its potential costs and the possibility of workers' associations changing their role from organisations devoted to the class struggle to mere benevolent societies,[260] the unions faced a great deal of internal opposition to begin with. But, despite this, they increasingly began to provide their members with unemployment benefits from the late 1890s onwards, largely in an attempt to reduce their fluctuations in membership. The percentage of Germany's socialist free-trade-union members insured against unemployment was 12.9 in 1891, 34.4 in 1901 and 81.3, or 1.7 million members, in 1913.[261] The liberal Hirsch-Duncker unions and Christian trade unions also followed suit in providing their unemployed members with considerable financial assistance.[262]

The trade unions increasingly demanded that their struggle against the effects of unemployment be recognised by Germany's municipal

260. See Gerhard A. Ritter, *Die Arbeiterbewegung im Wilhelminischen Reich: Die sozialdemokratische Partei und die Freien Gewerkschaften, 1890–1900*, Berlin-Dahlem, 2nd edn 1963, pp. 157–61.

261. Schönhoven, 'Selbsthilfe', in *Archiv für Sozialgeschichte* 20 (1980), p. 174.

262. A. Faust in his 'State and Unemployment in Germany 1890–1918: Labour Exchanges, Job Creation and Unemployment Insurance', in Mommsen (ed.), *Emergence*, pp. 150–63, esp. p. 157, estimates that the inclusion of Germany's white-collar associations meant that approx. 3.2 million employees were insured against unemployment through their trade unions. For the growth and development of trade union unemployment insurance, *see also* Robert Michels and Gisela Michels-Lindner, 'Das Problem der Arbeitslosigkeit und ihre Bekämpfung durch die deutschen freien Gewerkschaften', in *Archiv für Sozialwissenschaft und Sozialpolitik* 31 (1910), pp. 421–97.

authorities, who were asked to provide supplementary benefits, modelled on the system first introduced in the Belgian town of Ghent in 1901. These additional payments were to be paid directly into trade union unemployment funds.[263] But, while the governments of Bavaria, Baden and Württemberg approved of the scheme in principle, few local authorities put it into practice in the period before 1914.[264] Most towns only took the trouble to provide support for the unemployed or improve their existing arrangements after the outbreak of the First World War in 1914 had for some months led to a dramatic rise in unemployment.[265] Local authorities now made government money available for the unemployed and, under pressure from the growing demand for labour caused by the expanding war economy, built up the system of public labour exchanges.[266] While this development was taking place, the idea that society as a whole was responsible for providing for the unemployed won increasing acceptance.

The social, economic and constitutional effects of social insurance before 1914

According to a survey produced in 1907–08, German working-class families spent on average 3 per cent of their total outgoings or 3.7 per cent of the husband's income from his main occupation (not taking into account any additional income) on insurance contributions.[267] Before

263. For the free trade unions' policy on the issue of state unemployment assistance, *see* the resolutions on 'Unemployment Statistics and Unemployment Insurance' in 1902 and 'Public Labour Exchanges and Unemployment Assistance' in 1911 at the German Trades Union Conferences (*Protokolle der Verhandlungen des vierten und achten Kongresses der Gewerkschaften Deutschlands*, 1902, pp. 188ff., 211; 1911, pp. 41, 337). See also *Die Arbeitslosenunterstützung in Reich, Staat und Gemeinde: Denkschrift der Generalkommission der Gewerkschaften Deutschlands für die gesetzgebenden Körperschaften des Reiches und der Bundesstaaten und für die Gemeindevertretungen*, 2nd edn, Berlin, 1914.

264. *See* Hansjoachim Henning, 'Arbeitslosenversicherung vor 1914: Das Genter System und seine Übernahme in Deutschland', in Hermann Kellenbenz (ed.), *Wirtschaftspolitik und Arbeitsmarkt*, Munich 1974, pp. 271–87; Ritter, *Staat*, p. 63.

265. *See* Woytinsky, *Arbeitsmarkt*, vol. 1, p. 102.

266. *See* Ludwig Preller, *Sozialpolitik in der Weimarer Republik*, reprint edn, Kronberg and Düsseldorf 1978, esp. pp. 6–8, 34f., 40, 43, 61ff.

267. *Erhebung von Wirtschaftsrechnungen minderbemittelter Familien im Deutschen Reiche*, compiled by the Kaiserliches Statistisches Amt, Abteilung für Arbeiterstatistik, Berlin 1909, reprint edn by Dieter Dowe with an introduction by Jens Flemming und Peter-Christian Witt, Berlin and Bonn 1981, p. 56*. The percentage figure includes private insurance companies. According to Reuter's calculations in his 'Verteilungs- und Umverteilungseffekte', in Blaich (ed.), *Staatliche Umverteilungspolitik*, p. 126, the costs of contributions paid by the insured worker into state insurance alone

1914 there was already an improvement in the general situation of working-class families as a result of the protection provided by sickness, accident, disablement and old-age insurance.[268] Compared with the workers' organisations we have known little up to now about the ordinary worker's reaction to social insurance.[269] In statements made by labour leaders and in the immediate reaction to new laws, such as that for disablement and old-age insurance, critical views tended to dominate at first. Bismarck's legislation did not, as he desired, produce a split between the workers and the socialist movement. To his and the employers' disappointment, the insurance laws merely made the workers' political and social struggle for emancipation more intense. Nevertheless, it is important to distinguish between the immediate effect the laws had and their long-term effect of creating mass loyalty for the existing political system by reducing the anxieties felt by working-class families.[270] Thus Bismarck's social insurance ultimately had the effect of furthering to some degree the workers' social emancipation and facilitating their political and social integration.

The actual benefits paid out under Germany's social insurance system were substantial. Total payments (not including the miners' provident societies) amounted to 850 million marks in 1912 at a time when the central government's budget was about two thousand million marks.[271] This fact, together with the generally encouraging experience of favourable legal decisions in social insurance matters, reinforced the workers' willingness to participate constructively in Germany's social

amounted to 2.7 per cent of his income. In 1902 the Krupp family's steelworks in Essen paid 858,520 marks into state insurance in respect of its workers and junior management. This sum represented 2.74 per cent of a total wage bill of 31,353,526 marks (Zahn, 'Arbeiterversicherung und Volkswirtschaft', in *Die deutsche Arbeiterversicherung*, p. 20). Because of rising medical costs, sickness insurance contributions had to be increased on several occasions during the period before 1914. In 1885 only 26.1 per cent of all sickness funds charged a contribution in excess of 2 per cent of local average daily wages or actual earnings. By 1900, 39.2 per cent of sickness funds did so (*Die Krankenversicherung im Jahre 1900, Statistik des Deutschen Reichs*, vol. 140, p. 47*f.*).

268. The East German historian Jürgen Kuczynski comes to a similar conclusion in his *Die Geschichte der Lage der Arbeiter in Deutschland von 1789 bis zur Gegenwart*, vol. III (1871–1900), Berlin (GDR) 1962, pp. 408f. Kuczynski sees Germany's social insurance as a 'palliative measure' which 'made several of the ever-worsening consequences of the new methods of exploitation somewhat more bearable'.

269. *See* Ritter, *Staat*, pp. 65f.

270. Michael Stolleis, 'Hundert Jahre Sozialversicherung in Deutschland: Rechtsgeschichtliche Entwicklung', in *Zeitschrift für die gesamte Versicherungswissenschaft* 69 (1980), pp. 155–75, esp. pp. 172f.

271. Based on figures in *Bevölkerung und Wirtschaft*, pp. 219–22; Peter-Christian Witt, *Die Finanzpolitik des Deutschen Reichs von 1903 bis 1913: Eine Studie zur Innenpolitik des Wilhelminischen Deutschland*, Lübeck and Hamburg, 1970, p. 380; idem, 'Finanzpoli-

welfare institutions, and this involvement signalled the workers' first steps towards establishing a new relationship with the state. Various legal rulings stressed the welfare component of the social security system and recognised the right to claim benefits in cases where individual employers had failed to keep up their share of contributions.[272] Such encouraging signs in the interpretation of labour law were further reinforced by the rulings of the industrial courts. Their work contrasted sharply with legal decisions in other areas, which were frequently interpreted as examples of biased 'class justice'.

It is difficult to estimate the effect which social insurance had on the medical health of Germany's workers. To begin with, there was a dramatic rise in the figures for life expectancy. A child born during the period in question could expect to live a full nine to ten years longer than his parents and a fifteen-year-old an extra 4.5 years. The chances of newly born male babies reaching the age of seventy or over also increased from 17.7 per cent in 1871–80 to 27.1 per cent in 1901–10.[273] However, it would certainly be wrong to attribute these figures either wholly or even predominantly to the effect of insurance benefits in the fields of medical care and the maintenance of the sick and infirm. There was also an improvement in people's diet, housing conditions and factory legislation, as well as increased welfare provision for workers and mothers. There were improvements, too, in town living conditions, social hygiene and child care, especially in the big cities.[274] The

tik und sozialer Wandel: Wachstum und Funktionswandel der Staatsausgaben in Deutschland, 1871–1913', in Hans-Ulrich Wehler (ed.), *Sozialgeschichte heute. Festschrift für Hans Rosenberg zum 70. Geburtstag*, Göttingen 1974, pp. 564–74, esp. p. 568.

272. Heinrich Rosin was instrumental in influencing legal developments. *See* his *Das Recht der Arbeiterversicherung: Für Theorie und Praxis systematisch dargestellt*, vol. 1, in 3 parts, Berlin 1890–93; vol. 2, Berlin 1905. *See also* Walter Kaskel, 'Geheimer Rat Professor Dr Heinrich Rosin', in *Monatsschrift für Arbeiter- und Angestelltenversicherung* 15 (1927), pp. 316–20; Göckenjan, 'Verrechtlichung', in *Leviathan* 9 (1981), pp. 31f. For a positive view of the work of the Reichsversicherungsamt, according to which it adopted 'the most liberal and sensible of attitudes' in disputes over compensation under the terms of the accident insurance law, *see* Grillenberger's Reichstag speech of 6 December 1888 (*Sten. Berichte des Reichstags*, VII, IV, vol. 1, p. 149). Bismarck and the employers' occupational associations, on the other hand, criticised the rulings of the Reichsversicherungsamt in accident cases as being too sympathetic towards the workers. Following Bödiker's departure as head of the Reichsversicherungsamt in 1897, the Imperial Office of the Interior instigated new administrative measures to apply criteria more rigorously in awarding disablement pensions which had initially risen sharply as a result of a disablement law of 1899 (Tennstedt, 'Sozialgeschichte der Sozialversicherung', in Blohmke (ed.), *Handbuch*, pp. 430, 450f.).

273. *See* the statistics on mortality in *Bevölkerung und Wirtschaft*, pp. 109f.

274. Between 1876/80 and 1913 infant mortality among legitimate offspring fell in Prussia only from 18.3 to 14.6 per cent in the countryside as opposed to a drop from

medical inspection of school-children by school doctors was introduced
and other forms of preventive medicine appeared, not forgetting, of
course, the progress made by medical research, especially in combating
infectious diseases, and the general improvement in medical training.
Taken together, these individual advances obviously had an even
greater combined effect and significance. But recent research has also
shown that 'social inequality in illness and death'[275] not only simply
persisted in the period of the Empire, but probably worsened.[276] For
instance, the decline in the infant mortality rate was at first confined to
the 'new middle class' of civil servants and white-collar workers and
was singularly more apparent here than among other groups right up
to 1913. In contrast, there was up to about 1900 only a small decline in
the figures of infant mortality for children of the self-employed. Up to
1900 there was even a rise recorded in the infant mortality rate of
children of skilled workers, unskilled workers and domestic servants in
the towns and the countryside; the last-named group, it should be
recalled, having a higher proportion of illegitimate children, among
whom infant mortality was particularly high.[277] Only after 1902–03
did the figures fall for all social groups. Even then, the slowest rate of
decline was still registered among unskilled workers, whose infants
were twice as likely to die in the first year after birth than the children
of civil servants.[278]

Contemporaries especially noted the greater tendency among certain

21.1 to 13.2 per cent in the towns. During the same period the comparable figures
for illegitimate offspring were a fall from 31.2 to 27.2 per cent in the countryside
compared with a drop from 40.3 to 24.1 per cent in the towns (Hohorst *et al.*,
Sozialgeschichtliches Arbeitsbuch II, p. 36).

275. Reinhard Spree's study, *Soziale Ungleichheit vor Krankheit und Tod. Zur Sozialgeschichte
des Gesundheitsbereichs im Deutschen Kaiserreich*, to be published in English as *Health and
Social Class in Imperial Germany*, Leamington Spa 1987, is indispensable for this
subject.

276. *See* Reinhard Spree, 'Zur Bedeutung des Gesundheitwesens für die Entwicklung der
Lebenschancen der deutschen Bevölkerung zwischen 1870 und 1913', in Blaich
(ed.), *Staatliche Umverteilungspolitik*, pp. 165–223, esp. p. 198. For the varying
mortality rates of Germany's social classes, *see also* the interesting figures for
Bremen between 1901 and 1910, in M. Mosse and G. Tugendreich (ed.), *Krankheit
und Soziale Lage*, Munich 1912/13, editor's introduction, pp. 16–18, and Arthur E.
Imhof, 'Mortalität in Berlin vom 18. bis. 20. Jahrhundert', in *Berliner Statistik* 31
(1977), pp. 138–45, esp. 141f.

277. *See* Reinhard Spree, 'Strukturierte soziale Ungleichheit im Reproduktionsbereich:
Zur historischen Analyse ihrer Erscheinungsformen in Deutschland 1870 bis 1913',
in Jürgen Bergmann, Klaus Megerle und Peter Steinbach (eds.), *Geschichte als
politische Wissenschaft: Sozialökonomische Ansätze, Analyse politikhistorischer Phänomene,
politologische Fragestellungen in der Geschichte*, Stuttgart 1979, pp. 55–115; ibid., p. 72.

278. Ibid., p. 73. Prussia's infant mortality rate in 1912/13 came to 14.8 per cent for the
total population. The figures for children among the following occupational categories were 12.3 per cent for the self-employed, 9.3 per cent for public servants, 13.1

social groups to contract or die from tuberculosis and recognised that the incidence of the disease was related to jobs, housing and diet. In Prussia, for example, special care centres were set up to try and combat the spread of tuberculosis by educating the population in matters of hygiene and preventive care. These centres also provided help for sufferers in their own homes. The importance of the sanatoria — set up by the regional insurance offices in charge of disablement insurance — in combating tuberculosis was almost certainly overestimated at first. However, of the 16,053 available beds in 1915 in Germany's 158 sanatoria, the regional insurance offices were responsible for 5,494 beds in forty-one centres.[279] Between 1876 and 1910 the sanatoria and, more importantly, the increased isolation of sufferers and a general improvement in the economic situation of the poorer classes, helped reduce the annual figure for TB cases by half, from 30.9 to 15.3 per 10,000 inhabitants.[280] Yet even after the turn of the century tuberculosis was still by far and away the most common cause of death among adolescents and young and middle-aged adults of all ages. In Prussia, for example, according to the figures for 1910, tuberculosis was still the cause of more than 40 per cent of all recorded deaths between the ages of fifteen and thirty.[281] The great interest shown by the disablement insurance funds in promoting preventive measures, as well as in restoring the patient's physical fitness, was, of course, connected with the fact that this disease was by far the single most important cause of premature disablement among young workers, thus placing a long-

per cent for skilled workers, 17.4 per cent for unskilled workers and 22.5 per cent for domestic servants. These groups were categorised on the basis of the father's social position, or, in the case of illegitimate children, the mother's.

279. Tennstedt, 'Sozialgeschichte der Sozialversicherung', in Blohmke (ed.), *Handbuch*, p. 454. Between 1897 and 1903, disablement insurance was responsible for placing 78,329 people under constant medical care on account of pulmonary tuberculosis. The average annual costs in 1903 came to 373.84 marks for each male patient and 350.30 marks for each female patient. These figures were about two and a half times the average disablement pension figure of 152 marks (Bielefeldt, 'Arbeiterversicherung und Volksgesundheit', in *Die deutsche Arbeiterversicherung*, p. 23). For a criticism of the way in which the effect of sanatoria was exaggerated, *see* Alfred Grotjahn, *Erlebtes und Erstrebtes: Erinnerungen eines sozialistischen Arztes*, Berlin, 1932, pp. 136–8. The growth and development of sanatoria became a matter of prestige for the regional insurance offices and helped increase their popularity. Grotjahn relates the content and reception of a lecture entitled 'The Crisis in the Sanatoria Movement', which he gave to the Society for Social Medicine (Gesellschaft für Soziale Medizin) on 11 April 1907.

280. M. Mosse 'Einfluss der soziale Lage auf die Tuberkulose', in Mosse and Tugendreich (eds.), *Krankheit und soziale Lage*, pp. 551–607, esp. p. 563. *See also* Dirk Blasius, 'Geschichte und Krankheit: Sozialgeschichtliche Perpektiven der Medizingeschichte', in *Geschichte und Gesellschaft* 2 (1976), pp. 387–415, esp. pp. 397–402.

281. Mosse, 'Einfluss', p. 557.

term strain on their funds. For instance, figures for the period 1896–99 show that of every 1,000 disabled male workers in industry and handicrafts, 624 in the 20–25 age group, 576 in the 25–30 age group and 505 in 30–35 age group suffered from TB. The figures for female workers, classified according to the same age groups show 597, 472 and 373 cases for every 1,000 persons receiving benefits. In all, tuberculosis accounted for 15 per cent of disablement among male workers and 9.5 per cent among female workers.[282]

Contemporaries were fully aware of the fact that, compared with Germany's better-off social classes, the incidence of the disease was much higher among the poorer classes in society and the areas they inhabited.[283] Increasing attention was paid to the relative frequency with which illness occurred in connection with specific types of employment. A generally greater recognition of the problem of occupational diseases among male and female workers was reflected in the extensive literature available on the subject from the 1870s onwards, including factory inspectors' reports, official inquiries, studies by social reformers and publications specifically dealing with social health problems. The most important of these investigations was the analysis of the files held by the Leipzig and district local sickness insurance office for the period between 1 January 1887 and 30 April 1905. This study, which was financed under the auspices of the Imperial Statistical Office by way of a generous special government grant,[284] resulted in a methodical and detailed analysis of the role of sex, age and occupation as regards the incidence of illness and the mortality rate. The purpose behind this investigation was to see what lessons could be learnt for the way in which workers' protective legislation should develop in the future.

The direct and indirect effects of social insurance on the general health of the population, especially that of the workers, cannot be viewed in isolation from other factors. We can, however, safely say that sickness insurance helped bring about the more successful treatment of illnesses. For many members of the poorer classes sickness insurance meant that they received proper medical treatment for the first time ever. The effectiveness of all the various branches of social insurance together played an essential part in helping identify the causes of illness and disablement, together with means of combating them by preven-

---

282. *Atlas und Statistik der Arbeiterversicherung*, p. 34.
283. Mosse, 'Einfluss', pp. 573ff.
284. *Krankheits- und Sterblichkeitsverhältnisse in der Ortskrankenkasse für Leipzig und Umgebung: Untersuchungen über den Einfluss von Geschlecht, Alter und Beruf*, compiled by the Kaiserliches Statistisches Amt, 4 vols. in 1 vol., Berlin 1910.

tive measures. One such measure was provided by the accident prevention regulations which were worked out in ever greater detail by the
employers' occupational associations established under the accident
insurance law. Even though, as a result of intensified work-methods
and the increasing use of machines, the number of accidents at work
showed an upward trend, these measures, together with improved
medical care for those injured at work, helped bring about a relative
decline in the figure for fatal accidents.[285]

In the years directly preceeding the outbreak of the First World War,
working-class families still experienced the breadwinner's premature
disablement or a family member's chronic illness as a major blow,
especially since sickness benefits only partially compensated for loss of
earnings. Moreover, the need to stay at home and look after the sick
worker frequently meant that the mother of the family could no longer
go out to work. Medical benefits were only gradually extended to the
other members of the family. However, problems caused by illness or
disablement were no longer accepted as fatalistically as had been the
case before sickness insurance was introduced. The interesting obser-
vations of the factory inspectorate in Baden appear to be typical of the
time. One of the inspectors wrote in 1892 that:

> the social insurance laws have resulted in a situation where, in cases
> involving sick and injured workers one notices less distress among working-
> class families, with all that entails. Visiting workers' apartments, one gets
> much less of an impression of gloominess and indifference when coming
> across cases of illness or victims of accidents. The workers also appear to
> maintain a sense of holding onto their accustomed living conditions in this
> situation.[286]

Sickness insurance not only made it possible to provide appropriate
medical treatment at an early stage of a patient's illness. It also had a
socially educational effect in that the worker became accustomed to
taking better care of his own health, as well as taking precautions to
prevent the onset of short or long-term disablement. This meant that
workers were more able to adapt to the conditions of modern industrial
society.[287] At the same time, the typical middle-class values of culti-

285. Lotte Zumpe, 'Zur Geschichte der Unfallverhältnisse in der deutschen Industrie
   von 1885–1932', Wirtschaftswiss. Diss. (MS), Berlin (GDR) 1961, esp. pp. 221,
   316.
286. *Jahresbericht der Grossherzoglich Badischen Fabrikinspektion für das Jahr 1892*, Karlsruhe
   1893, p. 126.
287. Spree in *Soziale Ungleichheit* speaks of a 'spread of medical provision (*Medikalisierung*)
   among the lower sections of society in the form of an 'enforced socialisation'
   (p. 157) and concludes that 'a consequential process which unified values, attitudes

vating a healthy, 'moral' and sensible life-style, originally aimed against
an aristocratic culture viewed as moribund and degenerate and reflected
in middle-class goals, percolated through to the poorer classes from the
sickness funds and their forerunners — the journeymen's and factory
workers' voluntary self-help organisations.[288] From around the turn of
the century, official statements justifying the system of compulsory
state insurance gave increasing prominence to the idea that it provided
a vehicle for educating the workers. Thus Friedrich Zahn, one of
Germany's leading contemporary experts on social insurance, thought
that the idea of workers' insurance having crippled the workers' awareness of personal responsibility was completely wrong. In his opinion, it
was precisely the compulsory nature of social insurance which had
succeeded in rousing the workers, who could not be reached through
voluntary schemes, to rise above their attitude of lethargy and helplessness. It had educated them in 'social policy and public hygiene values',
but without weakening their own self-help organisations. Workers' insurance, on the whole, had resulted in the emergence of 'a physically and
mentally more efficient and capable workforce, which was happier at
work, more capable of consumption and, at the same time, enhanced in its
social standing'.[289]

The East German historian Jürgen Kuczynski has argued that the
per capita increase in the number of working-days lost through illness
and incapacity, from 6.1 in 1885 to 8.7 in 1913,[290] is evidence of a
general deterioration of health caused by increased demands on people's work-effort, deteriorating housing conditions, greater distances to
work and the growing use in the productive process of materials likely
to cause damage to health.[291] In my opinion, this is not a convincing
argument. The rise in the number of days lost through illness is much
more likely to be a result of the improvement in sickness benefits which
resulted from later legislation. For instance, the maximum term of
benefit payments was increased from thirteen to twenty-six weeks and

and behaviour patterns in respect of health was introduced which influenced
important areas of private reproduction (in everyday life). The structures of social
inequality showed a tendency to be reflected less and less on the level of values and
attitudes, which instead — as a result of being partly shaped by this spread of
medical provision in society — resulted in a progressive levelling out of differences
between the various social strata and sub-cultures' (p. 162).

288. See Frevert, *Krankheit als politisches Problem*, pp. 336f.
289. Zahn, 'Belastung durch die deutsche Arbeiterversicherung', in *Zeitschrift für die
gesamte Versicherungswissenschaft* 12 (1912), p. 1141.
290. Spree, 'Bedeutung des Gesundheitswesens', in Blaich (ed.), *Staatliche Umverteilungspolitik*, p. 179.
291. Kuczynski, *Lage der Arbeiter*, vol. 3, pp. 386f., vol. 4 (1900–17/18), Berlin GDR
1967, pp. 407f.

payment no longer withheld in cases where an illness was attributed to the patient's 'sexual excesses'.[292] Also, workers learnt to make fuller use of the benefit funds and paid more attention to their health. Since loss of earnings was so keenly felt, the point at which they were prepared to register themselves sick was only reached at an exceptionally late stage at first. But the general improvement in living conditions apparently led to the lowering of this threshold, and, as the increase in the average length of a registered illness — from 14.0 days in 1885 to 20.6 in 1913 — would appear to indicate,[293] there was a growing tendency to stay at home until the illness had been completely cured.

Social insurance had a number of important effects on the medical profession and developments in the field of medicine. As a body, doctors were almost completely ignored when it was first introduced in the 1880s, even though the successful operation of the entire system depended on their cooperation. Once it had been established that a patient's injury was the result of an industrial injury, it was their expert opinion which ultimately decided on whether and to what extent an accident merited compensation. They also decided on whether or not a disablement pension should be awarded, and, in cases where a patient was unfit for work as a result of illness, the payment of sickness benefits also depended ultimately on the medical certificates which they supplied. The sickness funds tried at first to keep a check on feigned illnesses, reduce the costs of medicine as well as medical treatment and streamline their administration by employing doctors on individual contracts in their central or branch offices or doctors who were heavily dependent on them because of their receipt of a lump sum for each fund member.[294]

With the growth in the system of sickness funds, these doctors were, to a great extent, soon able to corner the market provided by sickness insurance, especially in the big cities and industrial centres. The effect of this was to undermine the economic viability of those doctors' practices which were excluded from the system. Among the many objections to the system, the patient's restricted choice of doctor and

292. Tennstedt, 'Sozialgeschichte der Sozialversicherung', in Blohmke (ed.), *Handbuch*, p. 389. *See also* A. Blaschko's article on 'Geschlechtskrankheiten', in Alfred Grotjahn and J. Kaup (eds.), *Handwörterbuch der Sozialen Hygiene*, 2 vols., Leipzig 1912, vol. 1, pp. 397–405, esp. p. 404; Friedrich Prinzing, *Handbuch der medizinischen Statistik*, 2nd edn, 2 vols., Jena 1930/31, vol. 1, pp. 205–9.

293. Spree, 'Bedeutung des Gesundheitswesens', in Blaich (ed.), *Staatliche Umverteilungspolitik*, p. 179.

294. *See* Claudia Huerkamp, 'Ärzte und Professionalisierung in Deutschland: Überlegungen zum Wandel des Arztberufs im 19. Jahrhundert', in *Geschichte und Gesellschaft* 6 (1980), pp. 349–82, esp. pp. 369f.

the 'terrorism of the fund managers' were especially singled out for criticism, although widespread accusations concerning their nepotism and vetting of doctors' political views were to a great extent unfounded.[295] However, the social insurance system's neglect of doctors' interests helped speed up the process whereby the medical profession organised itself in order to put forward its views. On 13 September 1900 doctors formed the so-called Hartmann League (*Hartmannbund*) with the aim of representing doctors' interests, and a Prussian law passed in 1899 set up 'courts of honour' which made it easier for them as a professional body to bring court cases against the sickness funds.[296]

After bitter arguments, which even went as far as boycotts, strikes and other actions on the part of the doctors, the Hartmann League succeeded in having the principle of collective agreements for doctors' services recognised. This was contained in the so-called Berlin agreement signed between the League and the various federations representing the sickness insurance funds in 1913.[297] Funds still concluded individual contracts with doctors, but the ground rules for such contracts were explicitly set out in this collective agreement. The right of funds to employ doctors at their own discretion — one doctor had to be hired for every 1,350 members — was replaced by new legal procedures governing the admission of doctors to treat fund members.[298]

All in all, sickness insurance positively benefited doctors economically. Payments made by the funds to practising doctors rose from an average of 786 marks per annum in 1887 to 2,777 marks in 1909.[299] Together with the rise taking place at the time in patients' real wages and the general drift to the cities, the new system enabled them to increase their panel of regular patients quite considerably.

If we take the increase in the number of doctors, from 35 to 51 for every 100,000 members of the population between 1885 and 1913,[300]

---

295. *See*, for example, Otto von Bollinger's inaugural address as Rector of Munich University, *Wandlungen der Medizin in den letzten 50 Jahren: Rede beim Antritt des Rektorats der Ludwig-Maximilians-Universität gehalten am 28. November 1908*, Munich 1908, p. 37.

296. *See* Huerkamp, 'Ärzte', in *Geschichte und Gesellschaft*, esp. pp. 367–79.

297. For the setting up of sickness insurance associations (*Krankenkassenverbände*) by the local sickness insurance funds (*Ortskrankenkassen*) and their effectiveness before 1914, *see* Tennstedt, *Soziale Selbstverwaltung*, esp. pp. 83–104.

298. *See* ibid., pp. 75–82; Feige, *Sozialpolitische Analyse*, pp. 79–87.

299. Huerkamp, 'Ärzte', in *Geschichte und Gesellschaft*, p. 373. The figure for 'practising doctors' is arrived at after subtracting the figure for army doctors and those employed only in hospitals from the total number of doctors. Doctors' fees paid by the miners' provident societies' (*Knappschaftskassen*) and state sickness insurance rose from 10 million marks in 1885 to 36 million marks in 1900, 76 million in 1909 and 100 million in 1913 (Reuter, 'Verteilungs- und Umverteilungseffekte', in Blaich (ed.), *Staatliche Umverteilungspolitik*, p. 163).

the increase in the number of hospital beds per head of the population by almost two and a half times between 1882 and 1913,[301] the more intensive care of patients by hospitals, no longer regarded with terror as just another form of poorhouse,[302] and the rapid growth in dentistry — the number of dentists in Prussia rose by twenty times between 1887 and 1913 from 548 to 11,213[303] all of this would have been inconceivable without social insurance. This is borne out by a comparison with Britain and the USA during the same period. While the number of doctors in Germany increased by 56.2 per cent between 1889 and 1898 alongside a population rise of 11.5 per cent, the number of doctors in Great Britain rose only by 16 per cent between 1891 and 1901 alongside a 12.8 per cent rise in population. In the USA the figure for the period between 1890 and 1900 was 25.9 per cent alongside a population rise of 20.7 per cent.[304] Certainly, the fact that Germany's agricultural labourers were completely incorporated into the system only in 1914[305] meant that, as regards medical provision, there was a distinct bias which favoured the towns at the expense of the countryside. In 1911, for example, there were 9.6 doctors for every 10,000 inhabitants in towns with a population over 100,000. Communities with under 10,000 inhabitants, on the other hand, had only 2.7 doctors.[306] The geographical distribution of doctors also showed wide variations throughout the country. In 1906, for example, Prussia's predominantly agricultural provinces of Posen, East Prussia and West Prussia had 3.08, 3.51 and 3.22 doctors, respectively, for every 10,000 inhabitants. The respective figures for Berlin and Hamburg were, in contrast, 12.88 and 7.82 doctors for every 10,000 inhabitants.[307]

300. Tennstedt, 'Sozialgeschichte der Sozialversicherung', in Blohmke (ed.), *Handbuch*, p. 403.
301. From 27.9 to 69 for every 10,000 inhabitants (*Bevölkerung und Wirtschaft*, p. 125).
302. Spree, 'Bedeutung des Gesundheitswesens', in Blaich (ed.), *Staatliche Umverteilungspolitik*, pp. 184–8. Between 1887 and 1909 the number of female and male nurses rose from 3.1 to 10.8 for every 10,000 inhabitants (*Bevölkerung und Wirtschaft*, p. 124).
303. *Bevölkerung und Wirtschaft*, p. 124.
304. Henry Ernst Sigerist, 'Von Bismarck bis Beveridge. Entwicklungen und Richtungen in der Gesetzgebung der Sozialversicherung', in Erna Lesky (ed.), *Sozialmedizin: Entwicklung und Selbstverständnis*, Darmstadt 1977, pp. 186–214, esp. p. 213.
305. The number of workers insured against sickness was also much lower in rural areas than in the big cities and industrial centres. In 1897, for example, only 62.3 per thousand of East Prussia's and 67.5 per thousand of West Prussia's population were members of a state-approved sickness insurance funds. The comparative figure for Berlin was 266.1 per thousand (Tennstedt, 'Sozialgeschichte der Sozialpolitik', in Blohmke (ed.), *Handbuch*, p. 164).
306. Wilhelm Thiele, 'Zum Verhältnis von Ärzteschaft und Krankenkassen 1883 bis 1913', in *Das Argument, Sonderband 4: Entwicklung und Struktur des Gesundheitswesens: Argumente für eine soziale Medizin* (V), Berlin 1974, pp. 19–45, esp. pp. 36f.

Social insurance also eventually brought about specific changes in the nature of the medical practitioner's job inasmuch as doctors were called upon as referees and experts to provide statistical data in their role as 'agents of state institutions' and 'joint administrators of the nation's resources and work-efficiency'. This meant that they now spent some of their time performing civil service functions.[308] As regards the direct and indirect effects which social insurance had on medicine in general, the intensified efforts which were made to combat tuberculosis have already been mentioned. To these must be added the medical profession's improved knowledge of measures to tackle the causes of occupational diseases, the more effective treatment of accidents and increased efforts after the turn of the century to combat venereal diseases (whereby attitudes of moral condemnation gave way to a more enlightened matter-of-fact attitude and appropriate medical treatment), as well as attempts to eradicate alcoholism, seen both as a dangerous illness and one which was costly in its effects on the national economy. Social insurance was also instrumental in encouraging the intensive growth of paediatrics[309] and reducing by half the mortality rate among children between the ages of one and fifteen years. Between 1871 and 1880 one in five children in this age group died. Between 1901 and 1910 it was only one in ten.[310] The reason was that children from the poorer classes, where the low value placed on children's lives led to sickness and death being more readily accepted as nature taking its course, now received more medical attention when they fell ill. Mothers, who had previously seen no need to call in a doctor, were now also given medical advice on how best to prevent children's illnesses.

In addition, the statistical information supplied by social insurance institutions helped deepen medical knowledge of the connections which existed between a patient's social background, occupation and the illness he or she contracted. This made a significant contribution to the growth of a specialist field of medicine concerned with the social causes of diseases, medical statistics and, more especially, social hygienics. During this period, the latter emerged alongside experimental hygienics as an independent field of research at German universities.[311] In

---

307. *Verhandlungen des Reichstags*, XII, II, vol. 274; *Anlagen zu den Sten. Berichten*, p. 758. Water-supply systems and sewage systems, which had important effect on standards of hygiene, were also much more advanced in the big cities compared with small towns or rural districts (*see* Spree, 'Bedeutung des Gesundheitswesens', in Blaich (ed.), *Staatliche Umverteilungspolitik*, pp. 199–214).
308. J. Rubin, *Grundzüge der internen Arbeiterversicherungs-Medizin*, Jena 1909, p. 1. *See also* Bollinger, *Wandlungen der Medizin*, p. 35.
309. *See* Bollinger, *Wandlungen der Medizin*, pp. 7f.
310. *See* mortality statistics in *Bevölkerung und Wirtschaft*, pp. 109f.

1887 the Imperial Insurance Office ruled that it was not necessary for an 'injury resulting from an accident' to be judged 'the sole cause of incapacity for work' before a worker could qualify for accident insurance benefits. Instead, it 'sufficed to see [the injury] as only one of several contributory causes and, as such, was to be the primary consideration'.[312] This decision, together with the recognition of 'traumatic neuroses' as illnesses causing incapacity — on the basis of which pensions could be awarded under the terms of the accident insurance law — led to a heated controversy on the causes and significance of psychiatric illnesses.[313] The reason why so many of these cases were falsely diagnosed as 'faked illnesses' was seen by a Königsberg doctor — no doubt rightly — 'in the lack of comprehension with which doctors from the well-to-do classes encounter the psyche of the destitute worker, whose only form of capital is his health'.[314]

Impoverishment resulting from old age and premature disablement was a fate which most workers could not avoid in spite of the social security net which at first still had large gaps. The average pension was still too small and required such a high degree of disablement and advanced years before a worker could qualify for one that most workers, especially in industry and handicrafts, had already lost the jobs for which they were originally qualified. Many had already gone through the painful process of working at less skilled jobs or suffered temporary

311. Thus Dr Alfred Grotjahn, one of the founders of social hygiene in Germany, collaborated with the economist, demographer and later town councillor F. Kriegel in publishing from 1902 onwards the 'Jahresberichte über soziale Hygiene, Demographie und Medizinalstatistik, sowie alle Zweige des sozialen Versicherungswesens' (Jena 1092–15, Berlin 1916–23). He was also one of the main figures behind the founding in 1905 of the 'Verein für soziale Medizin, Hygiene und Medizinalstatistik'. For a summary of his work in this field, *see* his *Soziale Pathologie: Versuche einer Lehre von den Sozialbeziehungen der menschlichen Krankheiten als Grundlage der sozialen Medizin und der sozialen Hygiene*, Berlin 1912. The *Handwörterbuch der Sozialen Hygiene* referred to in note 292, above, gives a good insight into the state of research in this field before the First World War. *See also* the chapter entitled 'Die Sociale Hygiene als Sonderfach', in Grotjahn, *Erlebtes*, pp. 123–46.
312. 'Rekursentscheidung des Reichsversicherungsamts, Nr. 323 der Rekursentscheidungen, Bescheide und Beschlüsse', in *Amtliche Nachrichten des Reichs-Versicherungsamts 1887*, pp. 133f.
313. The funds' financial interests obviously played a part here. Thus, according to Rubin in his *Grundzüge* (p. 19), 'in the case of traumatic neuroses especially. . ., the authorities liable for the payment of treatment found themselves obliged to protest in the course of time, in order to prevent the term losing its original purpose and being interpreted too widely. For the doctor as well, a limited application of this term would be desirable for reasons of the national economy'.
314. Siegfried Stern, 'Traumatische Neurose und Simulation', in *Festschrift zur Feier des 60. Geburtstages von Max Jaffe. Chemische und medizinische Untersuchungen*, Braunschweig 1901, pp. 81–100, esp. p. 100. Stern sees a parallel in the judiciary's ill-considered judgements *vis à vis* the working class.

or chronic unemployment long before they came into a pension —
assuming they ever lived to see one.

The results of studies which have monitored the chronological
development of individual working-class budgets over a considerable
period of time have revealed that the workers' true situation cannot be
gauged accurately from 'snapshot' studies of domestic family budgets.[315] Instead, the worker's true material situation depended to a
great extent on the different phases he went through in life, different
periods affecting his income and the rhythm of the family cycle.[316] For
instance, the financial situation of an unmarried male worker or a
young married childless couple, where the wife could work to help set
up a home, was better than that of a married couple which, at a later
stage, had to look after several small children whose needs increased as
they grew older. In such cases, the potential earning capacity of the
wife, who was stuck at home, was either wholly lost or limited to her
working at home to earn some extra money. Some years later, the
children, who were by now old enough to work, could make a significant contribution to the family budget through their wages, assuming,
of course, that they had not set up their own home in the meantime.

Physical exhaustion, illness and partial or total disablement could
easily result in a worker losing his job at a relatively early stage in life,
forcing him to take on less skilled work[317] or resign himself to unem-

315. Before they can be regarded as having been calculated on a methodologically sound
    basis, domestic budgets, as they exist for Germany from the 1880's onwards,
    require that a strict record of all income and expenditure be kept over a minimum
    period of one year (*see* Ernst Engel, *Das Rechnungsbuch der Hausfrau und seine Bedeutung
    im Wirtschaftsleben der Nation: Ein Vortrag*, Berlin 1882; idem, *Die Lebenskosten belgischer
    Arbeiterfamilien früher und jetzt, ermittelt aus Familienhaushaltsrechnungen und vergleichend
    zusammengestellt*, Dresden 1895, esp. pp. 10–15). As a result, the families of workers
    with poor school qualifications, irregular work, low income, advanced age or
    frequent change of residence are naturally underrepresented compared with the
    élite of younger and middle-aged skilled workers. Therefore, these budgets can not
    be regarded as representative of the overall situation, especially of old age and
    disabled workers.
316. B. Seebohm Rowntree had already drawn attention to these connections in his
    pioneering study of poverty in York, published in 1901 (*Poverty: A Study of Town Life*,
    reprint of the 1922 edition, New York 1971, esp. pp. 169–71). As far as German
    research on this subject is concerned, these questions have been taken up by
    Heilwig Schomerus, *Die Arbeiter der Maschinenfabrik Esslingen, Forschungen zur Lage der
    Arbeiterschaft im 19. Jahrhundert*, Stuttgart 1977, esp. pp. 143ff., 267ff., *See also* note
    318, below.
317. On the process of a worker sinking in the labour market as a consequence of old
    age, *see* Friedrich Syrup-Gleiwitz, 'Der Altersaufbau der industriellen Arbeiter-
    schaft', in *Archiv für exacte Wirtschaftsforschung* (= *Thünen-Archiv*), 6 (1914), pp. 14–115,
    esp. p. 96; 'Diskussionsbeitrag von Alfred Weber', in *Verhandlungen des Vereins für
    Sozialpolitik in Nürnberg 1911* (*Schriften des Vereins für Sozialpolitik* 138), pp. 147–56,
    esp. p. 156; idem, 'Das Berufsschicksal der Industriearbeiter: Ein Vortrag', in *Archiv*

ployment. In some parts of industry and in certain occupations it was already difficult for a worker over forty to keep his job, let alone find a new one. Redundancy often meant the start of the worker's slide into poverty, leading to his parting with many household luxuries beyond his essential needs, such as jewellery, furniture and items of clothing acquired along the way as a kind of 'indirect provision for old age'.[318] The high proportion of older workers in unskilled and low-paid jobs, especially in agriculture and the textile industry,[319] was not just the result of these workers' degradation. Nor was it simply a result of older workers drifting into the textile industry from other parts of industry or returning to the countryside from work in the towns; that is, from industry to agriculture. The explanation also lies in the fact that, unlike unskilled workers, it was not uncommon for skilled workers to set up their own small craft business or find themselves taken on the staff in a factory workshop. If this happened, they were included in statistical surveys under the categories of the self-employed or white-collar workers. In addition, both textiles and agriculture were stagnating industries, which, in contrast to the expanding sectors of the economy, hardly, or at most only temporarily, took on young workers in any great numbers. The sources provide us with sufficient evidence of the below-average wage earned by most older workers[320] as well as their generally lower qualifications. Nevertheless, this evidence does not necessarily indicate that they were sinking lower in the job market. Instead, their apparent impoverishment may well have been the result of changes taking place in the structure of the workforce and the fact that qualified workers were moving into the self-employed and white-collar worker categories.

A 'hypothetical curve of life-earnings', based on a comparison of

für Sozialwissenschaft und Sozialpolitik 34 (1912), pp. 377–405, esp. pp. 387f.; Marie Bernays, 'Berufswahl und Berufsschicksal des modernen Industriearbeiters', in *Archiv für Sozialwissenschaft und Sozialpolitik* 35 (1912), pp. 123–76, esp. pp. 125–59; ibid., 36 (1913), pp. 884–915; Goetz Briefs, 'Das gewerbliche Proletariat', in *Grundriss der Sozialökonomik, IX. Abteilung, Das soziale System des Kapitalismus, 1. Teil: Die gesellschaftliche Schichtung im Kapitalismus*, Tübingen 1926, pp. 142–240, esp. pp. 208f.; Reif, 'Soziale Lage', in *Archiv für Sozialgeschichte* 22 (1982), esp. pp. 32–7.

318. Heilwig Schomerus has discussed the connection between life earnings curves and family and domestic cycles in her study on Württemberg which compares 'inventories' and 'divisions' of property on marriage or the death of a spouse: *see* Schomerus, *Arbeiter*, esp. pp. 221–49, 258–62; and idem, 'Lebenszyklus und Lebenshaltung in Arbeiterhaushalten des 19. Jahrhunderts', in Werner Conze and Ulrich Engelhardt (eds.), *Arbeiter im Industrialisierungsprozess. Herkunft, Lage und Verhalten*, Stuttgart 1979, pp. 195–200.

319. *See Berufsstatistik von 1907*, in *Statistik des Deutschen Reichs*, vol. 211, esp. pp. 259–265; Syrup-Gleiwitz, 'Altersaufbau', in *Thünen-Archiv* 6 (1914), esp. p. 87.

320. For example, see Syrup-Gleiwitz, 'Altersaufbau', p. 96.

workers' wages according to different age groups within, say, an
individual firm or trade union at a given point of time, would give us a
very gloomy picture of workers sinking at an early stage into the acute
poverty associated with old age. But if, instead, we take as our basis a
'curve of real life-earnings', based on the wages of individual workers at
different stages of their working life, a quite different picture emerges.[321]
Nevertheless, it was still true that incapacity resulting from old age and
disablement meant a considerable drop in living-standards for most
German workers before 1914. If they had no savings laid aside or were
not taken into their children's homes, workers or their widows had to
turn to poor relief to supplement the benefits paid out under disablement and old age insurance. Even then, this only provided them with
the barest standard of living.[322]

Bismarck had hoped that the disabled worker, by virtue of the cash
he brought into a household with his pension, could count on being
shown more respect, given better treatment and generally pushed
around less than before, especially in the countryside.[323] Whether this
hope was ever realised is, of course, something we will never know for
certain.

As managing director of Westphalia's regional insurance office between 1899 and 1925, Dr Hermann Althoff, one of the leading civil
servants in charge of administering Germany's disablement and old-age
insurance, noted in his memoirs dealing with the early days of this
insurance:

> One has to admit that, as a rule, pensions did not match the cost of living.
> This was certainly the case in the towns. In the countryside, on the other
> hand, where payment in kind was still normal and hard cash often not
> available, there was evidence that pensions were very important for covering
> people's living expenses. The old and the disabled, who at most could still be
> useful in lending the odd hand and looking after their family's children, were
> often an undesirable burden on their relatives. Yet they won amazing respect
> and love if they could contribute a reasonable amount of cash each month to
> the household budget.[324]

321. *See* Hermann Schäfer, 'Die Industriearbeiter: Lage und Lebenslauf im Bezugsfeld
    von Beruf und Betrieb', in Hans Pohl (ed.), *Sozialgeschichtliche Probleme in der Zeit der
    Hochindustrialisierung (1870–1914)*, Paderborn 1979, pp. 143–216, esp. pp. 185f.,
    196–202; and idem, 'Arbeitsverdienst im Lebenszyklus: Zur Einkommensmobilität
    von Arbeitern', in *Archiv für Sozialgeschichte* 21 (1981), pp. 237–67.
322. 'Die Einwirkung der Versicherungs-Gesetzgebung auf die Armenpflege', in Kai-
    serlich Statistisches Amt, *Vierteljahreshefte zur Statistik des deutschen Reichs 1897. H. II*,
    esp. p. 7. *See also Haushaltungs-Rechnungen Nürnberger Arbeiter: Ein Beitrag zur Aufhel-
    lung der Lebensverhältnisse des Nürnberger Proletariats. Bearbeitet im Arbeiter-Sekretariate
    Nürnberg (von Adolf Braun)*, Nuremberg 1901, pp. 2, 6f.
323. *See* ibid., p. 35f.

In his careful study of older factory workers in the Ruhr, Heinz Reif also comes to the conclusion that state pensions were inadequate to help realise the ideal many workers had of being able to afford the independent upkeep of their household without outside assistance. However, pensions did 'without doubt' reduce conflicts within the family caused by the children's obligation to pay their way, and so actually helped strengthen the tradition of caring for the old within the family structure. Finally, they no doubt also helped single men and married couples to avoid being sent to the dreaded poorhouse or local authority homes, which were often the only alternative to starvation and homelessness for widows and single women.[325]

Although, strictly speaking, pensions on their own were generally unable to provide the old and disabled with a decent standard of living up until the pension reforms of 1957, there was in fact a tangible improvement in the situation of older persons compared with previously. It is certainly significant that the number of people living off savings and pensions showed an almost threefold increase between 1882 and 1907, rising from 810,458 to 2,278.022 alongside a population rise of only 36.5 per cent during the same period.[326] Doubtless these figures were to a great extent the result of disablement and old-age insurance and partly also an indication of a general improvement in living conditions. At the same time, it must be noted that the proportion of the total male population in work remained fairly constant at 61 per cent, while the percentage of employed males in the over-70 age group fell by a sixth, from 47.3 to 39 per cent, and those in the 60–70 age group by about a tenth, from 78.9 to 71.2.[327] This decrease is even more apparent if one excludes 'family members employed in family enterprises', who, in contrast to the 1907 census, were only partially included in the census for 1895.[328]

324. *See* Althoff, 'Erinnerungen', in *Zentralblatt für Reichsversicherung und Reichsversorgung*, Oct. 1940, nos. 19/20, p. 181.
325. *See* Heinz Reif, 'Soziale Lage', in *Archiv für Sozialgeschichte*, 22 (1982), pp. 93f.; *see also* Tennstedt, 'Vorgeschichte', in *Zeitschrift für Sozialreform* 27 (1981), p. 677.
326. *See Berufsstatistik von 1907*, in *Statistik des Deutschen Reichs*, vol. 211, pp. 47, 13–17. The increase in the number of pensioners cannot be explained in terms of a change in the population's age structure. The percentage of people over sixty years of age actually declined during the period between 1882 and 1907, from 7.7 to 7.0 among men and from 8.4 to 8.2 among women.
327. Ibid., pp. 16, 41. Of all pensioners (men and women) 18.4 per cent had some form of supplementary income in 1907. This was true of 30.2 per cent of pensioners living in rural districts, 14.2 per cent in small and medium-sized towns and 4.9 per cent in the big cities. About three-quarters of all cases where pensioners were able to supplement their income by earnings occurred in the agricultural sector (pp. 51f.).
328. Thus, in 1895, out of a total of 303,528 male wage-earners over the age of seventy

Certainly, we can only speculate as to whether, alongside the declining number of older workers in employment, the dramatic fall in Germany's emigration figures before the economic upswing of 1895, from more than 200,000 people each year in 1881–82 (still over 100,000 in 1891–92) to between 20,000 and 30,000 per year after the mid-1890s[329] should be seen, alongside other, probably more important factors, as partly a result of the relative improvement in the level of social security arrangements and people's general unwillingness to give up social insurance claims.

What is certain, however, is that, according to figures for 1893–94, sickness, disablement and old-age insurance (less so, accident insurance) had the intended effect of greatly relieving the burden on poor relief,[330] though the latter continued to function as the basis of the social security system[331] for groups who were inadequately or not at all covered by social insurance. Despite this effect, however, the estimated figure of between 2 and 4 per cent of the population living on poor relief in the cities showed no sign of decreasing.[332] Nor was there any decrease in the amount of poor relief expenditure. What happened was that the system of public poor relief was extended in scope and improved as higher individual payments were awarded and claimants accepted who would previously have been turned down owing to lack of funds.[333]

21,666 workers (7.14 per cent) belonged to the category of *mithelfende Familienangehörige*, (family members workihg in family enterprises). In 1907 the figure was 30,750 (10.9 per cent) out of a total of 280,404. In 1895, out of a total of 932,957 male wage-earners between the ages of sixty and seventy, 28,221 (3.02 per cent) were assisting family members. In 1907, out of a total of 987,199 wage-earners 44,010 persons in this age group (4.46 per cent) belonged to this occupational category (ibid., p. 227*).

329. Emigration figures taken from *International Migration*, vol. 1, *Statistics*, New York 1929; reprint edn 1969, pp. 700f.

330. 'Einwirkung der Versicherungs-Gesetzgebung', in *Vierteljahreshefte zur Statistik des Deutschen Reichs*, 1897, vol. II, esp. pp. 5–7. Richard Freund, *Armenpflege und Arbeiterversicherung: Prüfung der Frage, in welcher Weise die neuere soziale Gesetzgebung auf die Aufgaben der Armengesetzgebung und Armenpflege einwirkt*, Leipzig 1895. Freund's book is based on the findings of a study carried out by the 'Deutscher Verein für Armenpflege und Wohltätigkeit', of 1893/94. *See also* the analysis of the reports of several city magistrates on the effects of social insurance on the costs of poor relief borne by the local authorities, in H. von Frankenberg, 'Die Gemeinden und die Arbeiterversicherung', in *Schmollers Jahrbuch*, Neue Folge, 21 (1897), pp. 871–98, esp. pp. 890ff.

331. Sachße and Tennstedt, *Geschichte der Armenfürsorge*, p. 263.

332. Lass and Zahn, *Einrichtung*, p. 230.

333. 'Einwirkung der Versicherungs-Gesetzgebung', in *Vierteljahreshefte zur Statistik des Deutschen Reichs*, 1897, vol. II, esp. pp. 1, 10f.; Freund, *Armenpflege*, p. 83f.; Dr Flesch, 'Die sociale Ausgestaltung der Armenpflege', in his and Dr Soetbeer's *Sociale Ausgestaltung der Armenpflege (Schriften des deutschen Vereins für Armenpflege und Wohltätigkeit*, no. 54), Leipzig 1901, pp. 1–30, esp. p. 2. For the effect of social insurance on

As long as we still lack agreed criteria for defining what constitutes poverty, we must not assume, therefore, that the continuing rise in poor-relief payments in most areas of Germany[334] meant that there was also a corresponding increase in the number of people experiencing hardship and poverty. On the contrary, it can be shown that the opposite was the case in Germany before 1914. The number of citizens on poor relief[335] was related to the general level of wealth among the population, tending to increase rather than decrease alongside it. The poorer a community, the more stringent its means test tended to be. Consequently, the amount deemed to be the minimum necessary to live on was usually fixed lower, as was the approved rate of poor relief.[336]

Thus, alongside the increased cost of living after 1896, the reasons for the rise in poor relief expenditure, despite the extent of social insurance benefits, are mainly to be found in the greater willingness on the part of Germany's increasingly affluent classes to permit greater expenditure on social welfare. The process of urbanisation likewise contributed to the rising costs of poor relief, since payments were substantially greater in the cities compared with the countryside.[337] Finally, the government's social insurance policy also had the effect of putting pressure on Germany's federal states and local authorities to increase the level of their social welfare arrangements.[338] Better provi-

---

poor relief, *see also* the publication from the Wilhelmine period, *Sozialversicherung und öffentliche Fürsorge als Grundlagen der Alters- und Invalidenversorgung, Schriften des Deutschen Vereins für öffentliche und private Fürsorge*, Neue Folge, no. 14, Karlsruhe 1930, esp. pp. 1–12. *See also* Wolfram Fischer's study, *Armut in der Geschichte: Erscheinungsformen und Lösungsversuche der 'Sozialen Frage' in Europa seit dem Mittelalter*, Göttingen 1982, pp. 83–90.

334. *See* 'Einwirkung der Versicherungs-Gesetzgebung', in *Vierteljahreshefte zur Statistik des Deutschen Reichs*, 1897 vol. II, pp. 12f.; Friedrich Zahn, 'Arbeiterversicherung und Armenwesen in Deutschland (unter Mitberücksichtigung der neuen Reichsversicherungsordnung)', in *Archiv für Sozialwissenschaft und Sozialpolitik* 35 (1912), pp. 418–86, esp. p. 464.

335. One of the weaknesses of the voluminous contemporary source material on poor relief is that it does not deal with poverty *per se*, but always takes the supported poor as its reference point. In addition, it mainly documents the activities of public institutions for the care of the poor. For a discussion of the methodological problems which arise from this, especially with regard to statistical data on the poor, *see* Ernst Mischler, 'Die Methode der Armenstatistik', in *Bulletin de l'Institut International de Statistique* XIV, 2e livraison, Berlin 1904, pp. 108–42, esp. 111ff.

336. *See* Paul Kollmann, 'Armenwesen (Armenstatistik)', in *Handwörterbuch der Staatswissenschaften*, 3rd edn, vol. 2, Jena 1909, pp. 173–96, esp. pp. 179ff.; Schumann, 'Armenlast', in *Jahrbücher für Nationalökonomie und Statistik*, Neue Folge, 17 (1888), esp. pp. 617f.

337. In Bavaria, for example, the average annual amount of poor relief for each member of the population in 1909 amounted to 1.2 marks in communities of up to 500 inhabitants and 3.7 marks in communities of over 20,000 inhabitants (Zahn, *Arbeiterversicherung*, p. 463).

sions for the care of the poor, which began to assume the character of modern welfare arrangements, especially in the wealthier big cities, can also be seen in Germany's improved medical care. This followed growing recognition that poverty and disease were related. It can also be seen in the increasing number of doctors per head of the population.[339] Dreaded older-style institutions for the sick, which imposed a strict regime on their patients, increasingly gave way to modern hospitals. The treatment of orphans and the elderly living on their own also saw a slow improvement. Poorhouses and infirmaries for the very old were gradually replaced by more sympathetic old people's homes. The poor-relief authorities and the voluntary charitable organisations which supplemented their efforts increasingly took the view that the best and, in the long run, cheapest way of helping the poor lay in restoring their ability to work and their economic self-reliance. By kindling and reinforcing a new spirit of social awareness, social insurance legislation gave rise to a tendency in German society to replace the traditional style of disciplinary poor relief with a social welfare policy aimed more at preserving the poor's sense of self-respect and self-confidence. Though this attitude by no means dominated before 1914, it was nevertheless noticeable. One of the reasons for the appearance of this thinking was that, alongside social insurance, efforts to improve provisions for the poor also lay in the interests of the economy and the state, especially in the case of children. Increasing the workers' efficiency meant increasing the German economy's competitiveness and preventing any weakening of the nation's 'capacity to defend itself'.[340] This general change in thinking was especially evident during the First World War when relieving the distress of war widows, war orphans and soldiers' wives and the treatment of war invalids was recognised as the object of a non-discriminatory welfare policy for which society as a whole was responsible. The so-called 'war welfare' provisions were regarded as something separate from the traditional system of poor relief and the curtailment of civic rights which this involved.[341]

338. *See* Tennstedt, *Vom Proleten zum Industriearbeiter*, pp. 573ff.; Zahn, 'Belastung', in *Zeitschrift für die gesamte Versicherungswissenschaft* 12 (1912), pp. 1152–56.

339. *See* 'Einwirkung der Versicherungs-Gesetzgebung', in *Vierteljahreshefte zur Statistik des Deutschen Reichs*, 1897, vol. II, p. 9; Lass and Zahn, Einrichtung, pp. 229f.; Zahn, *Arbeiterversicherung*, pp. 468–81; Emil Münsterberg, 'Die leitenden Ideen der modernen Armenpflege', in Peter Schmidt (ed.), *Am Born der Gemeinnützigkeit. Festgabe zum 80. Geburtstag des Herrn Geh. Reg.-Rat Prof. Dr jur. Victor Böhmert*, Dresden 1909, pp. 102–11, esp. 103f.

340. Lass and Zahn, *Einrichtung*, p. 214; Greißl, 'Wirtschaftliche Untersuchungen', in *Schmollers Jahrbuch*, Neue Folge, 23 (1899), esp. pp. 857–59.

Prior to 1914, social insurance certainly affected the older system of poor relief which was legally administered outside the control of Germany's central government.[342] But the reverse was also true. The various public welfare and private charitable organisations which combined in 1880 to form the German Association for the Care of the Poor and Charitable Work (*Deutscher Verein für Armenpflege und Wohltätigkeit*), renamed the German Association for Public and Private Welfare Work after 1919 (*Deutscher Verein für öffentliche und private Fürsorge*), were instrumental in supporting the expansion of Germany's welfare system. Of course, their contribution was also accompanied by efforts from other quarters and should not be regarded as the sole or even the main impetus behind the reforms which took place during the period under discussion. Nevertheless, the Association was important in supporting a large number of measures, which included broadening the scope of insurance liability and increasing maternity protection. It also advocated taking the size of family into account when calculating disablement and old-age benefits — something which came into effect only in 1911 — as well as introducing unemployment insurance; though its efforts here proved unsuccessful before the war.[343]

341. See Carl Ludwig Krug von Nidda, 'Entwicklungstendenzen und gegenseitige Beziehungen der öffentlichen und freien Wohlfahrtspflege in Deutschland in der Epoche des Übergangs von der Armenpflege zur Fürsorge', in Hans Muthesius (ed.), *Beiträge zur Entwicklung der Deutschen Fürsorge: 75 Jahre Deutscher Verein*, Cologne and Berlin 1955, pp. 133–349, esp. pp. 205–20.

342. Even after the founding of the Empire in 1871, the North German Confederation's law of 6 June 1870 concerning the place of residence of poor-relief claimants, together with its amendments of 1894 and 1908, did not apply to the whole of Germany. In Bavaria, where poor relief was governed by a law of 29 April 1869, it first came into effect after 1 January 1916 and in Alsace-Lorraine, where French law still applied after, 1 April 1910. It was possible, therefore, for the much called-for legal regulation and reform of the poor-relief system to be delayed on the grounds that it was desirable to wait and see what the effects of social insurance would be.

343. See for example, the resolutions and recommendations passed at the annual meetings of the Deutscher Verein für Armenpflege und Wohltätigkeit in 1897, 1898, 1901, 1902 and 1908, in Heinrich Braun, 'Der Deutsche Verein im Geschehen seiner Zeit: Eine synoptische Darstellung', in Muthesius (ed.), *Beiträge*, pp. 1–131. For an account of the work of the Deutscher Verein in Wilhelmine Germany, which in September 1913 put forward detailed 'guidelines' for a future poor-relief law, see Eberhard Orthbandt, *Der Deutsche Verein in der Geschichte der deutschen Fürsorge*, Frankfurt 1980, pp. 148–53. See also the report by its General Secretary between 1892 and 1911, Emil Münsterberg, *Generalbericht über die Tätigkeit des deutschen Vereins für Armenpflege und Wohltätigkeit während der ersten 25 Jahre seines Bestehens 1880–1905 nebst Verzeichnissen der Vereinsschriften und alphabetischen Register zu den Vereinsschriften*, Leipzig 1905; and Florian Tennstedt, 'Fürsorgegeschichte und Vereinsgeschichte. 100 Jahre Deutscher Verein', in *Zeitschrift für Sozialreform* 27 (1981), pp. 72–100, esp. pp. 73–8; Carl Ludwig Krug von Nidda, *Wilhelm Polligkeit, Wegbereiter einer neuzeitigen Fürsorge*, Cologne 1961.

Social insurance and the expansion of social welfare also had the effect of making the workers distance themselves much more from Germany's *Lumpenproletariat* of beggars, vagrants and antisocial elements. Day-labourers, casual workers and navvies, who inhabited the slums of the 'wilder districts' of towns or workers' barracks and barns in the countryside, spreading diseases and indulging in spontaneous and often violent protests, were regarded as 'the lowest of the low.' Partly because of the growth of the police force, the activities of the labour movement and general improvements to housing and living conditions, these groups now began to settle down into regular work.[344] This is not to ignore the fact that, for example, the emergence of new types of youth culture in the rapidly growing cities gave rise to new problems of a similar kind. But the notion of collective self-responsibility in place of a regimented social discipline imposed from above gradually gained ground at this time and, by stressing the encouragement of self-help, began to change the character of poor relief. This was a result not only of the state's social legislation and the ideas of middle-class reformers, but has to be seen mainly as a consequence of the increased self-confidence and sense of self-responsibility which the German labour movement encouraged among broad sections of the poorer classes.

Social insurance was also important in Germany for encouraging the growth of economic and social statistics. The first ever comprehensive survey on the occupational and social structure of the German population was undertaken in 1882. This, together with parallel figures for all business undertakings and later surveys made in 1895 and 1907, provides the basis of any analysis of Germany's social and economic structures during the Wilhelmine Empire, together with the changes these underwent between 1882 and 1907. This wealth of available material had its direct origins in Bismarck's wish to gather reliable statistical data for accident and old-age insurance.[345] According to a passage added to the royal message of 17 November 1881 and written in Bismarck's own hand, 'The prerequisite for any further decisions on forthcoming social and political reforms consists in producing reliable statistical information on the Empire's population, for which there has been no sufficient and dependable information up until now'.[346] The great importance of social insurance statistics and related information

344. *See also* Tennstedt, 'Sozialgeschichte der Sozialpolitik', in Blohmke (ed.) *Handbuch*, pp. 64–7.
345. *See* his letter to Boetticher of October 1881, quoted at length in Peters, *Geschichte*, p. 69.
346. *See* facsimile reprint of the draft for the Emperor's message in *Zeitschrift für Sozialreform* 27 (1981), pp. 711ff.

for providing a clearer understanding of Germany's social problems, together with the growing willingness to find ways to solve these, has already been mentioned with regard to medicine.[347] Georg Zacher was of the opinion that compulsory insurance was leading to less emphasis on 'therapy and more on preventive medicine.' The comprehensive social statistics provided by social insurance 'clearly revealed the various kinds of harm done to the nation', but 'its many different institutions, capabilities and means also offered the possibility . . . of introducing preventive care on a major scale'.[348] This opinion was certainly borne out by developments taking place in Germany before 1914.

At the same time, social insurance also profited considerably from the world of research.[349] An example of the fruitful interaction which proved mutually beneficial to both spheres were the studies of workers' career patterns in modern industrial society, instigated by the Social Policy Association a few years before the outbreak of the First World War.[350] By demonstrating the early point at which industrial workers left the productive process, these studies helped in the success of efforts during the First World War to lower the pensionable age from seventy to sixty-five years. Emil Lederer's brilliant sociological studies on white-collar workers was stimulated by the discussion concerning the introduction of a separate pension insurance for white-collar workers.[351] The view of Heinrich Rosin, Germany's leading expert on social insurance law, that the worker's claims under the social insurance system did not correspond to those of someone insured through a private company but derived from the 'worker's individual right under

347. *See* above, p. 108f.
348. 'Die Arbeiterversicherung auf der Weltausstellung in St. Louis 1904', in Zacher, *Arbeiter-Versicherung*, vol. 5, no. XIX, p. 145.
349. *See also* Florian Tennstedt, 'Sozialwissenschaftliche Forschung in der Sozialversicherung', in *Kölner Zeitschrift für Soziologie und Sozialpsychologie*, Sonderheft 19/1977, *Soziologie und Sozialpolitik*, ed. by Christian von Ferber and Frank-Xaver Kaufmann, Opladen 1977, pp. 483–523.
350. See *Untersuchungen über Auslese und Anpassung (Berufswahl und Berufsschicksal) der Arbeiter in den verschiedenen Zweigen der Grossindustrie*, 6 vols., 1910–1912, vols. 133–5 of the *Schriften des Vereins für Sozialpolitik*; the study's findings were summarised by Heinrich Herkner for the Association's annual conference in 1911. They covered the structure of the German working class, its social and cultural life and work effort ('Probleme der Arbeiterpsychologie unter besonderer Rücksichtnahme auf Methode und Ergebnisse der Vereinserhebungen', in *Verhandlungen des Vereins für Sozialpolitik in Nürnberg 1911*, pp. 117–38; discussion with remarks by Marie Bernays, Alfred Weber and others pp. 138–203.
351. *See* esp. Emil Lederer, *Die Privatangestellten in der modernen Wirtschaftsentwicklung*, Tübingen 1912; idem, *Die Entwicklungstendenzen in den Organisationen der Angestellten: Vortrag in der Versammlung des Allgemeinen Verbandes der Deutschen Bankbeamten in Berlin am 13. Dezember 1913*, Heidelberg 1914, and his article cited in note 236, above.

public law' based on his social existence, came to form part of the legal basis on which Germany's social welfare system was subsequently built.[352] Social insurance data similarly helped bring about a greater understanding of the cost-effects of work and incidental labour costs.

Social insurance also contributed to the growth of private insurance, whose benefits often completely matched those paid out by the state's insurance funds. The example provided by the worker's sickness insurance scheme stimulated the demand for similar protection on the part of groups not liable for state contributions, such as civil servants, the self-employed and senior- and middle-management white-collar workers.[353] Life assurance associations were also able to increase their business since the Prussian income tax reforms of 1891 granted favourable concessions on contributions in order to give those social groups excluded from old-age pensions and civil service superannuation an incentive to make provision for their old age.[354] The benefits paid out by private life assurance companies rose from 153 million marks in 1901 to 370 million in 1912 and were thus considerably greater than those of the state's disablement and old-age insurance schemes. The latter paid out 91 million marks in 1901 and 177 million marks in 1912. As previously pointed out,[355] private accident and liability insurance also continued to operate effectively despite the state's accident insurance law of 1884. The benefits paid out by private insurers in respect of damages and accident insurance rose from 207 million marks in 1907 to 273 million marks in 1913, while, compensation payments made for the same period under the state's accident insurance scheme only rose from 150 to 175 million marks.[356]

The accumulation of capital savings, especially in the case of pension insurance, led to a substantial amount being earmarked for 'preventive' social policy measures. In 1913, for example, state social insurance had reserves at its disposal amounting to more than 3 billion marks. As well as being able to satisfy agriculture's need for credit, the money was used to build hospitals, convalescent homes, sanatoria, public baths, homes for the blind and nursery schools, new town

352. Hugo Sinzheimer, 'Philip Lotmar', in his *Jüdische Klassiker der deutschen Rechtswissenschaft*, Frankfurt 1953, pp. 207–24, esp. p. 210.
353. Peter Koch, 'Wechselseitige Auswirkungen der Entwicklung von Individual- und Sozialversicherung', in *Zeitschrift für die gesamte Versicherungswissenschaft* 69 (1980), pp. 199–213, esp. pp. 212f.; Alfred Manes, 'Über die Grenzen der Privat- und der Sozialversicherung', in *Zeitschrift für die gesamte Versicherungswissenschaft* 12 (1912), pp. 499–524.
354. Koth, *Auswirkungen*, p. 210.
355. *See* above, p. 38.
356. All figures taken from *Bevölkerung und Wirtschaft*, pp. 217, 221f.

water-supply systems and sewage and drainage systems. The money was also used to promote the construction of modest workers' dwellings by giving relatively low-interest mortgages to building society cooperatives.[357] It appears that up to the First World War the regional insurance offices responsible for disablement insurance helped finance the construction of around 300,000 to 400,000 dwellings, a figure which represented one and a half to two years' demand for new housing in the German Empire. This helped mitigate the desperate housing shortage which existed, especially in the big cities.[358]

Though its anti-cyclical effects should not be exaggerated, social insurance also had an unintended effect on the economic cycle. It provided the elderly, sick and disabled with 'purchasing power beyond the "natural" distribution of economic wealth', and thus helped revive and stabilise the economy by 'creating, stabilising and normalising people's needs'.[359]

The effect which the new legislation had on the constitutional and administrative structure of the German Empire was also considerable. It increased the tendency of the bureaucracy to develop from an administration supervising the maintenance of law and order to one providing services. Also, the large number of white-collar workers employed by the various institutions of social insurance led to a corresponding growth in the overall number of public servants. In 1913 accident insurance employed 5,378 officials and disablement insurance a further 6,939.[360] Since the personnel and administrative costs of the public sickness insurance scheme amounted to about three-quarters of the combined costs of accident and disablement insurance, we can deduce that sickness insurance must have employed something approaching another 9,000 officials. If we ignore white-collar insurance, Germany's various social insurance services altogether employed over 21,000 people. As well as the effect this had in strengthening the bureaucracy, new institutions of co-administration and self-administration also came into existence, in which workers played a decisive part alongside the employers.

357. Reuter, 'Verteilungs- und Umverteilungseffekte', in Blaich (ed.), *Staatliche Umverteilungspolitik*, pp. 137–9. Between 1895 and 1913 disablement insurance alone paid out 1,245 million marks for measures designed to improve the infrastructure (p. 162).

358. *See* Tennstedt, 'Sozialgeschichte der Sozialversicherung', in Blohmke (ed.), *Handbuch*, p. 460; Ulrich Blumenroth, *Deutsche Wohnungspolitik seit der Reichsgründung: Darstellung unk kritische Würdigung*, Münster 1975, pp. 75f., 80.

359. Christian von Ferber, *Sozialpolitik in der Wohlstandsgesellschaft: Was stimmt nicht mit der deutschen Sozialpolitik?* Hamburg 1967, p. 47.

360. Reuter, 'Verteilungs- und Umverteilungseffekte', in Blaich (ed.), *Staatliche Umverteilungspolitik*, p. 158.

By extending the scope of its insurance legislation, setting up an Imperial Insurance Office as a superior supervisory body to rule on social insurance cases and creating an Imperial Insurance Board to administer white-collar insurance directly, Germany's imperial government strengthened its position at the expense of the federal states, though these were still able to influence policy through their regional insurance offices and administrations.

The fact that social insurance took over certain responsibilities associated with traditional forms of poor relief did indeed remove some of the financial burden on the local authorities. At the same time, however, they lost some of their former purpose and paid for this with a decline in importance.[361] Contrary to Bismarck's designs,[362] the strength of the Reichstag's position tended to gain by virtue of its considerable involvement in introducing the country's social insurance laws. Furthermore, social insurance greatly accelerated the process by which social and economic groups organised themselves for the collective representation of their interests. This could clearly be seen in the legally compulsory formation of employers' assocations in different parts of industry, which strengthened moves within German industry to organise itself on the basis of cartels.[363] It was also evident in the medical profession's creation of its own organisation in response to the sickness insurance law, the organising of white-collar workers to demand their own pension insurance and the strengthening of the workers' political and trade union organisations, however unintended the latter development may have been.

The creation of special judicial arrangements for social welfare, the granting of legal powers to the Imperial Insurance Office, the growth in legal arbitration and the increased involvement of lay-judges — all these developments led to an expansion of Germany's legal system. As additional arrangements, however, they must have inevitably resulted in restricting the legal powers of the normal courts.

But, above all, the acceptance of the view that social security was a responsibility of government had the effect of stressing anew the state's involvement in social and economic affairs, which had been eclipsed by the *laissez-faire* liberalism of the nineteenth century. Germany was thus placed irrevocably on its path towards becoming a modern welfare state, one of the characteristics of which is the redistribution of society's wealth in favour of the materially worse-off groups in the population. If

---

361. Benöhr, 'Verfassungsfragen', in *Zeitschrift der Savigny-Stiftung für Rechtsgeschichte, Germ. Abt. 97*, 1980, pp. 137–42.
362. *See* above, p. 62.
363. *See* Erich Maschke, *Grundzüge der deutschen Kartellgeschichte*, Dortmund 1964, p. 23.

we leave aside the problematical interpretation (for which no proof can be found) that employers' contributions to compulsory sickness, accident, disablement and old-age pension insurance schemes represent earnings which would otherwise be paid to the employee, or that wages are reduced by the amount of the employer's share,[364] the levying of contributions and premiums has in itself a certain redistributive effect.

In 1901, after pension insurance had come into full effect, Germany's Imperial Statistical Office published figures on the composition of social insurance revenue. Of its total amount, the share paid in by insured employees amounted to 37.64 per cent, while that of employers (including, of course, state and other public authority employers) made up of 45.2 per cent. The government's supplementary benefits accounted for a further 6.43 per cent and interest and other revenue 10.73 per cent.[365] However, social insurance was still relatively insignificant in terms of its effect on the total economy. Between 1885 and 1913, payments to insured workers suffering permanent or temporary disablement (or, in the case of deceased workers, to their close relatives) rose from around 0.2 to 2.0 per cent of the net domestic social product.[366] The total amount for social insurance services and benefits increased from 0.3 to about 3.0 per cent of the net domestic social product, but this came nowhere near to exploiting the possibilities social insurance offered of redistributing income and relieving the burdens on the lower classes, suffering particularly at this time from the high tariff duties on imported foodstuffs.

In contrast to private insurance practice, where contributions and benefits were calculated on the basis of specific risks, a certain amount of redistribution of wealth did take place through the system of earnings-related (as opposed to risk-related) contributions in sickness and disablement and old-age insurances. It was also partly achieved through the payment of government supplementary benefits in disablement and old-age pensions. This had the effect of levelling out differences in awards. At the same time, improved medical benefits became equally available to all persons covered by the state's social security system and free medical care was increasingly extended to the families of insured workers. The redistributive effect of these measures was reinforced by

364. *See* Reuter, 'Verteilungs- und Umverteilungseffekte', in Blaich (ed.), *Umverteilungspolitik*, p. 125.
365. *Atlas und Statistik der Arbeiterversicherung*, p. 16. In his 'Verteilungs- und Umverteilungseffekte', p. 126, Reuter estimates the amount paid by the insured at an average of 47 per cent per annum before 1914. This figure is based not on the total sum of revenues but the total sum of contributions.
366. Reuter, 'Verteilungs- und Umverteilungseffekte', in Blaich (ed.), *Umverteilungspolitik*, pp. 131, 134.

the terms of the government's insurance code of 1911, which granted additional allowances for children under fifteen in disablement insurance and extended supplementary benefits to the orphans and disabled widows of workers paying pension contributions. The extent of this redistribution remained limited, however, at least compared with Britain. This was largely because of the strong opposition to the idea of central government subsidies, which was to some degree reinforced by Germany's federal states which feared an encroachment by the Empire on their tax resources. In Britain, in contrast, the principle of state subsidies was accepted after the turn of the century by all the major political parties. Social security payments were much more readily calculated according to people's real needs, compared with Germany, where their calculation was still based on the equivalent sum of contributions paid into the system.

CHAPTER 3

Mass Poverty and Social Reform in Britain at the Turn of the Century

The main impetus behind Germany's social insurance legislation before 1914 was the attempt to combat the danger to the political and social order from a socialist workers' movement which was widely regarded by contemporaries as a revolutionary threat. This was to be achieved by making material concessions to the socialists' main body of support in the shape of the industrial workforce, particularly its skilled workers. Britain's social reforms, on the other hand, were primarily aimed at solving the problem of mass poverty.[1]

Compared with other European countries, Britain had a relatively strong trade union movement.[2] Before 1889 this consisted mainly of skilled workers, textile workers and miners. As a movement which espoused the principle of self-help, it won positive acceptance and the government earnestly sought its cooperation in the framing of social legislation. If we ignore the relatively small and insignificant socialist

1. For the causes and scope of urban poverty and attempts to combat its effects, *see* James H. Treble, *Urban Poverty in Britain, 1830–1914*, New York 1979.
2. For the state of the British trade union movement at the end of the 1880s, *see* H. A. Clegg, Alan Fox and A. F. Thompson, *A History of British Trade Unions since 1889*, Oxford 1964, vol. 1 (1889–1910), ch.1, pp. 1–54.

parties founded in the 1880s and 1890s, an independent political movement representing organised labour only emerged in Britain after the turn of the century with the founding of the Labour Party as a federation of various socialist organisations and trade unions.[3] Working in close cooperation with the Liberals before 1914,[4] this party did not pursue a socialist programme in the years before 1918 and was, therefore, not regarded as a revolutionary threat.

Among the motives behind Britain's social legislation was the desire to pre-empt the sometimes radical demands of the labour movement, which included pressing for a state guarantee of the 'right to work' and a statutory minimum wage. Britain's welfare measures were introduced in order to hold on to the support of working-class voters, who before 1914 mainly voted Liberal or Conservative, partly because the Labour Party was unable to field its own candidates in nine-tenths of Britain's parliamentary constituencies.[5] A classic example of this can be seen in the favourable terms granted to the trade unions in the Trades Dispute Act of 1906.[6] But before the introduction of national insurance in 1911, which was aimed at skilled workers and their unions, Britain's social reforms were mainly directed at improving the lot of the poor, the elderly, the weak and destitute. These groups could prove potentially troublesome to the government and, hence, constituted a potential problem of law and order, but were relatively unimportant as far as party politics were concerned.

Behind Britain's welfare legislation lay a new awareness that poverty, including that of able-bodied workers, was not a condition necessarily caused by laziness, alcoholism, an immoral life-style or lack of adequate provision for old age, for which the worker himself was to blame. It therefore saw its main task as one of protecting the nation's

3. *See* for the origins and founding of the Labour Representation Committee in 1900 and its development into the Labour Party of 1906; Henry Pelling, *The Origins of the Labour Party*, 2nd edn, Oxford 1965; Philip P. Poirier, *The Advent of the Labour Party*, London 1958; Frank Bealey and Henry Pelling, *Labour and Politics, 1900–1906: A History of the Labour Representation Committee*, London 1958.

4. *See* Gerhard A. Ritter, 'Zur Geschichte der britischen Labour Party 1900–1918: Die Umbildung einer parlamentarischen Pressure Group in eine politische Partei', in idem, *Parlament und Demokratie in Grossbritannien: Studien zur Entwicklung und Struktur des politischen Systems*, Göttingen 1972, pp. 125–81, esp. pp. 139f., 142–51.

5. In the January (and December) elections of 1910 — the last elections to be held before the war — the Labour Party fielded its own candidates in only seventy-eight (resp. fifty-six) of the 670 parliamentary constituences. Of the forty (resp. forty-two) elected M.P's, none (resp. two) had been opposed by Liberals. The other two seats which Labour gained in December 1910 were constituencies which the Conservatives did not contest (ibid., p. 144).

6. *See* Adolf M. Birke, *Pluralismus und Gewerkschaftsautonomie in England: Entstehungsgeschichte einer politischen Theorie*, Stuttgart, 1978, pp. 106–15.

human resources by alleviating social distress. By replacing the old Poor Law with non-discriminatory welfare provisions, it aimed at preventing large sections of the population from sinking into the demoralised condition of paupers incapable of self-help.

The delayed development of state social insurance

Despite its advanced level of industrialisation and urbanisation and the relatively advanced stage reached by its workers' protection and trade union legislation, there were a number of reasons why Britain's state welfare system was introduced at a relatively late stage in comparison to Germany's. There was no powerful political movement to represent British workers and, unlike Germany's constitutionally dualist monarchy, the legitimacy of the British parliamentary system remained relatively unchallenged right up to 1910–11. This was partly because Britain had a much stronger tradition of political and economic liberalism based on ideals of *laissez-faire*. In addition to this, older forms of state welfare other than poor relief were a far less significant factor.

Certainly, nineteenth-century Britain also saw the state intervene in social and economic affairs in a number of different areas. After 1834 the English system of poor relief was rationalised and placed under state control. Health services and, to a lesser extent, housing were also made subject to state supervision. In addition, factory inspection and work-safety regulations led to increased government intervention in the field of working conditions, and the 1870 Education Act saw the state assume overall responsibility for primary education. But, apart from the educational system and the growth of free medical services for the poorer sections of the population, developed from the system of medical care under poor relief, government intervention limited itself almost entirely to protecting society against major evils by applying legal regulations in various fields.[7] Beyond this, however, Britain had no effective state bureaucracy which would have allowed the state to perform a more constructive role outside of the work of its local authorities. Apart from the postal services, customs officials, tax inspec-

---

7. *See* Eric J. Evans (ed.), *Social Policy 1830–1914: Individualism, Collectivism and the Origins of the Welfare State*, London, 1978, esp. pp. 2ff.; Derek Fraser, *The Evolution of the British Welfare State. A History of Social Policy since the Industrial Revolution*, London 1973; for developments between 1833 and 1854 and, in particular, the growth and activities of a body of civil servants concerned with social problems, *see* David Roberts, *Victorian Origins of the British Welfare State*, New Haven 1960.

tors, inspectors of government dockyards and officials responsible for seeing that local authorities applied government measures, Britain's civil service at the end of the nineteenth century was still mainly limited to central government in London. According to reasonably reliable statistics, the number of government civil servants rose from 27,000 in 1821 to 39,147 in 1851, 53,874 in 1871 and 79,241 in 1891. It was only after the turn of the century that the civil service began to undergo rapid expansion. The number of civil servants in Britain rose to 280,900 in 1914, many of whom were employed in the various branches of the social services.[8] The English legal system of Common Law with its emphasis on private property and the law of contract, as well as the late development of public law in general, also delayed the introduction and development of a social security system.[9]

A factor which is of even greater importance in explaining why Britain was slow in developing public institutions for a social security system was the country's strong tradition of self-help. This was particularly strengthened by the Friendly Societies,[10] and also to some extent by trade union benefit funds.[11] The law encouraged the activities of the Friendly Societies, and private charitable organisations also played an important part. A detailed study by Wilhelm Hasbach on 'The British System of Workers' Insurance', which appeared in Schmoller's *Series of Studies on the Political and Social Sciences* in 1883, came to the conclusion that compulsory state insurance schemes of the kind proposed by the German government at this time were being constantly countenanced, but did not stand the slightest chance of ever being adopted in Britain: 'With the active support of sympathetic upper classes, rich nations can achieve that for which poor nations have to make use of the entire wherewithall of the state'.[12] Hasbach's study was relatively critical of the Friendly Societies and Britain's 'poor social welfare legislation',[13]

---

8. W. J. M. Mackenzie and J. W. Grove, *Central Administration in Britain*, London 1957, p. 7.
9. *See* Anthony Ogus, 'Conditions in the Formation and the Development of Social Insurance: Legal Development and Legal History', in Zacher (ed.), *Bedingungen*, pp. 337–48, esp. pp. 343f.
10. For the development, activities and internal structure of the Friendly Societies, their guiding principles and relations with the government and attitude to poor relief, *see* P. H. J. H. Gosden, *The Friendly Societies in England 1815–1875*, Manchester 1961; and his *Self-Help: Voluntary Associations in the 19th Century*, London 1973.
11. *See* Wolfgang Krieger, 'Das gewerkschaftliche Unterstützungswesen in Grossbritannien in den zwanziger Jahren', in *Archiv für Sozialgeschichte* 20 (1980), pp. 119–46, esp. pp. 119–27.
12. Wilhelm Hasbach, *Das Englische Arbeiterversicherungswesen: Geschichte seiner Entwicklung und Gesetzgebung*, Leipzig 1883, p. 447.
13. Ibid., p. 446.

thus betraying his distinct preference for state-administered insurance schemes.

But this view did not remain unchallenged for long. A few years later a much more careful study by J. M. Baernreither appeared on 'English Workers' Associations and Their Legal Basis'. Baernreither was strongly influenced by Lujo Brentano's view of Britain's trade unions as a model worthy of emulation by the Germans. This study generally came to a much more positive conclusion as regards the Friendly Societies, which were seen as a 'grand institution' and 'an important part of working-class self-administration'. 'As a result of the combined efforts of various working-class organisations' they 'had won a place in British society'. As Baernreither explained, the Friendly Societies 'perform great educational tasks, extend the worker's knowledge and teach frugality and prudence. They heighten the individual's sense of duty towards himself and his family, but at the same time increase the working-classes' sense of social cohesion'. It was 'a piece of good fortune for a country if reform came about mainly through the moral strength and organising power of that class, the organisation and improvement of whose living conditions constitutes the main goal of this reform'.[14] In Baernreither's view, British labour conditions showed 'that the activities of government should be seen as the props surrounding a building during its construction which are to be pulled away once it has reached the stage where it is firmly in place and likely to stay put. The great lesson which Germany ought to learn from studying labour conditions in Britain is the necessity and duty to arouse and educate the working-class to self-help simultaneously and systematically in all matters where the state has to step in.[15] Both Hasbach and Baernreither belong to the tradition of German social reformers who made a close study of English conditions at this time. Because of her pioneering lead in the processes of industrialisation, England was widely regarded as the model which anticipated Germany's own future development. As a result, many Germans attempted to profit from the English experience and avoid mistakes by steering their own country's industrial development. How this experience should be assessed and what lessons should be drawn from it was, however, the subject of much controversial debate. From a desire to avoid the kind of social problems which had accompanied Britain's industrialisation, conservative reformers in Germany favoured a greater degree of state intervention along the lines of

14. J. M. Baernreither, *Die Englischen Arbeiterverbände und ihr Recht: Ein Beitrag zur Geschichte der sozialen Bewegung in der Gegenwart*, Tübingen 1886, pp. 446–50.
15. Ibid., pp. VIIIf.

the Prussian monarchy's traditional policy of intervention in social and economic affairs. Liberal reformers, on the other hand, sought to strengthen the nation's potential for self-help.

Finally, in explaining the reasons behind the relatively late emergence of state social insurance in Britain, the capacity of England's traditional Poor Law to adapt itself to the new economic and social conditions created by industrialisation and urbanisation should not be underestimated. Modern studies on British social history no longer take the view that a rigid poor-relief system based on the principles established by the Poor Law Amendment Act of 1834 confronted all the able-bodied poor with the choice of being sent to the poorhouse, which was often little better than a prison, or losing their poor relief. Instead, it has been shown that the able-bodied poor were able to find various other forms of relief.[16] Recent studies have stressed both the wide geographical variations in the poor relief system and the changes it went through in the course of the nineteenth century. At the same time, it has been emphasised that with the growth and gradual acceptance of bureaucratic regulations,[17] the Poor Law also anticipated the welfare state, which, to some extent, was created in reaction to the older system of poor relief.

During the 1860s, the Poor Law, which in 1834 was still intended to operate in a predominantly agricultural society, reached a crisis point. Several severe winters brought great distress to vast numbers of casual and seasonal workers, suffering increasingly from unemployment, particularly in London. In Lancashire the cotton industry was almost completely shut down when supplies of imported raw materials were cut off between 1862 and 1864 as a result of the American Civil War.[18]

16. The total number of persons in receipt of poor relief in England and Wales fell from 1,009,000 or 5.7 per cent of the population, in 1850 to 797,000, or 2.5 per cent of the population, in 1900. Although the number of indoor paupers increased from about one in eight to more than one in four of the total number during the same period and continued to rise in the years before 1914, poor relief was still granted in larger amounts in cases involving outdoor relief (*see* Karel Williams, *From Pauperism to Poverty*, London 1981, Table 4.5 pp. 158–63 and Table 6, p. 179.). At 21 per cent of the total of supported poor in England and Wales in 1849 and 13.5 per cent in 1874, the proportion of able-bodied adults was relatively small. Of the total number of male adults receiving relief, the percentage on indoor relief was 19.2 per cent in 1849 and 28.6 per cent in 1874 (Derek Fraser, 'The English Poor Law and the Origins of the British Welfare State', in Mommsen, *Emergence*, pp. 9–31, esp. pp. 22f.). It was certainly a result of the 1834 Poor Law Amendment Act that the previously widespread practice of supporting the unemployed or underemployed able-bodied was only rarely encountered after about 1850 (*see* Williams, *From Pauperism to Poverty*, pp. 179–95; Harris, *Unemployment*, p. 373). In Germany also, poor relief was rarely given to the unemployed (*see* above, p. 40.).

17. Fraser, 'English Poor Law', in Mommsen (ed.), *Emergence*, esp. pp. 19f.

In London attempts to combat the resultant distress were made more difficult as a result of the increasing segregation of the social classes into their own residential areas within the city. This destroyed the balance which had previously existed between rich and poor in smaller local communities; a balance that was necessary if the poor-relief system was to function properly in each local authority area charged with administering poor relief. It was, therefore, precisely the poorest districts of London which were left with the greatest burden on poor relief and, conversely, the richer districts which enjoyed the lightest.[19] At the same time, the work of the various private charitable organisations was poorly coordinated. By the late 1860s, in London alone, their financial assistance outstripped that of the poor-relief authorities by three and half times and almost equalled the amount the country spent on the navy.[20] Some skilful types managed to procure assistance from several different sources, thus providing them with support in excess of that earned in wages by the normal labourer, while others had to go completely without help.

The economic crisis, however, together with revelations concerning the lack of adequate treatment for the sick, led to a change in middle-class thinking. This in turn led to the law of 1865 which transferred the costs of poor relief from the parishes to the larger poor-law unions, thus restoring the balance between rich and poor communities within the poor law union.[21] The Metropolitan Poor Act of 1867, which was copied by other cities, improved the medical care available to the London poor, distinguished between poor relief as such and medical care for the poor, and transferred a considerable part of the financing of poor relief to a central fund. It also strengthened the influence of the Poor Law Board on the administration of poor relief.[22] Finally, the founding of the Charity Organisation Society (COS) in 1869[23] created

18. M. E. Rose, 'The Crisis of Poor Relief in England, 1860–1890', in Mommsen, *Emergence*, pp. 50–70, esp. pp. 54–8; Gareth Stedman Jones, *Outcast London: A Study in the Relationship between Classes in Victorian Society*, Oxford 1971, esp. pp. 241–50. For the development of the Poor Law, *see also* the compilation of source material by Michael E. Rose in idem (ed.), *The English Poor Law, 1780–1930*, Newton Abbot 1971.

19. Jones, *Outcast London*, pp. 249f.

20. Ibid., pp. 244f.

21. Rose, *Relief of Poverty*, p. 36.

22. Jones, *Outcast London*, pp. 253f.; M. W. Flinn, 'Medical Services under the New Poor Law', in Derek Fraser (ed.), *The New Poor Law in the Nineteenth Century*, London and Basingstoke 1976, pp. 45–66, esp. pp. 64–6. Among other things, the law recognised for the first time the government's obligation to provide hospitals for the poor.

23. For the origins and work of this organisation, *see* Charles Loch Mowat, *The Charity Organisation Society, 1869–1913: Its Ideas and Work*, London 1961; Jones, *Outcast London*,

an effective instrument for organising and coordinating the work of Britain's separate private charities.

These reforms, parallel to which, however, there was a strict reduction in the payment of outdoor relief, especially in the case of women after 1871,[24] led to a noticeable revitalisation of Britain's system of poor relief. Not least, they contributed to the application of scientific methods in the study of the poor-relief system. A growing interest was shown in schemes involving individual care of the poor through a system of voluntary workers like that adopted at Elberfeld in the Rhineland. This system had virtually revolutionised Germany's system of poor relief after 1850 and was widely seen in England as a system worth emulating. Initial moves towards making a detailed study of this system came from two men in particular. The first was Charles B. P. Bosanquet, a London lawyer, who published a book in 1868 containing the first detailed information in England on the Elberfeld system. In 1869 Bosanquet was appointed the first head organiser of COS. The other was the Liberal MP and founder of the Liverpool Central Relief Society, William Rathbone, who persuaded the head of the Local Government Board, James Stansfeld, to send a study commission to Elberfeld. Despite similar goals — that is, a desire on the part of the better-off classes to educate the poor towards economic self-reliance by imposing forms of social discipline and raising them morally and ethically, while at the same time reducing the burden on poor relief — the Elberfeld system had next to no chance of being adopted by the public authorities in Britain. Part of the reason for this was the aversion many felt in England towards a system which involved outside interference in the everyday life of the poor and their families; but it was mainly because there were simply not enough sufficiently committed helpers in Britain who could have replaced the state's officials and given individual attention to the poor on a voluntary basis.[25] A later initiative by Rathbone, which led to the Local Government Board organising a further field-trip to Germany for three English poor-relief experts in 1887, did nothing to alter the position.[26]

esp. pp. 254–61, 268–80; David Owen, *English Philanthropy, 1660–1960*, Cambridge, Mass. 1965, pp. 215–46.

24. Pat Thane, *The Foundations of the Welfare State*, London and New York 1982, pp. 34f.
25. Charles B. P. Bosanquet, *London: Some Account of its Growth, Charitable Agencies, and Wants*, 1868. One year previously, William Rathbone had called for a major reform of the British system of poor relief in his *Social Duties, Considered in Reference to the Organisation of Effort in Works of Benevolence in Public Utility*, 1867. He was especially in favour of an extension of 'friendly visiting' of the poor.
26. On the discussion of the Elberfeld system of poor relief in Great Britain, I am mainly indebted to Jürgen Reulecke for the information contained in his lecture on

Thanks, however, to the influence of leading circles within COS, the Elberfeld system of poor care, which on the whole was judged very favourably by these British observers, did have some effect on the work of Britain's private charities.[27]

The causes of social and political reform efforts at the turn of the century

From the 1880s onwards, as Britain gradually lost the position it had once enjoyed as the world's leading industrial nation, the effect of economic crises and their social consequences strengthened those ideas and forces in English society which worked towards a greater degree of state intervention in economic and social affairs.[28] It was significant that, with the help of the empirical social sciences, contemporaries now had a more sophisticated knowledge of the complex causes and true extent of poverty.[29] This branch of learning rapidly expanded and, at the same time, improved its methodology. Its research findings also struck a responsive chord among the general public. As early as 1883 a

'Formen bürgerlich-sozialen Engagements in Deutschland und England in 19. Jahrhundert', which is due to be published in 1986 in a collection of articles edited by Jürgen Kocka, entitled *Arbeiter und Bürger im 19. Jahrhundert. Varianten ihres Verhältnisses im europäischen Vergleich*'. More information regarding the Elberfeld system's reception in Britain can be found in Rose, 'Crisis', in Mommsen (ed.), *Emergence*, pp. 6f.

27. The members of the 1871 study group were Rathbone, the British Poor Law Inspector, Andrew Doyle, and the Foreign Office expert on trade, J. A. Crowe. Charles Loch, the influential Secretary of COS, James Stewart Davy, a Local Government Board inspector and A. F. Hanewinckel of the Liverpool Central Relief Society visited Germany in 1887.

28. *See* Jones, *Outcast London*, esp. pp. 281–321. E. P. Hennock, however, in his article 'Poverty and Social Theory in England: The Experience of the Eighteen-Eighties', in *Social History* 1 (1976), pp. 67–91, challenges the argument that the 1880s constitute a watershed in English social theory and contemporary awareness of social problems. He stresses, instead, the continuity of ideas between the 1860s and the early 1890s. It is certainly true that important shifts of emphasis took place in the discussion after 1895 which played a major part in laying the theoretical basis of the Liberal social reforms after 1906. But it would be wrong to underestimate the importance of the 1880s and the early 1890s as a period which witnessed a sudden general awareness of poverty, its many causes and effects and growing recognition that it constituted a major problem in Britain's domestic politics.

29. Anthony J. Ogus, 'Landesbericht Grossbritannien', in Köhler and Zacher (eds.), *Ein Jahrhundert Sozialversicherung*, pp. 269–443, esp. pp. 303–6; O. R. McGregor's article, 'Social Research and Social Policy in the Nineteenth Century', in *The British Journal of Sociology* 8 (1957), pp. 146–57, deals mainly with the earlier evolution of social studies.

pamphlet entitled *The Bitter Cry of Outcast London* drew the attention of its wide readership to the social misery, vice, moral degradation and extreme overcrowding of London's slums and was soon followed by a profusion of similar pamphlets, parliamentary inquiries and press reports on the ·subject.[30] A few years later, widespread hardship and unemployment gave rise to the violent London riots of February 1886 and November 1887.[31] These disturbances had a profound impact on the middle classes, who feared the incalculable effects of mass poverty on the safety of their property and feared that the 'decent' workers among the working-class would be infected by the 'dregs of humanity' in the shape of casual workers, alcoholics and the work-shy.

The change in middle-class thinking which now came about eventually led to the questioning of *laissez-faire* liberalism and traditional methods of dealing with poverty. On the one hand, it provided new inspiration for the social sciences, while the findings of social science research in turn reinforced the new change in attitudes.

The first two volumes of Charles Booth's famous study on the *Life and Labour of the People in London*, made a significant contribution to this development after their publication in 1889 and 1891. Booth discovered that 30.7 per cent of London's total population and around 35.2 per cent of the city's East End area lived in conditions of poverty.[32] At about the same time that Booth's study appeared, the great strike of 1888–89 brought London's grave social problems to light, particularly those of its casual labourers, who for a while managed to improve their level of trade union organisation.[33] Against this background, Booth's findings gave rise once more to fears of renewed social disturbances,

30. Andrew Mearns, *The Bitter Cry of Outcast London: an Enquiry into the Conditions of the Abject Poor*, London 1883; *see also* Jones, *Outcast London*, esp. pp. 222–30, 282–5.
31. For an account of the riots and the unusually fierce reaction of middle-class groups, *see* Jones, *Outcast London*, pp. 290–7.
32. Charles Booth (ed.), *Life and Labour of the People in London*, 2 vols., London 1892, vol. 1, p. 35, 62; vol. 2, p. 21. This was in fact the 2nd edition of Booth's study. The 1st edition, which appeared in London in 1889 and 1891, was entitled *Labour and Life of the People*. The 3rd edition of 1902/03 eventually ran to eighteen volumes, divided into three series: *Poverty* (4 vols.), *Industry* (5 vols.) and *Religious Influence* (7 vols.), accompanied by two separate volumes, one containing maps, the other a summary. The volumes on *Poverty* caused the greatest stir among contemporaries. For an account of Booth's life and work, *see also* T. S. Simey and M. B. Simey, *Charles Booth: Social Scientist*, Oxford University Press 1960.
33. For account of the 'New Unionism', which, following its initial appearance after 1885, first made headway as a result of the wave of strikes, *see* Clegg *et al.*, *History*, pp. 55ff., 87ff.; A. E. P. Duffy, 'New Unionism in Britain, 1889–1890: A Reappraisal', in *Economic History Review* 14 (1961), pp. 306ff. The effects of the economic crisis during early 1890s in weakening this New Unionism and the employers' move to resist the spread of its influence are dealt with in E. J. Hobsbawm, 'General Labour Unions in Britain 1889–1914', in *Economic History Review* 1 (1949), pp. 123ff.

but at the same time shook people's consciences and led to an increased level of social commitment. Beatrice Webb, who had helped Booth in his investigations, was, alongside her husband Sydney, one of the few important social researchers of the period able to exert direct influence on the government's social policy. Writing to her husband in September 1891 in connection with their combined researches into the British trade union movement, she had the following to say: 'I get so sick of these ugly details of time-work and piece-work, over-time, and shop-rent, and the squalid misfortunes of defaulting branch officers or heckling by unreasonable members. Who would choose to imprison the intellect in this smelly kitchen of social life if it were not for the ever-present '30 per cent' with the background of the terrible East End streets?'.[34]

Booth, to whose study she referred, distinguished between four main categories of poverty:

A. The lowest class: occasional labourers, loafers and semi-criminals — 0.9 per cent
B. The very poor: casual labour, hand-to-mouth existence, chronic want — 7.5 per cent
C and D. The poor: including alike those whose earnings are small, because of irregularity of employment, and those whose work, though regular, is ill-paid — 22.3 per cent[35]

He concluded that the 8.4 per cent of London's population belonging to classes A and B were essentially living 'in distress' or 'in want'. He did not, however, explain their poverty solely on the basis of objective economic factors, large size of family or unforeseen circumstances. He also took a more traditional view of its causes, often ascribing the condition to the individual's own inadequacy and personal blame in cases of drunkenness or lack of thrift.[36] Despite this, his study drew attention to the high number of workers who were only able to find occasional work and also highlighted other causes of chronic poverty, such as the effects of the economic cycle, seasonal unemployment, old age, sickness and disablement. Booth's findings on the scale of the

34. Quoted in Mary Agnes Hamilton, *Sidney and Beatrice Webb: A Study in Contemporary Biography*, London 1932, p. 97.
35. Booth, *Life and Labour*, vol. 2, pp. 20f.
36. This is also pointed out in two new interpretations of Booth's study: Wolfgang Mock, 'Die Wiederentdeckung der Armut in der Phase der "mature economy": Das Beispiel Charles Booth', in Mommsen and Schulze (eds.), *Elend der Handarbeit*, pp. 418–41, esp. pp. 430–2; Hennock, 'Poverty', in *Social History* 1 (1976), pp. 80–4.

problem were confirmed by Rowntree's study of poverty in York, which employed more refined methods and was published in 1901.[37] Both Booth's and Rowntree's investigations showed clearly that the traditional system of poor relief, which affected 2.7 per cent of the population (i.e. only a fraction of the poor) was an inadequate method of dealing with poverty and its consequences. Many young intellectual social reformers during this time subscribed to the belief that the social sciences could help fight poverty, just as medicine could help combat the problem of infectious diseases.

The government was faced with a difficult choice. It could carry out a radical reform of the finances of local poor-law administration, so as to re-establish the balance which had previously existed between rich and poor districts, while at the same time imposing general standards in welfare.[38] The alternative was to depart from the practice of previous centuries, during which the responsibility for social welfare had been

37. Rowntree, whose study covered a total of 11,560 families comprising 46,754 individuals — that is, practically the whole of York's wage-earning population (excluding domestic servants) — discovered that 27.84 per cent of the city's population of 76,000 and 43 per cent of its wage-earners were living in poverty (*Poverty: A Study of Town Life*, pp. 150f.). Unlike Booth, whose results were mainly based on the impressions of HM School Inspectors and not supported by actual income figures, Rowntree and his helpers established the details of each family's income and by calculating the basic minimum expenditure of each household, defined poverty as the lack of sufficient means to maintain health and bare physical efficiency. According to his calculations, which took family size into account, 9.91 per cent of the population, or 15.46 per cent of members of working-class families, were living in conditions of 'primary poverty' (i.e below the poverty line), 'based upon the assumption that every penny earned by every member of the family went into the family purse, and was judiciously expended upon necessaries' (p. 144). 17.93 per cent of the population, or 27.94 per cent of members of working-class families, were living in 'secondary poverty' (i.e. Rowntree's helpers gained an impression of poverty), even though the family's income would have been sufficient 'for the maintenance of merely physical efficiency were it not that some portion of it is absorbed by other expenditure useful or wasteful' (pp. 150f., 118). Certainly, the percentage of 'primary poverty' compared with all poverty would have risen from 35.6 per cent to 47 per cent, had the poverty line been fixed at a level of only 2 shillings per week more (p. 175). The main cause of 'primary poverty' was low pay for regular work (51.96 per cent), with the result that those demanding that the government introduce a minimum wage were in future able to use Rowntree's survey to support their arguments. Other main causes of poverty were family size (22.16 per cent) and the death (15.63 per cent), old age or illness of the main breadwinner (5.11 per cent). In contrast to Booth's findings, unemployment (2.31 per cent) and irregular employment (2.83 per cent) were relatively minor factors (p. 153). For an extremely interesting biography of Rowntree, whom Lloyd George appointed Head of the Ministry of Munitions' Welfare Department at the beginning of 1916, *see* Asa Briggs, *Social Thought and Social Action: A Study of the Work of Seebohm Rowntree, 1871–1954*, London 1961.
38. J. R. Hay, *The Origins of the Liberal Welfare Reforms, 1906–1914*, London and Basingstoke 1975, esp. pp. 40–2.

almost entirely left to local authorities,[39] and, using the institutions of central government, intervene on a massive scale to solve the social problem, for which the traditional system of poor relief was proving inadequate. A reform of the existing system was, however, unlikely to succeed in view of the opposition of wealthier authorities to sharing the costs involved with poorer authorities, and there was also a strong tradition of lay administration by local civic dignitaries which had to be overcome. In view of this, the government eventually decided on the second course. However, this failed to bring about the abolition of the traditional system, which finally broke down only under the strain of mass unemployment during the 1920s. The institution of poor-law unions under the supervision of poor-law guardians was not abolished until 1929, when their duties were finally taken over by the county and county borough councils. In 1934 an Unemployment Assistance Board was set up for the unemployed, before the Poor Law finally disappeared with the setting up of the National Assistance Board in 1948.

Between 1905 and 1909 the reform of England's Poor Law was the subject of a detailed investigation by a royal commission. However, neither the proposals by the majority of the commission's members nor the minority report submitted by Beatrice and Sydney Webb were taken up by the government. The Webbs argued for an idea they had developed during the 1890s that the state should guarantee all citizens a minimum living standard beyond the barest essentials necessary for survival in a civilised society. As a result of their minority report, which was widely distributed, their views now reached a wider public[40] and

39. One result was that the local government's share of public expenditure rose from 38.36 per cent in 1890 to 51.14 per cent in 1905, before returning to 44.76 per cent in 1913 following the growth of central government controlled social services. The share of local government spending on social services rose from 38.7 per cent in 1890 to 47 per cent in 1913. During the same period, total expenditure on social services increased from 27.3 to 100.8 million pounds per annum and its share of total public expenditure rose from 20.9 per cent to 33 per cent. Public expenditure accounted for 8.9 per cent of Britain's GNP in 1890 and 12.4 per cent in 1913 (Alan T. Peacock and Jack Wiseman, assisted by Jindrich Veverka, *The Growth of Public Expenditure in the United Kingdom*, Princeton 1961, pp. 166, 184, 201, 207).

40. *Report of the Royal Commission on the Poor Laws and Relief of Distress, British Parliamentary Papers* (BPP), Cd. 4499, London 1909. Both reports, which were partly based on a large number of interviews give an excellent insight into the problems of poor relief in Britain during this period. For a summary of the more important reform proposals contained in the reports, *see* pp. 646–70 (Majority Report) and pp. 1218–38 (Minority Report). The extensive Minority Report was published separately in two parts by Sidney and Beatrice Webb. These were entitled, *Break Up the Poor Law and Abolish the Workhouse*, and *The Remedy for Unemployment*. The Report's recommendations were disseminated by the 'National Committee to Promote the Break-up of the Poor Laws' which Beatrice Webb founded for the purpose. It later became the 'National Committee for the Prevention of Destitution'. According to

increased pressure on the government to instigate social reforms. The successful introduction of compulsory schooling between 1870 and 1880 had a similar effect. It successfully demonstrated how illiteracy might be gradually eliminated. In 1891 the percentage of London's population between the ages of twenty-five and fifty-five who had attended a proper school was only 23 per cent and already stood at 78 per cent by 1911.[41] Education also enabled unskilled workers, who wavered between attitudes of deference towards the upper classes and irrational forms of protest, to gain respectability and self-confidence. They could be put to greater use in the industrial process, while they, for their part, learnt how to represent their interests more effectively.

The higher civil servants employed in the Labour Department of the Board of Trade, which developed from the Labour Statistical Bureau, provided one of the main driving forces behind reform. Unlike the staff of other ministries, these civil servants were not recruited in open competition against other university graduates possessing a general education. Instead, they were recruited from among people who were already experts in their own field, comprising mainly statisticians from the social sciences, economic experts and specialists on labour affairs and the trade union movement. These experts were able to use their influence to oust the Local Government Board, which was fairly inflexible and scarcely amenable to new changes, from its dominant position in determining social policy.[42]

From the end of the nineteenth century onwards, major changes were also discernible in the sphere of social ideas and their political application. *Laissez-faire* ideals and the belief in the individual's ability to improve his situation through his own efforts increasingly gave way to socialist and collectivist attitudes, which were not just confined solely to the labour movement.

At the same time, there were also calls to increase national productivity. This demand has to be seen against the background of the

G. D. H. Cole, *A History of Socialist Thought*, vol. 3, *The Second International, 1889–1914*, London, 1956, p. 207, the Minority Report contained 'the first full working out of the conception and policy of the Welfare State'.

41. E. H. Phelps Brown, *The Growth of British Industrial Relations: A Study from the Standpoint of 1906–1914*, London 1959, p. 45.

42. *See* Roger Davidson and Rodney Lowe, 'Bureaucracy and Innovation in British Welfare Policy, 1870–1945', in Mommsen, *Emergence*, pp. 263–95, esp. pp. 264–77; Roger Davidson, 'Llewellyn Smith, the Labour Department and government growth 1886–1909', in Gillian Sutherland, (ed.), *Studies in the Growth of Nineteenth-Century Government*, London 1972, pp. 227–62; and Davidson's article 'The Ideology of Labour Administration, 1886–1914', in *Society for the Study of Labour History, Bulletin*, no. 40, Spring 1980, pp. 29–35; Jose Harris, *William Beveridge: A Biography*, Oxford 1977, esp. pp. 144–6.

Boer War, which showed up Britain's military incompetence. It was also partly due to the ground lost by the British economy to its rivals, Germany and the United States. The demand was taken up by socialist, liberal and conservative academics, civil servants, writers and leading politicians, who were consciously turning away from the old, Gladstonian-style of Liberalism with its traditional emphasis on the involvement of non-specialists in politics, government and the economy.[43] Among the many political figures who advocated this were the Conservative Prime Minister, A. J. Balfour (1902–05), the leading Liberal imperialist, R. B. Haldane, and the guiding spirit of the socialist Fabian Society, Sidney Webb. Typical of Webb's views was an article he wrote, entitled 'Lord Rosebery's Escape from Houndsditch', the idea for which came from George Bernard Shaw, who revised the text before publication.[44] The aim of the article, in which the leaders of the socialist Independent Labour Pary were castigated for their views on the Empire as 'administrative Nihilists — that is to say, ultra-Nationalists, ultra-Gladstonian, Old Liberal to the fingertips'[45] was to support the Liberals' growing rejection of Gladstonian principles with their stress on the individual and opposition to state intervention in social and economic affairs. This had to be done 'in order to clear the way for Fabian collectivism'.[46] As leader of the Liberal imperialists, Lord Rosebery had turned away from the old ideals of Gladstonian Liberalism. Now Webb called on the former Prime Minister to lead a revitalising progressive opposition to the government by adopting an extensive programme aimed at 'national efficiency in every department of life'.[47] As was the case with other figures who demanded an increase in 'national efficiency', the issue at stake for Webb was the modernisation of Britain's entire political, economic and social system, with the aim of adapting the country to the new demands of a scientifically and

43. *See* G. R. Searle, *The Quest for National Efficiency. A Study in British Politics and Political Thought, 1899–1914*, Oxford 1971. For the connection between imperialist and social reformist ideas frequently encountered in England and Germany (e.g. Max Weber, Friedrich Naumann), of which Searle makes no mention, *see* Bernard Semmel, *Imperialism and Social Reform: English Social-Imperial Thought 1895–1914*, London 1960, and the final two volumes of Elie Halévy's classic study, *A History of the English People in the Nineteenth Century*, vol. 5, *Imperialism and the Rise of Labour (1895–1905)*; vol. 6, *The Rule of Democracy (1905–1914)*, (first published in France, 1926 and 1932) London 1961.

44. Beatrice Webb, *Our Partnership*, ed. by Barbara Drake and Margaret Cole, London 1948, pp. 220, 224.

45. Sidney Webb, 'Lord Rosebery's Escape from Houndsditch', in *Nineteenth Century,* September 1901, pp. 366–86, esp. p. 372.

46. Webb, *Partnership*, p. 220.

47. Webb, 'Escape', in *Nineteenth Century*, September 1901, p. 375.

technologically advanced industrial society.[48] As far as these social reformers were concerned, the idea of social reform was closely bound up with the idea of strengthening the Empire, since imperial expansion, increased foreign settlement and the consequent growth of trade were primarily intended to bring about a decline in unemployment at home and provide the means for solving Britain's social problems. Conversely, measures intended to strengthen the working-class (e.g. improvements in health, education and the employment situation) were seen as a necessary prerequisite for improving imperial defence.

Typical of this kind of thinking was the new cult of experts, something which would previously have been viewed as quite 'un-British'. Businessmen were called upon to become actively involved in politics. The civil service and management in industry began to show signs of increasing professionalisation, and the prestige of the natural and social sciences began to grow with their importance to the economy and the military establishment. In the same way, the concept of 'social engineering' came to the fore. Although this was not accepted uncritically, more attention began to be paid to emulating the German example of technical schooling, technical universities and state patronage for science, as well as specific aspects of central and local government social policy.[49]

German social insurance, together with other aspects of German social policy and medical welfare, were initially brought closer to the attention of most Englishmen through the writings of William Harbutt Dawson, one of the most knowledgeable contemporary British experts on Germany.[50] Following the Liberals' election victory in 1906, Lloyd

48. For a time both the Webbs and Haldane saw in the Conservative Prime Minister, Arthur James Balfour, whom they held in high regard on account of his interest in scientific and educational affairs, the British statesman who could best be expected to bring about a realisation of their ideas. Their view was confirmed when Balfour carried out reforms in secondary and technical education, which they rightly saw as an attempt on his part to increase national efficiency (Searle, *Quest*, p. 144, 207–16).

49. *See* Günter Hollenberg, *Englisches Interesse am Kaiserreich: Die Attraktivität Preussen-Deutschlands für konservative und liberale Kreise in Grossbritannien, 1860–1914*, Wiesbaden 1974, pp. 230–7, 248–55. On Britain's selective adoption of German university research methods and scientific knowledge and the organisational structures of Germany's system of higher education, cf. Hollenberg, pp. 147–78; cf. also Frank R. Pfetsch, *Zur Entwicklung der Wissenschaftspolitik in Deutschland, 1750–1914*, Berlin 1974, pp. 314–47; Peter Alter, 'Staat und Wissenschaft in Grossbritannien vor 1914', in Helmut Berding *et al.* (ed.), *Vom Staat des Ancien Regime zum modernen Parteienstaat*, Munich and Vienna 1978, pp. 369–83, esp. pp. 373–6; and his *Wissenschaft, Staat, Mäzene: Anfänge moderner Wissenschaftspolitik in Grossbritannien, 1850–1920*, Stuttgart 1982, esp. pp. 121–6, 148–56, 181ff., 248ff.

50. *See* William Harbutt Dawson, *Bismarck and State Socialism: An Exposition of the Social and Economic Legislation of Germany since 1870*, reprint of the 1890 edn, New York 1973, esp. ch. 9, pp. 109–127. In this book Dawson unequivocally passes a

George appointed him to the post of research assistant at the Board of Trade, from whence he later moved to the Treasury in order to help in preparing the government's national insurance legislation of 1911.[51] He was married to the daughter of Emil Münsterberg, a Berlin city councillor and probably Germany's most prominent expert on the field of social welfare. Dawson advocated a Liberal social policy aimed at raising the workers' productive efficiency along the lines of Germany's example, but saw this only partially realised.[52] This was because of fundamental differences between his own ideas and those of Lloyd George and his closest advisors, as well as the need to compromise with the vested interests of the insurance companies, trade unions and Friendly Societies. It was, therefore, not surprising that with his appointment as Principal Clerk to the newly created National Health Insurance Commission for England, Dawson was excluded from participating any further in framing social welfare legislation within the ministry itself.

In the period between 1906 and 1914, successive Liberal governments were able to carry out an extensive programme of social reforms, thanks to the emergence of a 'new Liberalism', which arose partly in opposition to the Liberal imperialists and drew upon the older traditions of British radicalism. One of the central concerns of this new Liberalism was the creation of a better society, in which poverty and distress would be virtually eliminated. On 1 October 1908, Lloyd

---

favourable judgement on a pragmatic form of state socialism, a view which clearly reveals the influence of his Berlin University tutor, Adolph Wagner. He later dispensed with the term 'state socialism' and, influenced by internal British disagreements on a preferential tariff for the Empire, also gave up his earlier conditional defence of Germany's tariff system.

51. *See* Hollenberg, *Englisches Interesse*, pp. 235f. Peter Hennock warns us against overestimating Dawson's influence on the 1911 National Insurance Act in his article, 'The Origin of British National Insurance and the German Precedent, 1880–1914', in Mommsen, *Emergence*, pp. 84–106, esp. p. 98.

52. Dawson emphasised the preventive aspects of Germany's social insurance, which had no equivalent at first in Britain (William Harbutt Dawson, *Social Insurance in Germany, 1883–1911: Its History, Operation, Results. And a Comparison with the National Insurance Act*, 1911, New York 1912; reprint edn, Westport 1979, pp. 182–208.). The book was written in order to defend Britain's National Insurance Act of 1911 against Conservative criticisms, which repeatedly drew attention to the allegedly negative effects of Germany's social insurance system. The book also contains lengthy passages on the attitude of German employers towards the social insurance laws (pp. 238–58). These passages were extracts from material collected by Dawson and published by the government in order to counteract the opposition of British employers to the 1911 Act (see *Memorandum containing the Opinions of Various Authorities in Germany BPP*, Cd. 5869, London 1911; J. R. Hay, 'The British Business Community, Social Insurance and the German Example', in Mommsen (ed.), *Emergence*, pp. 107–32, ibid., pp. 123f.).

George, who, together with Winston Churchill, was the leading political representative of this modern brand of Liberalism, made a typical
speech expressing these ideas:

> British Liberalism is not going to repeat the errors of Continental Liberal-
> ism. The fate of Continental Liberalism should warn them of that danger. It
> has been swept on one side before it had well begun its work, because it
> refused to adapt itself to new conditions . . . British Liberalism has been
> better advised. It has not abandoned the traditional ambition of the Liberal
> Party to establish freedom and equality; but side by side with this effort it
> promotes measures for ameliorating the conditions of life for the multitude.
> The old Liberals in this country used the natural discontent of the people
> with the poverty and precariousness of the means of subsistence as a motive
> power to win for them a better, more influential, and more honourable status
> in the citizenship of their native land. The new Liberalism, while pursuing
> this great political ideal with unflinching energy, devotes a part of its
> endeavour also to the removing of the immediate causes of discontent.

In particular, the state should assist the poor, who through no fault of
their own find themselves in a position where they cannot earn their
daily bread:

> the aged and infirm, the broken in health, the unemployed and those
> dependent upon them. . . . Starvation is a punishment that society has
> ceased to inflict for centuries on its worst criminals, and at its most barbar-
> ous stage humanity never starved the children of a criminal . . . I have heard
> some foolish mutterings that much recognition of this fact [i.e. the workers'
> part in creating the country's wealth] in legislation may drive capital away.
> There is nothing capital need fear as much as the despair of the multitude'.[53]

This quotation highlights the sense of commitment among important
sections of British Liberalism to an active policy of state social reform
in the decade before the First World War.

The different character which social insurance assumed in Germany
and Britain and the different ways in which it developed were largely
determined by the differing positions occupied by the Liberals of both
countries during its formative phase. These can be explained mainly in
terms of the different stage reached in the development of political
liberalism in both countries. In Germany, in contrast to Britain, it had
long since passed the zenith of its power, but young politicians, such as
Friedrich Naumann and Theodor Barth, were also advocating a radical programme of social reforms from the turn of the century onwards.
Recent research on Britain has stressed the vitality and adaptability of

---

53. D. Lloyd George, *Better Times: Speeches*, London 1910, pp. 51–5.

its Liberal Party after the turn of the century by pointing to the remarkable Liberal election success of 1906, their retention of power in the two subsequent elections of January and December 1910 and their successful implementation of a comprehensive programme of social, political and financial reforms.[54] This contrasts with earlier interpretations, according to which Britain's political liberalism was already in decline from the end of the nineteenth century onwards, its place being gradually taken over by the advancing labour movement.

In fact, it was not until after the Liberals had shown themselves incapable of preventing the outbreak of the First World War, their departure from liberal principles during the war and the Party's split following Lloyd George's formation of a coalition Cabinet at the end of 1916, that the disintegration and political decline of the Liberal Party in Britain began. There were already clear indications before 1914 which pointed the way forward to the later emergence of the welfare state. British Liberals overcame their traditional reservations towards the state and attempted to combine the ideals of freedom and individualism with those of social welfare and collectivism.[55] There was also a greater willingness to tackle the social effects of poverty and strengthen the legal position of the trade unions.

That the government actually carried out an active social policy was, of course, partly governed by political and tactical considerations. In 1911 the number of adult males entitled to vote still stood at only 60 per cent of the adult male population,[56] and, despite the growing strength of the suffragette movement before 1914, women were still denied the vote. However, in view of the gradual transition taking place towards class politics, which did not, however, produce a Parliament dominated by parties based on class before 1914,[57] the Liberals were forced to carry out an extensive social policy programme, which placed a

---

54. *See* esp. P. F. Clarke, *Lancashire and the New Liberalism*, Cambridge, 1971, esp. p. VII, 393–407. The spread of ideas on social reform and the activities of the 'Radicals' among the Liberal MPs in Parliament form the subject of H. V. Emy's study, *Liberals, Radicals and Social Politics, 1892–1914*, Cambridge 1973; for an account of the political ideas of New Liberalism and its connection with socialism, *see also* Michael Freeden, *The New Liberalism: An Ideology of Social Reform*, Oxford 1978; Peter Clarke, *Liberals and Social Democrats*, Cambridge 1978.

55. *See* Freeden, *New Liberalism*, esp. pp. 25–75; Clarke, *Liberals and Social Democrats*, esp. pp. 100–27.

56. Neal Blewett, 'The Franchise in the United Kingdom 1885–1918', in *Past and Present*, no. 32, 1965, pp. 27–56, esp. p. 27.

57. Clarke, *Lancashire*, pp. 406f. According to Henry Pelling, in his *Social Geography of British Elections, 1885–1910*, London 1967, 'social class was not as much of a political watershed as it has been in recent years. Nevertheless, social class was also a determinant of major importance in the period' (p. 418).

strain on their relations with their traditional sources of finance.[58] Such a programme was necessary if the Liberals were to keep a tight hold on working-class voters and not prematurely jeopardise the Lib–Lab electoral alliance of 1903, which was becoming increasingly precarious in the years before 1914.[59] Since the Conservatives' refusal to grant Irish Home Rule or their emphasis on the Empire could count on the support of the majority of voters, the Liberals wanted, above all, to place the Conservatives on the political defensive and prevent any change in government by concentrating on social and economic policy. In fact, the elections of 1906 and January and December 1910 were not fought primarily on the issue of individual reforms, which usually tended to gain in popularity only years after their introduction. But it did become generally clear to the electorate that the Liberals, more than the Conservatives (who similarly defended their proposed programme of preferential tariffs for the Empire as a way of creating the means to implement a comprehensive state social policy), were more committed to reforming social ills and combating poverty.[60] Since too many interests were involved in the traditional system of poor relief, reform was brought about, not by abolishing or basically changing the traditional system but, as in Germany, by excluding more and more social groups and categories of risk from poor relief until it was gradually dismantled.

Liberal reform policy between 1906 and 1914

One of the first concrete results of state intervention during the period of Liberal government between December 1905 and the First World War was the extension of employers' liability for industrial injuries, first introduced by the Workmen's Compensation Act of 1897 and carried through against employer opposition. A law of 1906 extended cover to further occupational groups and also took account of occupational diseases, something which went beyond current German practice at the time. For employers in trades affected by the laws of 1897 and 1906 the legal defences of contributory employee negligence and common employment were swept away and the individual em-

58. Emy, *Liberals*, pp. XI, 101–3.
59. Ritter, 'Geschichte der britischen Labour Party', in idem, *Parlament und Demokratie*, pp. 139f., 146–53; Ross McKibbin, *The Evolution of the Labour Party, 1910–1924*, Oxford 1974, pp. 48–71.
60. Clarke, *Lancashire*, esp. pp. 398–406.

ployer made liable for compensation amounting to half the worker's weekly wage in cases where an accident had not resulted from a serious, premeditated infringement of safety regulations on the part of the employee. Even where this was judged to have been the case, the employer was still liable for compensation if the accident proved fatal or resulted in injury leading to permanent disablement.

Not to have opted for a compulsory accident insurance along the lines of Germany's example, which was discussed as a serious alternative,[61] proved to be a mistake, because, unlike Germany's compulsory employers' occupational associations, Britain's new voluntary societies did not cover all employers. Also, claims by injured parties could often only be settled via the courts. As had been the case with Germany's liability law of 1871, this produced strained relations between both sides of industry and resulted in high administrative and legal costs. Since no machinery existed to support employees' claims, they frequently felt cheated and forced to accept an unfair flat-rate settlement, unless represented by their trade union or other organisations. In view of the ever-present danger of bankruptcy, there was no guarantee that legal rates of compensation would be paid out. Finally, it was extraordinarily difficult to assess liability in the case of occupational diseases, which workers often contracted over a long period of time with a number of different employers. Other disadvantages were that the laws gave no incentive to restore the injured party to physical health and the costs of medical treatment were borne either by the workers or private charitable and public welfare organisations. Since in most cases a lump sum was paid in settlement in place of a pension,[62] many workers eventually felt forced to turn to poor relief. A comparison of the actual results of the British and German system of providing for the victims of accidents at work is difficult, since many cases were not covered in the very incomplete British statistics.[63] According to these, workers' compensation in Britain amounted to 3,362 million pounds in 1913.[64] This was barely 40 per cent of the 175 million marks paid out during the same year by Germany's compulsory accident insurance. Despite the strongly sensed inadequacies of the law, it was replaced only in 1946

61. Emy, *Liberals*, p. 148.
62. On the Act's weaknesses, *see Der Beveridgeplan. Sozialversicherung und verwandte Leistungen. Bericht von Sir William Beveridge. Dem britischen Parlament überreicht im November 1942*, Zurich and New York 1943, pp. 55–9.
63. Peter Hennock, 'Arbeiterunfallentschädigung und Arbeiterunfallversicherung: Die britische Sozialreform und das Beispiel Bismarcks', in *Geschichte und Gesellschaft* 11 (1985), p. 20.
64. *Eighteenth Abstract of Labour Statistics of the United Kingdom*, 1926, BPP, Cmd. 2740, pp. 166f.

with the introduction of state insurance for industrial accidents and occupational diseases. This ended the previous practice, whereby, in contrast to Germany, workers' compensation was not included in the system of obligatory social insurance.

The introduction of school medical inspection and free school meals for poor children in 1906–07 fitted into the new concept of state assistance for the socially disadvantaged. One of the reasons for the introduction of these new measures was the fact that recruitment during the Boer War had brought to light the different standards of medical health among the youth of Britain's different social classes. But, in addition, there was a basic tendency at the time, probably connected with the fall in the birth-rate, to place a higher value on children's lives.[65] Another move towards protecting the weak can be seen in the creation of Trade Boards in 1909. These bodies were entrusted with fixing minimum statutory rates of pay in areas of business with particularly poor working conditions or where workers were scarcely in a position to form a trade union.[66]

State pensions were also introduced for old people in need above the age of seventy in the Old Age Pensions Act of 1908. The state thereby acknowledged its responsibility to support a section of the community beyond the provisions of traditional poor relief. The principle involved in this Act thus constituted a major step forward in the direction of the later welfare state.

The problem of poverty in old age, which was aggravated by industry's lack of concern for elderly workers, together with the introduction of old-age pensions, formed the subject of almost continuous discussion in Britain from the end of the 1870s onwards.

In 1878 the proposals of the Anglican churchman W. L. Blackley that compulsory contributions from workers between the ages of eighteen and twenty-one should provide the basis of sickness insurance benefits and a modest old-age pension for those over seventy[67] had no hope of being taken up. In 1891 Charles Booth and Joseph Chamberlain developed alternative plans for old-age provision, which was to be independent of the existing Poor Law. Booth took as his starting point his own investigations into poverty in old age. According to his calculations, probably more than 40 per cent of all those who died aged sixty-five years and over had been living on poor relief in one form or

65. Hay, *Origins*, pp. 43f. For the effects of occupation and social class on the mortality of workers and their children, *see* Phelps Brown, *Growth*, pp. 33–43.
66. For the Act's minimal effect on this area, *see* Phelps Brown, *Growth*, pp. 309f.
67. William Lewery Blackley, 'National Insurance: A Cheap, Practical and Popular Means of Abolishing Poor Rates', in *Nineteenth Century* 4, November 1878, pp. 834–57.

another during the last years of their life. Since no more than a ninth of these had drawn poor relief before the age of sixty, it would be possible to reduce considerably the extent of poverty in old age and the burden on poor relief if the state paid a pension to all citizens over the age of sixty-five.[68] Joseph Chamberlain, who, even after his break with the Liberal Party, was keen to preserve his image as one of Britain's leading social reformers, advocated instead a voluntary old-age insurance supplemented by government funds.[69]

However, all these projects ran up against stiff opposition from Britain's private charitable organisations and Friendly Societies, which by the end of the nineteenth century insured about a half of all males over the age of nineteen, especially against sickness.[70] Old-age pensions, on the other hand, were only very rarely provided by Friendly Societies. State subsidies for old-age insurance, whether voluntary or solely financed by the state, were seen as restricting the business interests of the Friendly Societies. Moreover, they ran counter to the basic principles of the Friendly Societies' membership, which was mainly drawn from skilled workers and artisans. For these groups, membership of a Friendly Society, which also provided members with a social life, had long been a status symbol which demonstrated their independence and respectability. They also feared that giving up the principle of individual or collective self-help would lead to the workers' morals being corrupted.[71]

The campaign for state provision for old age increasingly gained ground from the end of the nineteenth century onwards. This followed the introduction in 1898 of relatively generous state pensions for people over sixty-five in New Zealand and the founding in England of an Old Age State Pension League. Booth's plans were eventually taken up and

68. Charles Booth, 'Enumeration and classification of Paupers, and State Pensions for the Aged', in *Journal of the Royal Statistical Society* 54, December 1891. pp. 600–43. For more information, *see* his *Pauperism, a Picture; and the Endowment of Old Age, an Argument*, London 1892; and his *The Aged Poor in England and Wales: Condition*, London and New York 1894; Williams, *Pauperism*, esp. pp. 341–4.

69. For Chamberlain's plans for reform, their modification in the years that followed and his unsuccessful attempts to win the support of the Friendly Societies, *see* Gilbert, *Evolution*, pp. 180–6. In his testimony to the Royal Commission on the Aged Poor, which sat between 1893 and 1895, Chamberlain expressed the view that Germany's system of compulsory insurance — which entailed high costs and would be extremely unpopular with British workers — was 'inapplicable to English habits and feelings' (Gosden, *Self-Help*, p. 271).

70. *See* Gilbert, *Evolution*, p. 167. Gilbert bases his figures on an estimated membership of between 4.25 million and 4.5 million for the Friendly Societies.

71. James. H. Treble, 'The Attitude of Friendly Societies towards the Movement in Great Britain for State Pensions, 1878–1908', in *International Review of Social History* 15 (1970), pp. 266–99, esp. pp. 269–80.

supported by the British trade union movement, whose representatives played a leading part in setting up a National Committee of Organised Labour for Promoting Old-Age Pensions. Efforts such as this led in turn to the setting up of a House of Commons Committee, which at the end of July 1899 made the first official proposals for old-age pensions for the needy and deserving poor, to be financed from state funds and local poor rates. The criteria for granting pensions were to be very precisely defined. For instance, anyone claiming a pension was not allowed to have received poor relief in the previous twenty years and his or her income had to be less than 10 shillings per week.[72]

Even the Friendly Societies, which were ridden with considerable internal disagreement after 1900 on the subject of state pensions,[73] gradually gave up their original opposition. This was because they found themselves in considerable financial difficulties. The average life expectancy of their members was increasing. At a time when the birth-rate was declining, the death rate for members of the bigger societies between the ages of twenty and eighty was, according to later surveys, about a third below the national average.[74] The result was a drop in income and a relative increase in the amount of benefits paid out to the Societies' older members, who were especially vulnerable to sickness and frequently disabled.

That the introduction of old-age insurance was delayed until 1908 was mainly a result of the Boer War, which broke out in October 1899 and lasted until 1902. It temporarily relegated public interest in the question of old-age pensions to the background. In addition, the high costs of the war caused the government to shrink back from any increase in welfare expenditure.

Britain's old-age provisions differed from Germany's in that pensions were borne by the state rather than jointly financed by the employers, the insured and the state. Also, in Britain pensions were granted to women who were not in employment. Finally, compared to the average size of pension in Germany, Britain's benefits for single people were more than half as much again and married couples' pensions more than three times as much. Single persons received 5 shillings per week (i.e. about 260 marks per year) and married couples 10 shillings, if both partners were over the age of seventy. The more generous provisions in Britain were, of course, largely the result of the country's greater wealth and the higher wages paid to British workers. The British

72. *Report from the Select Committee on the Aged Deserving Poor*, House of Commons Papers, no. 296, 1899, pp. III–XIII.
73. Treble, 'Attitude', in *International Review of Social History* 15 (1970), pp. 280–97.
74. Gilbert, *Evolution*, pp. 172f.

government's original intention of keeping costs down by limiting married couples' pensions to a maximum of 7 shillings and 6 pence per week was eventually abandoned. The full pension, which 94.6 per cent of all pensioners received before 1914,[75] was paid out to anyone with an annual income of less than 21 pounds per year. Anyone with an annual income over 31 pounds 10 shillings received no pension at all. Incomes in between qualified for weekly pensions of between 4 shillings and 1 shilling, calculated on a sliding scale. With these benefits, Great Britain still trailed well behind New Zealand, where pensions were guaranteed to all citizens over the age of sixty-five and where those with an annual income of less than 34 pounds received the full pension of 18 pounds per annum.

In contrast to Germany's old-age pensions, Britain's depended firstly on a means test and secondly on a vetting of the claimant's character and reputation. The latter approach was an example of that distinction made between the deserving and undeserving poor which was so typical of Victorian and Edwardian society. Anyone drawing a pension had to have no record of imprisonment in the previous decade and no propensity towards heavy drinking. Furthermore, he or she was obliged to show that their poverty was not the result of a habitual refusal to work according to their abilities and in the light of their opportunities and needs. As a result of pressure from the government's own backbenches, the originally proposed additional stipulation that pensions should not supplement poor-relief payments and that anyone receiving poor relief after the 1 January 1908 should fail to qualify was eventually dropped. The result was that only those who were residents of a poorhouse were excluded from state pensions.[76]

There was a great deal of controversial discussion at the time on the principles behind pension legislation. While the Labour Party's spokesman in the House of Commons took the same view as Charles Booth and the trade unions that all people over a certain age should be provided with assistance with no conditions attached,[77] R. B. Haldane, one of the Liberal government's leading figures, saw the law merely as the old Elizabethan Poor Law adapted to fit changed circumstances: 'The Bill does not profess to introduce any new principle. . . . It is perfectly clear there cannot be a universal system . . . nor can there be a contributory scheme, because it is an extension of the system of the

---

75. *Seventeenth Abstract of Labour Statistics of the United Kingdom*, 1915, BPP, Cd. 7733, p. 184.
76. Halévy, *Rule of Democracy*, pp. 283–5.
77. Speech to the House of Commons by J. W. Taylor on 15 June 1908, *Parliamentary Debates, House of Commons* [=*Parl. Deb.*, HC] 4 series, vol. 190, col. 654.

Poor Law'.[78] The one-time Conservative Minister of the Local Government Board, W. Long, spoke after Haldane. He thought the latter's interpretation of the Poor Law was mistaken. He pointed to the lack of agreement on basic principles among the bill's own advocates and recommended adopting the German system of old-age pensions based on the level of insurance contributions, which the government had already turned down.[79]

Whatever views existed on the relationship between the new provisions for old age and the old Poor Law, there were several basic differences. Receipt of an old-age pension did not involve any curtailment of the citizen's rights under the law. Another new factor was that, unlike the system under the Poor Law, clear, universally applied legal criteria could now be used to determine the merits of pension claims. When these were met, the individual had a legal claim on public assistance.[80] Unlike Germany's disablement and old-age insurance, on the other hand, there was no element of self-administration for the insured, since pensions were entirely a matter for the state, which alone financed them.

Alongside the problem of poverty in old age, the economic crises of the 1870s and the London riots of the 1880s led to a growing awareness that unemployment among the able-bodied was one of the main causes of poverty and distress, for which the individual could not always be held responsible.[81] In keeping with the ethos of the 1834 Poor Law, unemployment among the able-bodied had previously been put down to work-shyness. Before 1914, irregular work and unemployment were a much greater problem in Great Britain than in Germany. According to trade union statistics collected by the Board of Trade, the peak figures for unemployment in Great Britain were 10.7 per cent in 1879, 9.6 per cent in 1886 and 8.7 per cent in 1908 and 1909. Since a disproportionately high number of skilled workers were included in these statistics, the figures, if anything, underestimate the true extent of unemployment. With an unemployment rate of between 3 and 6 per cent annually, Britain's figures lay well above those of 1.1 to 2.9 per cent unemployment as recorded by the German trade unions after 1903.[82]

78. Ibid., cols. 661–3.
79. Ibid., cols. 673–5, 735.
80. *See* Ogus, 'Landesbericht Grossbritannien', in Köhler and Zacher (eds.), *Ein Jahrhundert Sozialversicherung*, p. 327.
81. *See* alongside Harris, *Unemployment*, esp. pp. 7ff., John A. Garraty, *Unemployment in History: Economic Thought and Public Policy*, New York 1978, esp. pp. 103–45, which mainly deals with the political effects of the economic debate in an international comparative framework.

From 1880s onwards, a whole range of measures to combat unemployment were discussed in Great Britain. Various ideas were considered. These included encouraging emigration, introducing emergency relief work, to be financed by the state and local authorities,[83] and establishing workers' colonies within the country in order to improve labour market conditions. Among the supporters of colonies for workers were the Fabian Society, the Salvation Army[84] and leading contemporary socialists such as William Morris, Robert Blatchford, George Lansbury and Keir Hardie.[85] Booth, too, had taken up the idea in his proposals concerning the extremely poor sections of society contained in his class B, which comprised 7.5 per cent of London's population. What was not clear about the concept of workers' colonies was whether these were intended only for Britain or were also to be sited in the overseas territories of the Empire. The majority and minority reports of the Royal Commission on the Poor Laws likewise favoured the setting up of such colonies as well as so-called compulsory or detention colonies.[86] According to the minority report, normal training establishments would cater for the various groups of chronically unemployed, while detention colonies would be intended for the recalcitrant and work-shy.[87] Similar proposals to establish workers' colonies had been made as far back as the first half of the nineteenth century by Robert Owen and the Chartists. Socialist and trade union calls for the introduction of the eight-hour day, a statutory minimum wage and the legal right to work[88]

82. Harris, *Unemployment*, p. 374. For Germany, *see* above p. 100, note 256.
83. *See* Harris, *Unemployment*, esp. pp. 73ff., 115ff., 135ff.
84. Victor Bailey, '"In Darkest England and the Way Out": The Salvation Army, Social Reform and the Labour Movement, 1885–1910', in *International Review of Social History* 29 (1984), pp. 133–71.
85. For Booth's classification of the poor, *see* above, p. 141. On the workers' colonies, *see also* Mock, 'Wiederentdeckung der Armut', in Mommsen and Schulze (eds.), *Elend der Handarbeit*, pp. 432–5.
86. Majority Report, pp. 633, 662f.; Minority Report, pp. 1204–8, in *Report of the Royal Commission on the Poor Laws.*
87. 'The Detention Colony, though it will be entered only upon commitment by a judicial authority, will not be a. . . convict settlement. . . [it] has necessarily to have the characteristic of compulsory detention. Its inmates are sent there to be treated for, and if possible cured of, a morbid state of mind, which makes them incapable of filling a useful place in the industrial world. . . . Enforced regularity of life, and continuous work, of a stimulating and not monotonous kind; plain food, with opportunities of earning small luxuries by good conduct and output of work; restriction of personal liberty; and power to those in charge to allow return to one of the ordinary Training Establishments on probation, as soon as ever it is believed that reformation has been effected — these features sufficiently indicate the outlines of the experiment. Repeated recalcitrance, and, of course, any assault on the persons in charge, would be criminal offences, leading to sentences of penal servitude in a convict settlement' [Minority Report, ibid., pp. 1207f.].

were also aimed at distributing available work as equitably as possible and combating the effects of a saturated labour market on wages.

The breakthrough of a constructive government policy on unemployment after the turn of the century was in the end decisively influenced by a number of individual experts. One of these was William Beveridge, who was widely acknowledged after 1905 as Britain's leading authority on unemployment. Through his publications, his testimony to the Royal Commission on the Poor Laws and his role after 1908 at the Board of Trade, where he was officially in charge of unemployment policy, he initially defined the main points which guided subsequent public discussion of the problem. It was Beveridge also who went on to elaborate the government's plans for tackling unemployment.[89]

Following the severe winter of 1904–05, the Conservative government introduced the Unemployed Workmen Act of 1905, which for the first time acknowledged the state's obligation to combat unemployment. But after this attempt to keep down unemployment — by making municipal funds available for emergency relief works, establishing workers' colonies and communal labour exchanges — had proved relatively unsuccessful, Beveridge saw in regulating the entire labour market through labour exchanges the essential first step towards constructing an effective government policy on unemployment.[90] His views were reinforced by a trip he made to Germany between August and October 1907. He was exceptionally impressed, especially by the efficiency of Germany's municipal labour exchanges.[91] In the minority report of the Royal Commission on the Poor Laws, which made Beveridge's call for a national system of labour exchanges a central feature of its plans for regulating the labour market, the German system was referred to in some detail:

> the utility of the labour exchange has been abundantly demonstrated. In nearly all the large towns of Germany such an institution has now been established; and we have available, in some cases, the testimony of ten, and even of twenty years' experience. Over 700 labour exchanges of one kind or another are now regularly reporting to the Imperial Statistical Office at

---

88. Harris, *Unemployment*, esp. pp. 58–73, 235–45; Kenneth D. Brown, *Labour and Unemployment, 1900–1914*, Totowa 1971.

89. Harris, *Beveridge*, esp. 108–58. For Beveridge's views on the causes of unemployment and methods to combat it during this period, *see* W. H. Beveridge, *Unemployment: A Problem of Industry*, London 1909, reprint of the enlarged edition of 1930, New York 1969.

90. Harris, *Beveridge*, p. 126.

91. Ibid., pp. 134–6. The first edition of Beveridge's book on *Unemployment* (see note 89) contained an appendix entitled 'Public Labour Exchanges in Germany', which first appeared in the March 1908 issue of the *Economic Journal*.

Berlin. They are filling about *two millions of situations annually*. These labour exchanges are of various sorts, but the most interesting to us are the Public General Exchanges, established by the municipal authorities in practically every town of 50,000 inhabitants.[92]

Even though the Labour Exchanges Act of 1909 departed from the German concept of municipal labour exchanges by setting up up a network of public labour exchanges directly responsible to the Board of Trade, British policy on unemployment was, apart from the experiences with the London unemployed scheme, considerably influenced by the German example. This was also studied by a British trade union delegation and leading labour members of the House of Commons.[93]

Certainly, the widespread emulation of Germany's model of labour exchanges was not without its critics. Sir (later Lord) George Askwith, the Board of Trade's chief arbitrator in labour disputes, accompanied Beveridge and Llewellyn Smith, head of the Board's Labour Department on a fact-finding mission to Germany in August 1909. It was hoped that the findings would be of use in the creation of Labour Exchanges in Britain, but as Askwith commented critically: 'It was this system, so suited to the German ideas of organisation and so useful to a nation which wanted to know where every man was and what every man could do, which was hastily imposed on this country. . . . Its suitability to the United Kingdom and the effects which it might have upon the relations of employers and employed were not thought out'.[94]

While still Prime Minister, Sir Henry Campbell-Bannerman had continued to subscribe to traditional liberal principles and had remained sceptical of state intervention in social and economic affairs. Following his resignation in 1908 on the grounds of ill-health, Lloyd George's rise to become Chancellor of the Exchequer and Winston Churchill's appointment to President of the Board of Trade meant that the call for effective state social reforms was taken up with renewed vigour in 1908–09. The representatives of the 'new Liberalism' had

92. Minority Report, in *Report of the Royal Commission on the Poor Laws*, p. 1181, original italics. The Majority Report also supported the creation of a national system of labour exchanges under Board of Trade control 'for the general purposes of assisting mobility of labour and of collecting accurate information as to unemployment' (p. 659); the difference being that the Majority Report gave this issue less emphasis.
93. Harris, *Unemployment*, p. 277. Both Churchill and Lloyd George were partly responsible for despatching the British delegation of trade union leaders. Minutes of the Labour Party's Executive Committee of 15 December 1908 (Labour Party Archive); George N. Barnes and Arthur Henderson, *Unemployment in Germany: A Report of Inquiry*, n.d. London.
94. Lord Askwith, *Industrial Problems and Disputes*, 1920; London 1974, p. 274.

strengthened their position of influence in the meantime. In the winter of 1907/08 social problems became more acute as a result of the high rate of unemployment, which furthered the state swiftly acknowledging its responsibility for the labour market. At the same time, there was a growing awareness that a fundamental reform of the poor-relief system, which was failing to cope in the crisis, could not be achieved as quickly as was generally hoped. The Liberals, moreover, went on the political offensive with their strategy of instigating a programme of social reforms in order to counter Conservative demands for protective tariffs.

In this situation, both Lloyd George and Churchill realised that any further expansion of the social security system was impossible without introducing some form of social insurance system. If one was to provide for the sick, the disabled and the unemployed, this could not be left to the existing practice of social benefits financed exclusively by the state and the local authorities. As can be seen from a memorandum he wrote on 7 March 1911, Lloyd George saw insurance purely as an emergency measure dictated by financial expediency:

> Insurance necessarily temporary expedient. At no distant date hope state will acknowledge full responsibility in the matter of making provision for sickness breakdown and unemployment. It really does so now through Poor Law, but conditions under which this system has hitherto worked have been so harsh and humiliating that working-class pride revolts against accepting so degrading and doubtful a boon.
>
> Gradually the obligation of the state to find labour or sustenance will be realised and honourably interpreted.
>
> Insurance will then be unnecessary, and a great accumulated fund would tempt to extravagant and futile progress of expenditure.[95]

Thus, like Bismarck in the 1880s, Lloyd George saw workers' insurance merely as a transitional phase on the way to a fully fledged welfare system, administered wholly by the state and financed by taxation. His willingness to provide massive state subsidies to supplement insurance contributions from both employers and employees was entirely in keeping with this concept. But he realised that for the present no improvement in social security was possible without a social insurance system. During a celebrated journey he made to Germany in August 1908, he was able to study at first hand the way Germany's social insurance worked. Although the impression it made on him has doubtless been somewhat exaggerated, it played an important part in

95. Quoted in *Lloyd George's Ambulance Wagon: Being the Memoirs of William J. Braithwaite, 1911–1912*, edited, with an introduction by Sir Henry N. Bunbury and with a commentary by Richard Titmuss, London and Southampton 1957, pp. 121f.

influencing the subsequent form taken by Britain's sickness, disablement and unemployment insurance of 1911. 'I never realised before', he declared shortly after his return from Germany, 'on what a gigantic scale the German pension scheme is conducted. Nor had I any idea how successfully it works. . . . You have to see it before you can understand it. It touches the great mass of the German people in well-nigh every walk of life'.[96] While in Germany he had met not only members of the German government and senior civil servants but also leaders of the Social Democrats and trade unions, as well as employers. Lloyd George's positive view of Germany's social security system was undoubtedly influenced by his belief that these groups would have been the first to agree that workers' insurance was one of industrial Germany's greatest institutions.[97] In December, after the previously mentioned delegation of British trade unionists had expressed their approval of Germany's social insurance system, Winston Churchill urged Prime Minister Asquith to take note that:

> There is a tremendous policy in social organisation. The need is urgent and the moment ripe. Germany with a harder climate and far less accumulated wealth has managed to establish tolerable basic conditions for her people. She is organised not only for war but for peace. We are organised for nothing except politics. The minister who will apply to this country the successful experiences of Germany in social organisation may or may not be supported at the polls, but he will at least have left a memorial which time will not deface of his administration. . . . Thrust a big slice of Bismarckianism over the whole underside of our industrial system, and await the consequences whatever they may be with a good conscience'.[98]

The implementation of the new policy, which was officially announced in April 1909, was, however, delayed on account of implacable opposition from the Conservative-dominated House of Lords. The conflict between the Commons and the Lords arose as a result of Lloyd George's 1909 budget and eventually led to two early elections, followed by legislation to curb the latter's power.[99] For many contemporaries the budget appeared revolutionary. It saw Lloyd George

96. *The Daily News*, 27 August 1908.
97. Budget speech by Lloyd George, *Parl. Deb. (Official Report)*, *HC*, 5th series, vol. 4, col. 485.
98. Churchill's letter to Asquith of 29 December 1908, in Randolph S. Churchill, *Winston S. Churchill*, vol. 2, Companion Part 2, 1907–11, London 1967, pp. 862–4.
99. For an account of the controversy surrounding the budget and the two elections of 1910, *see* Bruce K. Murray, *The People's Budget 1909–10: Lloyd George and Liberal Politics*, Oxford 1980; Neal Blewett, *The Press, the Parties and the People: The General Elections of 1910*, London and Basingstoke 1972.

adopt the principle of using direct taxes as a means of closing the gap between the different living standards of Britain's social classes, and it appeared to question the existing right of property in land. The budget's aims were to be achieved by introducing a progressive income tax, increasing death duties and imposing a tax on unearned wealth resulting from rises in the value of landed property.[100] Though the latter was still a moderate measure, it was widely seen as establishing a precedent for the future. The idea of a land tax went back to the economic theories of David Ricardo, John Stuart Mill, Henry George and the Fabians, who had advocated the taxing of ground-rent as a major source of government revenue.

Although extreme inequality continued to exist in Great Britain — between 1911 and 1913, 170,000 property owners (i.e. 0.85 per cent of the population owning property at all) controlled 65.5 per cent of the country's available capital[101] — it was typical of Britain that, unlike Germany, the expansion of its system of state social benefits was financed, not by raising indirect taxes, but by substantially increasing direct taxes. The proportion of total tax revenue accounted for by direct taxes rose from 50.3 per cent in 1905/06 to 57.6 per cent in 1912/13.[102]

With the National Insurance Act of 1911 the British government went beyond the German system by extending unemployment insurance to certain groups of workers. Unlike the government's proposed work-creation programmes, the question of a central or municipal unemployment insurance was hardly discussed in Britain before 1907. It was in the same year that Beveridge, in an article in the *Morning Post* and in his testimony to the Royal Commission on the Poor Laws, drew attention to the idea of using the government's proposed labour exchanges as a possible means of administering unemployment insurance.[103] In contrast, the trade union unemployment insurance schemes, which often only amounted to a travel grant to relieve pressure on local labour markets by removing competition from unmarried workers, had 682,000 subscribers in 1891 and 2,357,000 in 1908; that is, half and later virtually all of Britain's trade unionists.[104] The suggestion of the Webbs that the trade unions' unemployment

100. For the budget's individual terms and significance, *see* Lloyd George's five-hour-long budget speech of 29 April 1909 (*Parl. Deb., HC*, 5th series, vol. 4, cols. 472–548).
101. Sidney Pollard, *The Development of the British Economy, 1914–1967*, 2nd edn, London 1976, p. 2.
102. Bernard Mallet, *British Budgets, 1887–88 to 1912–13*, London 1913, p. 493.
103. Harris, *Unemployment*, pp. 298–300.
104. Ibid., pp. 297f.

benefits should be supplemented by additional local authority funds[105] along the lines of the Ghent model, as adopted in several European countries, such as Belgium, the Netherlands, Denmark and Norway,[106] received no support. This was because the employers, whose participation in its funding was regarded as indispensable, rejected the system on the grounds that it exclusively benefited the unions. In addition, the unskilled workers, who were especially vulnerable to unemployment but still largely unorganised, were largely excluded from the proposed scheme.[107]

The idea of developing unemployment insurance through labour exchanges under direct Board of Trade control and providing government supplements was eventually accepted by the leaders of the unions but not by the TUC. Its delegates wanted to make the unions the sole agencies responsible for administering the insurance and had to take heed of criticisms voiced by many unions concerning the workers' share of contributions and the amount to be paid by low wage-earners.[108] But, despite all, there was still relatively little opposition in Britain to the introduction of state unemployment insurance in 1911. This was because the government, in order to win trade union support, agreed that unemployment benefit, which could only be claimed for a maximum period of fifteen weeks, could in the case of trade unionists also be paid out by the trade unions as well as the labour exchanges. In addition, the unions were to receive from the government three-quarters of the amount they paid out in unemployment benefit, up to the government's proposed weekly amount of 7 shillings' unemployment benefit. Finally, it was proposed, along the lines of the Ghent system, that the trade unions would be reimbursed[109] for up to a sixth of benefits (up to 12 shillings) paid out to unemployed workers in branches of industry not yet covered by unemployment insurance. In 1914 more than a third of all insurance benefits were paid out by associations, usually trade unions. By 1915 it was a half.[110] In July 1914, Britain's unemployment insurance — financed by a three-eighths share of contributions from both employer and employee and a quarter subsidised by the state — covered some 2.3 million workers in seven

105. Sidney and Beatrice Webb, *Das Problem der Armut*, Jena 1912, pp. 123ff. The Minority Report in *Report of the Royal Commission on the Poor Laws* also rejected the idea of a compulsory workers' insurance in favour of the state encouraging voluntary insurance schemes administered by trade unions along the lines of the system developed in Ghent (pp. 1199–1201).

106. For the discussion in Germany, *see* above, pp. 102f.

107. Harris, *Unemployment*, pp. 303f.

108. Ibid., pp. 317f.

109. Gilbert, *Evolution*, pp. 279f.

different branches of industry, some of which were greatly affected by
seasonal and long-term unemployment. It therefore covered only a
sixth of employees in the industrial sector.[111] Of these, over 23 per cent
claimed benefits in the twelve months prior to that date.[112]

The workers now covered against unemployment, of whom only a
fifth had previously been insured, still represented only a fraction of the
number of potentially unemployed workers. Britain's unemployment
insurance did nothing to solve the particularly urgent problems of
irregular work, youth unemployment and the high rate of unemployment among unskilled workers. Among those who benefited by it, some
63 per cent belonged to the country's relatively highly-paid skilled
workers.[113]

As well as unemployment insurance, the government also introduced
a combined compulsory sickness and disablement insurance for all
manual labourers between the ages of sixteen and seventy and all other
employees in the same age group with an annual income below 160
pounds. This insurance took in approximately 14 million employees.
According to an official estimate of the time, owing to their position as
dependants, around three quarters of the population benefited directly
or indirectly from sickness benefits.[114] From the fourth day of an illness,
men received sickness benefit amounting to 10 shillings and women
seven shillings and 6 pence. This continued to be paid for the first
twenty-six weeks of an illness. Thereafter, in cases of long-term illness
or disablement, the insured worker was paid a sickness or disablement
pension of 5 shillings per week. There was also provision for a maternity allowance of 30 shillings, free medical treatment by GPs (i.e.
non-specialists), free medicine and — only for tuberculosis patients —
a period of hospitalisation at a sanatorium. Maternity allowance was
also paid to the wives of insured workers, even if they themselves had
not paid contributions. On the other hand, there was no provision for
medical care of dependants, payment for normal periods of hospitalisation or treatment by medical specialists. Additional benefits, such as
free medical treatment for dependants, free dental treatment and the

110. Ministry of Labour, *Report on National Unemployment Insurance to July 1923*, London
    1923, pp. 219f.
111. *See* ibid., p. 206, for a breakdown of figures on the number of workers insured in
    different industries. Of these, the engineering and construction industries, which
    together employed over two-thirds of insured workers, were by far the most
    important, followed by shipbuilding.
112. Thane, *Foundations*, p. 95.
113. Harris, *Unemployment*, p. 360.
114. *Report for 1912/13 on the Administration of the National Insurance Act, Part I (Health
    Insurance)*, *BPP*, Cd. 6907, London 1913, p. 1.

payment of benefit before the fourth day of an illness could, however, be granted at the discretion of the insurance authorities, if their financial situation allowed. In addition, the law allowed for the treatment of diseases other than tuberculosis in sanatoria and hospitals, if this was decided by the Local Government Board, subject to Treasury approval. Thus the basis was laid for the future possible expansion of hospital care without any necessary change in the law.[115]

Compared with the introduction of unemployment insurance, the part of the law dealing with sickness insurance encountered much more opposition. This was particularly strong among doctors, who were affected by the new system, though their attempts to boycott it by refusing to carry out its requirements collapsed owing to their own lack of solidarity.[116] The opposition of the commercial insurance companies and the Friendly Societies, which had been highly influential in shaping the law, was only overcome after long drawn-out and complicated negotiations. In order to avoid the disgrace attached to a pauper's burial, a large section of the population made regular payments into burial funds run by commercial insurance companies.[117] As had been the case previously with the Friendly Societies in the elections of January 1910,[118] the commercial insurance companies brought considerable pressure to bear on candidates in elections to the House of Commons in December 1910.[119] In all, 490 of the 670 MPs elected promised during the election to vote against any bill which harmed the interests of the Friendly Societies and commercial insurance companies or gave preferential treatment to certain societies and associations at the expense of others. By threatening to mobilise some 70,000 door-to-door insurance salesmen against the government, the burial funds forced Lloyd George to drop his original plan to include a widows' and orphans' pension in the legislation. In addition, he had to grant the commercial insurance companies the same status as that enjoyed by the Friendly Societies and trade unions as officially approved societies for administering the insurance system.[120]

---

115. Ibid., p. 3.
116. *See* the detailed documentation on the government's negotiations with the medical associations, in ibid., pp. 124–48, and Gilbert, *Evolution*, pp. 401–16.
117. In a speech to the House of Commons on 4 May 1911, Lloyd George reported that 'There are 42,000,000 industrial policies of insurance against death issued in this country . . . there is hardly a household in this country where there is not a policy of insurance against death' (*Parl. Deb., HC*, 5th series, vol. 25, cols. 609f.). He went on to say that, in contrast, less than half the workforce (6–7 million) was insured against sickness and less than 10 per cent (1.4 million) against unemployment (ibid.).
118. Gilbert, *Evolution*, p. 316.
119. Ibid., esp. pp. 332–6.

The British system of sickness insurance differed to some extent from the German system in the smaller share of contributions paid by insured workers, amounting to only four-ninths of the total sum involved. Women, for their part, were expected to pay three-eighths. In Germany workers had to pay two-thirds, the rest being covered by employers. In addition, the state provided a supplement in the case of sickness insurance contributions of two-ninths and two-eighths, respectively. The remainder was paid in by the employer. Apart from women, who were treated as a special case, and the employer's liability for the additional cost of the worker's share of contributions in the case of the low-paid, the amount of contributions and sickness benefits was, in contrast to the German system of graduated contributions and benefits, the same for all workers.[121] This was to show that the law was not intended to maintain specific living standards but to prevent insured workers sliding into the class of paupers and, in the interests of the nation, preserve the workforce's productivity, by combating poverty and partially replacing the Poor Law.

The law was to be centrally administered by four commissions which were created for England, Wales, Scotland and Ireland, as well as by a general commission for the whole of the United Kingdom. It proved highly significant for the development of the British health system that, in contrast to Germany, medical treatment was not regulated by the insured organisations themselves, but by local medical committees, on which the commercial insurance companies were also represented alongside doctors and civil servants. Thus, the earlier practice, prevalent among the Friendly Societies and other similar organisations, of paying doctors directly under individual contract, was ended.[122] Patients now had a free choice of doctor from among those declaring their willingness on principle to treat insured workers against a fixed annual sum per patient.[123]

Like Germany's compulsory sickness insurance, the National Insurance Act of 1911 led not only to improved medical treatment for workers but raised the standard of living for doctors practising in

---

120. Ibid., esp. pp. 318–43.
121. Gustav Schmoller criticised this as being 'somewhat unjust': 'If the worker with a weekly wage of 15, 20, 40 or 60 shillings produces and receives the same, this is problematical; a future change and graduation is already partly expected' (*Soziale Frage*, p. 421.).
122. Richard M. Titmuss, 'Health', in Morris Ginsberg (ed.), *Law and Opinion in England in the 20th Century*, London 1959, pp. 306–8.
123. Apart from a few exceptions, the practice, employed in some areas at first, of paying doctors according to their number of consultations, was soon given up (*Report for 1912/13 of the Administration of the National Insurance Act*, pp. 147f.).

poorer urban districts.[124] The idea, suggested by the Webbs[125] and often threatened by Lloyd George, of breaking the British Medical Association's organised opposition by transferring the medical care of insured workers to full-time appointed doctors, who would also be given the right to treat dependants,[126] came to nothing. This was because more than two-thirds of Britain's practising doctors eventually cooperated under the new arrangements.[127] Nevertheless, the law highlighted the fact that the influence of the municipal and state authorities on the health system, which was increasingly taking over the work of the poor law authorities, was being strengthened. For example, the number of available beds in the medical clinics of poor-houses or hospitals run by the poor-law unions fell sharply in comparison with the total number of beds becoming increasingly available in city hospitals.[128] Nevertheless, there was still a long way to go until the creation in 1948 of a National Health Service with its own full-time medical appointees.

Alongside the greater involvement of central and local government in the medical treatment of insured workers, there was one other fundamental difference between Britain's social insurance system and Germany's sickness insurance and disablement insurance. This was the way in which it was partly administered by approved societies.

The differences between the British and German systems were the result of deliberate policy on the part of W. J. Braithwaite, the civil servant responsible for working out and applying the terms of Britain's sickness and disablement insurance of 1911. The same was true of

124. Brian Watkin (ed.), *Documents on Health and Social Services 1834 to the Present Day*, London 1975, pp. 76f.; Titmuss, 'Health', pp. 310–13.

125. The Minority Report in the *Report of the Royal Commission on the Poor Laws* already argued in favour of combining existing medical services under the traditional system of poor relief and the existing structure of state health services in order to create a 'unified Medical Health Service on Public Health lines'. The responsibilities of the new system would be considerably extended in scope (pp. 846–91, 1223–5). For a highly critical view of Britain's contemporary health services and the National Insurance Act of 1911, which censured the imitation of Germany's example, criticised the inadequate acknowledgement of the population's general health problems and lack of preventive measures to avoid illnesses, while proposing, at the same time, a complete reorganisation of the public health services, *see* William A. Brend, *Health and the State*, London 1917.

126. Gilbert, *Evolution*, esp. pp. 410–15.

127. Gilbert, in *Evolution* (pp. 437f.), estimates that approximately 20,000 of Britain's 41,000 doctors were potentially eligible as resident practising GPs to provide treatment for insured workers. Of these, about 14,000 doctors were locally registered before 1914 as being prepared to treat insured workers.

128. *See* Julia Parker, Constance Rollett and Kathleen Jones, 'Health', in A. H. Halsey (ed.), *Trends in British Society since 1900: A Guide to the Changing Social Structure of Britain*, London and Basingstoke 1972, pp. 321–71, esp. p. 349.

Lloyd George, who continually contrasted Germany's sickness insurance with Britain's proposed system only to emphasise the latter's superiority.[129] Both men wanted to avoid what they saw as the German system's strong bureaucratic element by encouraging the tradition of self-management and self-help as embodied by the Friendly Societies. In fact, the internal structure of the commercial insurance companies, who participated in the system contrary to their original intentions and were particularly successful[130] in recruiting customers, resulted in Britain's insured workers having much less influence on sickness insurance compared with Germany's workers. The reason was that these companies were only interested in profits for their shareholders and commissions for their representatives. They therefore made no real provision for any participation by the insured in managing their affairs.

Contemporary observers in Germany were extremely impressed by Britain's legislation, which they took as proof of the country's capacity for reform. Gustav Schmoller, for example, in his posthumously published book *The Social Question* (*Die Soziale Frage*), described Britain's sickness and disablement insurance as a 'magnificent reform', marking Britain's

> definite break with the past principles of *laissez-faire*. The state, the employers and the workers are working together to preserve the nation's health and the strength of its people, as well as to increase living standards. . . . Britain's two major laws of 1909 [on labour exchanges] and 1911 have, as it were, eliminated Germany's lead as far as the level attained by its social insurance is concerned. Let us hope that the German Empire will soon be able to catch up and again overtake this island kingdom.[131]

129. See *Lloyd George's Ambulance Wagon*, esp. pp. 82–8; Hennock, 'Origins', in Mommsen (ed.), *Emergence*, esp. pp. 89–100.

130. In October 1912, Britain's Friendly Societies accounted for 44.7 per cent of the total number of employees insured through 'approved societies'. The trade unions accounted for 11.5 per cent, employers for 0.6 per cent and private insurers for 43.2 per cent. Over and above these, must be added those people who, because they were considered particularly bad risks, were either rejected or whose custom was not sought in the first place by any of the approved societies. (No one could be rejected purely on the grounds of old age.) In such cases, the employee's, employer's and the state's contributions were paid into a private post-office account. In the case of sickness or disablement, the amount of benefit due could be withdrawn up to the balance of the account. In reality, this was a form of compulsory savings scheme supported by the government and employers, and not a genuine form of insurance. The number of these so-called 'Deposit Contributors' (395,021 in October 1912) declined during later years and was even lower than the government had originally feared. Between 1912 and 1938 the number of persons insured with private commercial companies rose from 42 per cent to 47 per cent of the total number of persons insured (see *Report for 1912/13 of the Administration of the National Insurance Act*, pp. 606, 610f.; Gilbert, *Evolution*, p. 424; *Beveridgeplan*, pp. 39–41).

Britain's social legislation of 1911 was also very closely studied by the German bureaucracy. For example, the social policy section of the Imperial Office for the Interior systematically collected press cuttings on Britain's legislation and procured parliamentary reports and other publications via the German Embassy in London. The differences and common features of both systems were also closely analysed in an internal memorandum on Britain's sickness insurance, which was used as the basis for a presentation made to the Kaiser.[132] The compulsory character of the insurance, the introduction of contributions by employer and employee, the participation of voluntary insurance associations and the substantial similarity which existed between the type and extent of benefits paid out in both countries were all taken to be examples of Britain emulating Germany's social insurance. Differences between the two systems were, however, discerned in the strong element of 'existing independent structures', such as Friendly Societies and trade unions, and attributed to differing political factors. Additional differences were seen in the considerable extent of the government's financial involvement, the combining of sickness and disablement insurance and the strong 'element of socialist and communist ideas' detected in the substantial 'equalisation of contributions and benefits regardless of individual wage levels or differing needs, e.g. between town and country'. In somewhat irritated tones, the memorandum criticised the glowing reports on Britain's social legislation which were appearing in the German daily press and specialist journals. These were regarded as a 'sign that the German press still fails to take an independent line when dealing with foreign affairs'. The view, moreover, that Britain's institutions were somehow more 'social' than Germany's also encountered considerable scepticism. This memorandum provides us with yet more evidence of the keen interest observers in both countries showed towards developments taking place in each other's social legislation. By studying the other country's alternative system, they hoped to gain new ideas for solving the social question in their own country, whose social welfare would then figure internationally as particularly progressive.

---

131. Schmoller, *Soziale Frage*, pp. 420, 421f., 449. The Preface by Schmoller's wife is dated October 1918; that is, from before the end of the First World War. Schmoller himself died on 27 June 1917.
132. Detailed extracts from the 1911 Memorandum are contained in Florian Tennstedt's, 'Anfänge sozialpolitischer Intervention in Deutschland und England — einige Hinweise zu wechselseitigen Beziehungen', in *Zeitschrift für Sozialreform* 29, (1983), pp. 631–648, esp. pp. 643–645.

The supporters of social legislation and the effect of reform

The passage of the National Insurance Act of 1911, which meant that a reform of the poor-relief system could be postponed, witnessed all the interested parties cooperating on a major scale: the Friendly Societies, the trade unions, the commercial insurance companies and the British Medical Association. These organisations were the essential partners and, in some cases, the opponents of the government. No parallel existed in Germany for this 'novel form of parliamentarianism above and beyond the official parliamentary government'.[133] Bismarck had been practically able to ignore the opposition of Germany's private insurance companies to the introduction of state social insurance.[134] The trade unions, which had been rendered largely ineffective by the anti-Socialist law and were only cautiously built up again during the 1880s,[135] had no direct influence on the shape of Germany's legislation:

As far as I am aware, no detailed research has yet been done on the influence of Parliament and party-political considerations on the formation and character of Britain's social welfare legislation after 1906. It is unlikely, however, that this was any less than that exerted in Germany by the Reichstag and the political parties. It is generally known, for instance, that on the question of introducing old-age pensions the Liberal government was under considerable pressure from its own backbenchers and the labour movement. In contrast to the situation in 1906, after the two elections in 1910 the government depended on the votes of the Labour MPs and the Irish Nationalists for its majority in the House of Commons. As a result, the Liberals were forced to take account of MPs' views in these two parties, which were loosely allied with the government, over and above renewed pressure from its own backbenchers. Interested parties not only attempted to influence the government and the civil service directly, but benefited from the help of sympathetic MPs who used the House of Commons committee system to influence the final terms of the Act. In view of the apparent popularity of reform among the electorate, the Conservative Opposition decided to give its support to the Liberal government's initial measures. In the case of the government's proposed sickness insurance, the Conservatives, after initial hesitation, adopted a critical stance under the pressure of increasing public dissatisfaction. They did

133. Halévy, *Rule of Democracy*, p. 358; Gilbert (*Evolution*, p. 356) describes the lead-up to the 1911 National Insurance Act as 'an almost classic history of lobby activity'.
134. *See* Vogel, *Arbeiterversicherung*, pp. 47–50.
135. Ritter and Tenfelde, 'Durchbruch', in Ritter, *Arbeiterbewegung*, pp. 60–71.

not, however, force the issue and the Opposition allowed the bill to pass its reading in the House of Lords. Following pressure from Austen Chamberlain's supporters, who had no wish to see the Conservatives identified as opponents of reform, the Conservative Party leader, Bonar Law, eventually had to retract his threat, made at the beginning of 1912, that a future Conservative government would abolish sickness insurance.[136]

In the case of both countries, a few prominent government ministers played a crucial part in determining the basic features of social legislation and ensuring its passage. Lloyd George's influence on the introduction of Britain's old-age pensions and sickness and disablement insurance, in particular, bears comparison with Bismarck's influence on Germany's social insurance during the 1880s. According to Churchill, he was 'the greatest master of the art of getting things done and putting things through that I ever knew'.[137] After Lloyd George, Churchill himself has to be seen as one of the political figures who prepared the way for Britain's welfare legislation. His period of office as President of the Board of Trade between April 1908 and October 1911 witnessed the setting up of labour exchanges, the creation of Trade Boards to fix minimum wage-rates in certain branches of industry and the introduction of unemployment insurance.

Civil servants, particularly those at the Board of Trade, and several of Lloyd George's assistants were able to influence the government's measures to at least the same degree as Germany's senior bureaucrats had done. In the case of the government's policy on unemployment, their influence proved paramount. In both countries the social sciences and social statistics played a significant part in identifying social problems, working out suggestions for their solution and creating a favourable climate of public opinion for the passage of welfare legislation.

The employers' significant though ambivalent influence has recently been examined in more detail. As in Germany, their attitude to social legislation was not uniform. Nevertheless, there was a strong group among employers, who — following Birmingham's lead — turned the country's Chambers of Commerce into their effective mouthpiece in support of demands for the creation of a comprehensive system of social insurance against accident, sickness, disablement and old age along the lines of Germany's.

136. Robert Blake, *The Unknown Prime Minister: The Life and Times of Andrew Bonar Law, 1858–1923*, London 1955, pp. 139f.
137. Churchill goes on to say, 'In fact no British politician has possessed half his competence as a mover of men and affairs' (Winston S. Churchill, *Thoughts and*

A statement issued by the Association of Chambers of Commerce in 1907 was typical of this support in declaring that 'this association is of the opinion that the time has arrived when His Majesty's Government should take into serious consideration the subject of national insurance for the working classes against accident, sickness, invalidity, and old age on the lines, so far as is practicable, of the comprehensive system which has operated so successfully in Germany'.[138] Behind this declaration lay the employers' attempt to increase the efficiency of British industry by improving the workers' productivity, especially in the new areas of industry which depended on skilled workers and demanded a highly developed technology. They also hoped to use social insurance to impose a certain amount of social control on the workforce and counter pressure from labour organisations to introduce an eight-hour day, fix minimum wages and legally guarantee the right to work. In addition, they sought to abolish the existing law on employers' liability, which they regarded as unacceptable, by incorporating industrial accidents into the general scheme for sickness insurance. At the same time, they hoped to reduce the cost of social legislation for the British economy by making the workers pay their own share of contributions.[139]

Because of the high costs involved, especially in wage-intensive industries, and because it was expected that unemployment insurance would strengthen the unions and reduce the employers' scope for imposing discipline on the workforce, the majority of employers representing small and medium-sized firms rejected the National Insurance Act of 1911. The Employers' Parliamentary Association, which was eventually set up in December 1911 with the specific aim of fighting the Act, and which derived its main support from the centres of the textile industry, failed, however, to win the support of the Chambers of Commerce and remained without any real influence on government social policy before 1914.[140] Like other employers' organisations, the

---

Adventures, London 1932, p. 60).

138. The full text of the resolution can be found in J. R. Hay (ed.), *The Development of the British Welfare State, 1880–1975*, London 1978, pp. 35f.

139. *See* J. R. Hay, 'Employers and Social Policy in Britain: The Evolution of Welfare Legislation, 1905–1914', in *Social History* 2 (1977), pp. 435–55, and for the significance of Germany's example among certain groups of British employers, *see* idem, 'The British Business Community, Social Insurance and the German Example', in Mommsen (ed.), *Emergence*, pp. 107–32.

140. Hay, 'British Business Community', in Mommsen (ed.), *Emergence*, pp. 124f.; idem, 'Employers and Social Policy', in *Social History 2*, esp. pp. 440ff.; idem, 'Employers' Attitude to Social Policy and the Concept of "Social Control", 1900–1920', in Thane, (ed.) *Origins*, pp. 107–25, esp. pp. 113ff.

Chambers of Commerce successfully suggested various amendments to the original bill. If most employers eventually rejected the Act, the earlier massive support shown for social insurance by important groups amongst them substantially supported the change of direction in British social policy from one of pure state aid for the needy to a social insurance system covering the majority of employees.

Assessing the role of the labour movement and the workers in the emergence of Britain's social legislation has been at the centre of much controversy in British research. Henry Pelling, one of the most knowledgeable historians of the course of the British labour movement and British politics in the years before 1914, has put forward the view that the Labour Party, whose lack of interest in ideas and social programmes was typical for the working class of the time, had no clear concept of social policy. Like the Poor Law, slum clearance and compulsory education, social reform — as an aspect of the extension of state power — was, in his view, unpopular with the vast majority of workers. According to Pelling, Britain's social legislation played no significant part in the elections of the period. Nor was it the result of pressure from below. Rather, it resulted from objective administrative necessity, rising professional standards and the work of middle-class philanthropists who were not always pursuing selfless motives.[141]

In contrast, other researchers, like P. F. Clarke and H. V. Emy, partly agree with the earlier interpretation of the leading French historian Elie Halévy that social legislation was mainly a result of the older-established parties competing for the working-class vote.[142] They see the central problem of British politics since the turn of the century in the different positions adopted towards social policy.[143] Other historians take a middle position and emphasise the influence of labour organisations and the workers on specific welfare laws.[144] In my

141. *See* Henry Pelling, 'The Working Class and the Origins of the Welfare State', in idem, *Popular Politics and Society in Late Victorian Britain*, London 1969, pp. 1–18, esp. pp. 12–16; idem, 'The British Working Class's Attitude to the Extension of State Powers, 1885–1914', in *Society for the Study of Labour History, Bulletin*, no. 13, 1966, pp. 17f.; idem, 'State Intervention and Social Legislation in Great Britain before 1914', in *Historical Journal* 10, (1967), pp. 462–6. Harris argues (*Unemployment*, pp. 270f), that a constructive policy of social welfare legislation did not appeal to the majority of voters, even though many Liberal politicians thought otherwise from the beginning of 1908 onwards.

142. Halévy, *Rule of Democracy*, p. VII. In 1908 the American political scientist, Lowell, saw the competition of the two main parties for the working-class vote by means of preferential legislation as 'probably the most serious menace to which British institutions are exposed' (A. Lawrence Lowell, *The Government of England*, 2 vols., 1908; New York 1910, vol. 2, p. 535.

143. Emy, *Liberals*, pp. XIf.; Clarke, *Lancashire*, p. 399.

opinion, one has to draw a much stricter distinction than has usually been the case hitherto between the attitude of the organisations representing the labour movement, the position of organised and unorganised workers, the reaction of various groups within the working class and the positions adopted towards individual measures and social reform as a whole.

The Labour Party and the trade unions, it is true, had no coherent social programme. They were more interested in the question of prices and incomes and their own ideas on alleviating unemployment, which differed from those of the government. That the ideas of the Labour Party were quite close to those of their rivals, the Liberals, was revealed by the Secretary of the Labour Party, James Ramsey MacDonald, when he warned the Party in 1907 not to put forward its own programme since the 'radicals' within the Liberal Party would seize on its demands, making it difficult for Labour to preserve its separate identity.[145] Despite this, the contribution of Britain's labour organisations to the successful passage of social reforms cannot be ignored. The introduction of free school-meals for poor children was the result of a parliamentary motion by a Labour MP. The medical inspection of school-children, the setting up of Trade Boards to fix minimum wages in certain areas of industry, the creation of labour exchanges and greater central and local government controls on housing all received the support of Britain's labour organisations, who, above all, played a significant part in the successful campaign for state old-age pensions after the turn of the century.[146]

Britain's labour organisations were, it is true, divided over the National Insurance Act. While the majority of the Parliamentary Labour Party voted for it, partly in return for the successful introduction of the payment of MPs in 1911,[147] and the government eventually

---

144. See E. J. Hobsbawm's discussion of Pelling's book, 'Popular Politics', in *Society for the Study of Labour History, Bulletin*, no. 18, 1969, pp. 49–54, esp. p. 52; Arthur Marwick, 'The Labour Party and the Welfare State in Britain, 1900–1948', in *American Historical Review* 73 (1967/68), pp. 380–403, esp. pp. 382–6; Pat Thane, 'The Working Class and State "Welfare" 1880–1914', in *Society for the Study of Labour History, Bulletin*, no. 31, 1975, pp. 6–8.

145. J. Ramsay MacDonald, 'Sozialismus, Gewerkschaften, Arbeiterpartei', in *Sozialistische Monatshefte* 13 (1907), pp. 828–35, esp. p. 834. MacDonald made similar statements during the Labour Party Annual Conference of 1909 (*Report* p. 85).

146. Marwick, 'Labour Party', in *American Historical Review* 73 (1967/68), esp. pp. 380–7; Thane, 'Working Class', in *Society for the Study of Labour History, Bulletin*, no. 18, 1969, pp. 6–8; Gilbert, *Evolution*, pp. 112f., 189–96, 202–14.

147. See MacDonald's letter to Alexander Murray, dated 4 October 1911, quoted in, Frank Owen, *Tempestuous Journey, Lloyd George, His Life and Times*, London 1954, pp. 207f.

succeeded in winning over the trade union leaders,[148] the Act was strongly opposed by the syndicalist movement, which, with its anti-state, anti-party and anti-parliamentary leanings, was growing in importance in the years after 1910.[149] It is revealing that Hilaire Belloc's phrase, the 'servile state',[150] with its simultaneous criticism of capitalist anarchy and socialist collectivism, especially during the campaign against the 1911 Act, was readily taken up not only by militant syndicalists in the labour movement but also by many Conservative critics. The Webbs also rejected the Act on the grounds that the workers' contributions were a kind of personal poll-tax. They especially criticised the lack of measures taken to protect workers against unemployment and sickness and to prevent feigned illnesses.[151] The same critical stance was adopted by the Fabian Society and a minority in the Parliamentary Labour Party led by Philip Snowden, who objected to workers' contributions as a disguised poor rate.[152] The Labour Party Conference of 1913 endorsed this criticism, demanding that the law be repealed and provision made for the sick, disabled and unemployed which was not based on contributions.[153]

In contrast to France, where the workers' and peasants' old-age pension insurance, introduced in 1910, largely failed because of its boycott by workers and employers,[154] the introduction of national

148. Hamilton, *Henderson*, pp. 77f.; Harris, *Unemployment*, pp. 317f., 331–333; Lord Elton, *The Life of James Ramsay MacDonald (1866–1919)*, London 1939, pp. 207ff.; *see also* above, p. 163.

149. For the syndicalist movement, *see* R. Holton, *British Syndicalism, 1900–1914: Myths and Realities*, London 1976. On its rejection of the 1911 Act, *see* ibid., pp. 35, 137f., 145, 165, 176f.

150. Hilaire Belloc, *The Servile State*, London and Edinburgh 1912. Inspired by a fanatical hatred of Protestants and Jews, Belloc attacked the changes brought about through industrialisation and the trend towards the welfare state. As a contrast to modern industrial society, he held up an idealised picture, based on his view of Catholic France and Ireland, of a social structure built around small farms and craft enterprises. For his ideas and social philosophy, *see also Socialism and the Servile State: A Debate between Messrs Hilaire Belloc and Ramsay MacDonald MP*, London 1911. Belloc's views were also published in *The Daily Herald*, which first appeared on 15 April 1912. (The strike publication of the same name, produced by the newspaper's compositors between 25 January and 28 April 1911 must be ignored here.) Belloc was a regular contributor to *The Herald*, which became a platform and mouthpiece for groups within the working class opposed to official Labour Party policy.

151. Webb, *Armut*, pp. 100–29.

152. Halévy, *Rule of Democracy*, pp. 355–7. For the Fabian Society's opposition to the proposed bill, *see* The Fabian Society, *The Insurance Bill and the Workers, Criticisms and Amendments of the National Insurance Bill. Prepared by the Executive Committee*, June 1911; The Fabian Society, *The National Insurance Bill*, October 1911. For Snowden's criticisms, *see* his speech to the House of Commons of 6 July 1911 (*Parl. Deb., HC*, 5th series, vol. 27, cols. 1391–9).

153. Labour Party Conference 1913, *Report*, pp. 104–6.

insurance in Britain encountered next to no passive resistance.

There have been no detailed studies as yet on the attitude of ordinary workers to Britain's social welfare legislation, as distinct from that of their representative organisations. However, we can assume that, unlike organised labour, in which skilled workers dominated,[155] the unskilled workers, who were still largely unorganised and often had no vote or adequate schooling, remained more critical of the government and its legislation.

As regards the influence of social reform on the outcome of elections, it can certainly be argued that the Liberals' successes were not due to particular welfare laws. These played no significant part in elections or, at most, only a secondary role. This does not preclude the fact, however, that many working-class voters viewed the Liberals as the party of social reform and preferred them to the Conservatives, who also tried, with some degree of success, to compete for the working-class vote.

One of the effects of the 1911 Act was that it established the British trade unions as approved organisations allowed to administer national insurance. Compared with the very slight rise in German trade-union membership during the same period, the rapid increase in British trade-union membership from 2.6 million in 1910 to 4.1 million in 1913, which was a significant departure from the stagnation of previous years,[156] was, admittedly, mainly a result of the powerful wave of strikes between 1911 and 1912, in the course of which the unskilled workers, in particular, became better organised. On the other hand, the possibility of being insured by the trade unions against sickness and unemployment doubtless helped them attract new members[157] and strengthened the workers' loyalty towards their own organisations.

Finally, the National Insurance Act and the government's social policy in general bound the trade unions closer than ever to the state. This can be seen in the fact that between 1907 and 1913 374 trade union officials were given well-paid civil servant jobs in the new social insurance institutions.[158] This no doubt involved a danger of corrup-

---

154. *See* above, p. 13.

155. Hobsbawm's discussion of Pelling's book on 'Popular Politics', in *Society for the Study of Labour History, Bulletin*, no. 18, 1969, p. 51.

156. In Germany during the same period trade union membership rose only from 2.5 to 3 million. Between 1894 and 1910, in contrast, the figure increased eightfold from its former level of 300,000, while the figure for Britain's trade union membership rose from approximately 1,530,000 to 2,565,000 members; that is, by only two-thirds (figures from Henry Pelling, *History of British Trade Unionism*, Penguin Books, 1963, pp. 261f., and Hohorst *et al.*, *Sozialgeschichtliches Arbeitsbuch* II, pp. 135f.).

157. Pelling, *History*, p. 129; Halévy, *Rule of Democracy*, p. 479.

tion and the increasing estrangement of trade union leaders from their members, but the recruitment of trade unionists to the civil service almost certainly contributed to the close cooperation which came into existence between the government and many of the unions during the First World War.

The 1911 Act also indirectly strengthened the way in which the employers organised the representation of their interests. Two viable organisations were subsequently founded for this purpose in the shape of the Federation of British Industries and the British Confederation of Employers' Organisations. These organisations were intended to remedy the obvious weaknesses which had come to light, such as the lack of cohesion and effective representation of their interests during the preparatory stages of the passage of the insurance bill.[159].

The effect which Britain's social welfare legislation had on the general situation of the population at large is difficult to estimate, since the laws were in effect for only a short period before the First World War brought about fundamental changes. There was apparently a distinct improvement in living conditions for the over-seventies age group, of whom over three-fifths (i.e. almost a million people) received old-age pensions amounting to over 12 million pounds in all.[160] The number of those over seventy still claiming poor relief fell from 229,500 in 1906 to 57,800 in 1913; that is, to a quarter of the former figure. While the number of people over seventy receiving indoor relief fell only by about a fifth, from 61,400 to 49,200, only 8,600 remained of the 169,100 persons in this age group originally supported by outdoor relief (i.e. slightly over 5 per cent).[161] Although only published as late as in 1971, Robert Roberts, in his impressive book on his childhood in Salford, Lancashire, almost certainly gives a true insight into the feelings of many pensioners when he relates how old people spending their pensions in his mother's shop 'would bless the name of Lloyd George as if he were a saint from heaven'.[162]

Admittedly, many still saw the workers' contributions in sickness

---

158. Halévy, *Rule of Democracy*, pp. 446f.
159. Hay, *British Business Community*, in Mommsen (ed.), *Emergence*, p. 125.
160. *Seventeenth Abstract of Labour Statistics of the United Kingdom 1915*, pp. 184f. In 1913 Britain's 967,921 old-age pensioners accounted for 63.7 per cent of those over seventy as recorded in the population census of 1911.
161. Williams, *Pauperism*, p. 207.
162. Robert Roberts, *The Classic Slum: Salford Life in the First Quarter of the Century*, Manchester 1971, p. 63. Following the introduction of the 1911 National Insurance Act, people drawing sickness benefit would say 'they were on the "Lloyd George"', a compliment to the tremendous part he played in introducing that measure' (ibid.).

and disablement insurance as an indirect tax, even though they amounted to about only 1 to 2 per cent of the family income and were thus well below the insurance payments of German workers.[163] Since most employees previously excluded from earlier voluntary insurance schemes were now incorporated into sickness insurance, there was a general improvement in the standards of medical treatment. The 1911 Act protected many workers for the first time against the complete impoverishment associated with chronic illness and disablement.

Britain's welfare legislation during the period before 1914 also helped the country cope better than would otherwise have been the case, when it faced various emergencies during the First World War.[164] It generally helped to defuse tensions between the social classes. Although there was some opposition to the deterioration in workers' living and working conditions, especially from shop stewards in centres of the munitions industry, the unity of the nation during the war was never seriously endangered.[165]

163. *See* statistics on 'Relation between Contributions and Income in Working-Class Families 1912', in Harris, *Unemployment*, p. 380. The contributions for unemployment insurance affected only a small part of the workforce and amounted to between 0.59 per cent and 1.15 per cent of weekly incomes of between 35 shillings and 18 shillings. Harris calculated that the payment of indirect taxes through the purchase of grocery provisions, tobacco and alcohol amounted to 7.1 per cent of an income of 18 shillings and 3.65 per cent of an income of 35 shillings. For Germany, *see* above, p. 50, note 99; p. 103, note 267.
164. M. B. Hammond stresses this fact in his *British Labor Conditions and Legislation during the War*, New York 1919, p. 21.
165. *See* esp. James Hinton, *The First Shop Stewards' Movement*, London 1973.

CHAPTER 4

Germany and Britain: a Comparison of their Social Security Systems before 1914

The fact that nearly two and a half decades lay between the introduction of the German and British systems of social security immediately accounts for certain basic differences which existed between them and the motive forces that caused them. It is important to bear in mind that the view of the state as an agent responsible for social welfare only began to replace the earlier widely held Liberal belief in *laissez-faire* from about the turn of the century onwards. Against this background, it becomes clear why in Germany Liberals not only opposed social insurance and its institutions on the grounds of the German system's pronounced compulsory character but also on principle. In Britain, on the other hand, Liberal governments led the way in this area. Also, the idea that one could use social insurance to achieve greater productivity from the workers, raise consumption and increase the efficiency of the national economy played no significant part in shaping the final form of Germany's early legislation. Yet it was precisely considerations of this kind regarding the 'German model', which, in the wake of Germany's concrete experiences with social insurance, virtually guided reform efforts in Britain.

There was an obvious difference in the significance and character of the political considerations which lay behind the introduction of social insurance in both countries. True, the desire to integrate the workers

179

into the social and political order also played its part in Great Britain. Here, however, it was not the main priority which it had been for Bismarck and Germany's employers. In Great Britain, where the legislation took strong account of the interests of the trade unions and Friendly Societies, there was hardly any intention of using social welfare legislation to undermine the influence of the workers' representative organisations among the workforce. Certainly, the British government desired to take the wind out of the sails of the Labour Party and both the Conservatives and the Liberals promoted social reform measures to prevent their losing the working-class vote. However, unlike the German Social Democrats in the eyes of Germany's social and political élites, the Labour Party was not regarded as a revolutionary threat.

Another feature connected with the different political motives behind social insurance was the fact that German social insurance was mainly aimed at the skilled workers who qualified for cover and were the main group organised by the Social Democrats and the socialist free trade-unions. This group was to be won over to the existing monarchical system by the granting of a certain amount of protection against the effects of accident, sickness, invalidity and old age. In Great Britain, on the other hand, social policy, by supporting the efforts of the Friendly Societies, extending workers' protection, guaranteeing much greater rights regarding freedom of combination and strengthening the trade unions' position in law, always provided the workers with more scope to pursue the ideal of self-help. Up to the 1911 National Insurance Act the actual target groups of Britain's social security system, were, in contrast to Germany's, those in particular need — children, and workers who were unable to organise the effective representation of their interests. Compared with Germany, women were also incorporated on a much greater scale in Britain thanks to its system of old-age pensions, which constituted the starting point for a national welfare system.

In Germany's case, the political motives behind the organisation of the insurance system resulted in the trade unions being rejected as vehicles for administering insurance and the closely allied free benefit funds for the sick being relegated to a minor role after the late 1880s. Of even greater importance was the creation of a separate pension insurance for white-collar workers. Politically aimed at blocking any inroads the Social Democrats and the free trade unions might make into the 'new middle class', this insurance constituted one of the main differences between the German and British systems.

Social problems and the inadequacies of the existing systems of poor relief gave an essential impetus in both countries to the creation of new state welfare systems. Even if the intention of unburdening, extending and/or replacing the traditional system of poor relief was not regarded in Germany as possessing the same paramount importance as in Britain, a basic motive behind Germany's social welfare reforms was the desire — hitherto overlooked by research — to reduce the burden on the existing system. This was connected not least with the fact that the receipt of benefits under the traditional system of poor relief tied the claimant to a particular local authority and thus hampered the mobility of the workforce, while imposing the social costs of labour on the local authorities.

Great Britain eventually followed Germany's example in adopting the principle of compulsory insurance for specific sections of the population. On the other hand, the idea of forcing a person to subscribe to a particular insurance was rejected and the individual largely left to choose his own insurance organisation. In contrast to the principle of earnings-related contributions and benefits, introduced in Germany partly against Bismarck's original intentions, the British welfare system laid down standard rates in both cases. Benefits were, with a few exceptions, considerably higher on average and based on the principle of securing a minimum level of existence regardless of previous earnings. In contrast, Germany's benefits were often not even sufficient to provide the barest standard of living. However, the system of graduated contributions and benefits later made it easier to adopt the principle of preserving as far as possible the standard of living to which a worker had become accustomed during his working life.

Contrary to Bismarck's original intentions, Germany's state subsidies were much lower than Britain's.[1] This was mainly true of old-age pensions, which in Great Britain, unlike Germany, were entirely funded from government revenue up to 1925. It was also true, though

1. In the financial year 1913/14, the United Kingdom government spent an estimated total of nearly £20m on the country's new social services. Two-thirds of this was spent on old-age pensions (Bruce, *Welfare State*, p. 183; Gilbert, *Evolution*, p. 230). Between 1890 and 1910, the amount spent by central and local government on the total range of social services (including poor relief, education and health services) rose from £27.3m to £89.1m; that is, from 20.9 to 32.8 per cent of the total public expenditure (Peacock *et al.*, *Growth of Public Expenditure*, pp. 82, 86). While outdoor relief payments still accounted for 97.6 per cent of total expenditure on income maintenance in 1900, its proportion fell to 30.0 per cent in 1910 and 3.6 per cent in 1920 (Julia Parker, 'Welfare', in Halsey, (ed.), *Trends*, pp. 372–406, esp. p. 402). In Germany in 1913, the imperial government subsidised disablement and old-age pension insurance to the amount of 30.8 million marks in 1900 and 58.5 million marks in 1913 (Born *et. al.* (ed.), *Quellensammlung*, p. 152). The similar trend in Germany of increasing expenditure on social welfare services can be seen most clearly in the growing proportion of transfer payments to total expenditure by public agencies. These 'transfer payments' were made without a simultaneous or

to a lesser extent, of the 1911 sickness and disability insurance, which saw the state give up its previously costly system of solely financing social benefits in favour of also imposing considerable burdens on employers and employees.

Another significant difference was that state subsidies in Great Britain were mainly financed from direct and not indirect taxes, as was the case in Germany. For this reason the redistribution of wealth effected by social legislation in Britain before 1914 was considerably greater than that achieved in Germany. Here, all plans intended to strengthen the Empire by transferring some of the direct taxes raised by the federal states failed on account of massive Conservative opposition.[2] This opposition was also largely responsible for the stagnation of social reform in Germany after 1911.

The much greater participation of insured employees in financing Germany's social insurance also resulted in the fact that, contrary to the original intentions of Britain's policy-makers, the element of self-management in the system of social security was more obvious in Germany's constitutionally dualist monarchy than in Britain's parliamentary democracy.

In many respects, the part played by social forces and political institutions in the creation of the new social security systems was about equal, even though there were some significant differences. Individual politicians in both countries, like Bismarck in Germany or Lloyd George and Churchill in Britain, played an important part, and the influence of leading civil servants and contemporary social scientists was a significant factor in both countries. The influence of the political parties and Parliaments on the concrete shape of welfare legislation was apparently greater in Germany, where Bismarck had to accept crucial limitations to his original concept of an extensive workers' insurance, administered and financed by the state. In contrast, the British Parliament and public played a greater part in initiating welfare legislation, as can be seen by comparing the introduction of both countries' systems of old-age pensions. Certainly, this difference is true only of Germany's insurance legislation during the 1880s. As the

---

indeed any corresponding economic return; that is, they were pure subsidies of all kinds. In addition to civil service and servicemen's pensions, they were also intended to cover the costs of social insurance. According to Peter-Christian Witt's calculation ('Finanzpolitik und sozialer Wandel', in *Sozialgeschichte Heute* pp. 568f.) these 'transfer payments' rose from 5.6 per cent to 18.6 per cent of total expenditure by public agencies between 1871/74 and 1910/13.

2. *See* Peter-Christian Witt, *Die Finanzpolitik des Deutschen Reiches von 1903 bis 1913: Eine Studie zur Innenpolitik des Wilhelminischen Deutschland*, Lübeck and Hamburg 1970.

examples of Germany's widows' and orphans' insurance and the white-collar insurance law show, the subsequent development of Germany's social welfare legislation after 1900 was also decisively pushed forward by public campaigning and initiatives from the political parties. The same is true of the influence of those interests directly affected. In the legislation of the 1880s, the German government was able to ignore these interests almost completely — with the exception of those of the employers. However, as the massive and successful campaign for separate old-age pensions for white-collar workers particularly demonstrates, they, too, proved very important in influencing German social policy after the turn of the century.

Employers in both countries adopted an ambivalent attitude towards social insurance, in that those representing small and medium-sized firms were from the outset much more critical of the additional costs involved than those representing larger concerns. Alongside the burden of costs to the economy, which eventually came to prevail in both countries *after* the new systems of social security had been introduced, the employers' disappointed expectations regarding the legislation's intended weakening of the Social Democrats played a significant part in the increasing rejection of social legislation, especially by the employers of Germany's heavy industry.

The new systems of state welfare decisively encouraged the organisation of social forces in both countries. In Britain's case, this can be seen in the way that the introduction of the National Insurance Act of 1911 resulted in mobilising the country's doctors, strengthening its trade unions and producing a more effective representation of employers' interests. In Germany, social welfare legislation helped consolidate the employers' representative organisations, founded earlier in connection with the changeover to protective tariffs. Contrary to Bismarck's intentions, social insurance substantially strengthened the Social Democrats and the trade unions. It led to the medical profession's collective representation of its interests in the Hartmann League and helped consolidate the growth of the extremely heterogeneous white-collar movement into a mass organisation which had previously existed only in rudimentary form.

Taking each of the individual areas of social security in turn, it appears that, as far as employers' liability for industrial accidents was concerned, Germany's accident insurance was superior to the British system, which remained in force until 1946. Under the German system there was a much greater likelihood of an injured worker's claims being accepted, together with a stronger incentive to take precautions against accidents. However, after 1906, Great Britain went further than the German system in incorporating occupational diseases into the sphere of employers' liability. Despite detailed discussion of Britain's example, Germany's Imperial Insurance Code of 1911 rejected the idea of incorporating occupational diseases, though the Federal Council was given powers to extend accident insurance to cover such diseases in specific industries.[3]

In the case of sickness insurance, the 1911 National Insurance Act helped Great Britain more or less catch up with Germany, both as regards the number of workers insured and the level of benefits they enjoyed. Despite the different ways of financing the two systems (in Germany the costs had to be borne to a greater extent by the insured themselves) Britain's departure from the German system in combining sickness and disablement insurance, in granting special status to approved societies administering the system (which had a certain parallel in the German special sickness insurance funds) and in the much more prominent role of local and central government authorities in medical treatment, the concrete effect of both systems on insured employees was probably much the same in both countries. Certainly, the individual contributions paid by the German worker, to which the amount of sickness benefits was related, differed in amount compared with the British system of standard rates of contributions and benefits.

In the case of old-age pensions, the British system of paying a standard state pension to any deserving person over the age of seventy in need of assistance — thus standing in between the old system of poor relief and the new concept of a universal state welfare for all citizens — departed widely from the German system based on the principle of insurance and differentiated benefits. Although German pension insurance was more in keeping with the modern idea of preserving the living standard achieved by the individual during his working life, the fact that its level of benefits lay generally well below Britain's and that persons not in employment were excluded (especially the majority of women before the very limited introduction of widows' and orphans' pensions shortly before the First World War), meant that, compared to Britain's new arrangements, it was less able to replace the traditional system of poor relief.

In each country, the main vehicles for unemployment insurance were the trade unions. In the state regulation of the labour market, in which the German example of municipal labour exchanges played a significant role, as well as in the introduction of a state unemployment insurance which, admittedly, covered only a small section of the

---

3. Tennstedt, *Vom Proleten zum Industriearbeiter*, p. 516.

industrial workforce, Great Britain took the lead over Germany. This was probably largely due to the fact that unemployment in the last decade before 1914 was a much more serious problem in Britain than in Germany and that owing to the federal structure of Germany's political constitution it was difficult in that country to decide whether responsibility for the unemployed lay with the municipal authorities, the individual states or the central government.

While the German social insurance system deliberately created new state-controlled social institutions, Britain — apart from a few exceptions like the labour exchanges — managed to preserve the continuity of existing social institutions. The system based on 'approved societies' in sickness and disablement insurance as well as unemployment insurance did not, however, prove practical and was given up after the Second World War in favour of a unified state administration. In contrast, the German system, despite its complexity and diversity of organisation was able to operate efficiently on the whole. Also, the system of challenging decisions on disability and accident pensions by arbitration courts and the Imperial Insurance Office was more strongly developed in Germany, where it led to the emergence of a more precise legal framework for social welfare.

In both countries the traditional system of poor relief was relegated to a minor role, but by no means wholly replaced. The creation of new state welfare institutions increased the role of central over local government, enlarged the sphere of government intervention in social and economic life and strengthened the trend towards an expanding and increasingly professionalised state bureaucracy.

Without doubt, the main political aims of integrating the workers into the social and political order, overcoming social problems caused by industrialisation and urbanisation and heightening productivity were advanced in the long term, if not completely realised. The measure of social controls imposed on those receiving benefits and the expansion of the bureaucracy meant that the social welfare laws of both countries retained an element of social discipline *vis-à-vis* the working classes as had traditionally been the case under the Poor Law, albeit now in a milder form. This, however, was somewhat offset by the strengthening of the workers' self-organisation, which was equally typical for the modern welfare state. Thus, by liberating large sections of the population from the danger of extreme hardship, the modern social security systems of both countries contributed in the long-term to the political and social emancipation of the lower classes.

Since the First World War, Great Britain's social security system has undergone much greater changes than Germany's. As early as 1925 the system of old-age pensions for those in need over seventy years of age, financed by the state, has been expanded with the introduction of pensions related to insurance contributions and no longer dependent on a means test for anyone between the ages of sixty-five and seventy covered by national insurance. Unemployment insurance, which incorporated new occupational groups in 1920, largely broke down during the Depression. In the 1930s the British system of unemployment assistance was based on a clear distinction between insurance benefits awarded for a limited period and unemployment assistance dependent on a means test. When the Beveridge Report of 1942 was finally implemented after the war, the previous system of administering insurance through approved societies was also replaced by a largely unified system of social security and a national health service. With the introduction of additional earnings-related contributions and benefits in 1959, Britain departed to some degree from the principle that standard rates of benefits for all citizens should secure a national minimum for all in favour of the idea that pensions should be aimed at maintaining the former standard of living. In the German Empire and, subsequently, in the Federal Republic of Germany, the introduction of unemployment insurance in 1927, the inclusion of occupational diseases in accident insurance, the linking of pension insurance to the general state of the economy since 1957 by way of an index which calculates pension amounts on the basis of an individual's wages, the concept of a 'generational contract' and the view of pensions as a means of not only securing a minimum existence but preserving accustomed living standards has expanded the scope and benefits of the social insurance system to an extraordinary degree. Nevertheless, the basic features of this system and its organisation into separate branches have been essentially maintained now for over a hundred years. This continuity is all the more astonishing if one recalls the major political upheavals of 1918, 1933 and 1945 and the basic changes which have taken place in almost every other area of German society and politics.

Table 1. Sickness insurance in Germany

	Members[a] % of females	Members as % population	Contributions Figures (millions)	Contributions Per member in RM/DM per year	Figures (millions)	Cash benefits[c] as %	Benefits Benefits in kind[c] as %	Per member in RM/DM per year
Figures (000s)[b] 1	2	3	4	5	6	7	8	9
1885 4,294	18.1	9.2	56	13.1	47	56.8	43.2	11.05
1890 6,580	19.9	13.3	91	13.4	84	52.6	47.4	12.82
1895 7,256	22.4	14.4	117	15.6	105	48.5	51.5	14.03
1900 9,521	23.1	16.9	166	17.4	158	49.3	50.7	16.74
1905 11,184	25.3	19.6	250	22.4	232	49.0	51.0	21.05
1910 13,069	27.9	20.3	358	27.4	320	46.8	53.2	24.84
1914 15,610	36.9	23.0	524	33.6	445	46.4	53.6	28.49
1920 17,089	39.1	27.7	—	—	—	50.9	49.1	—
1938 23,983	33.5	32.9[d]	1,822	76.0	1,686	30.2[d]	69.8[d]	70.3
1950 15,709	33.5	31.2	2,129	135.5	1,868	—	—	118.9
1965 28,740	40.7	48.5	15,088	525.0	14,914	—	—	518.9
1982 35,699	45.6	—	96,515	2,703.3	92,676	—	—	2,596.0

a Insured members' dependants who were covered against sickness insurance have to be taken into account in two respects. In the case of cash benefits, it has been calculated that the payments made to each member of a sickness fund in 1913 also partly protected his on average two to three dependants against the economic effects of the breadwinner's ill-health. This meant that financial hardship caused by ill-health was alleviated for around 62.5 per cent of the Reich's population. Benefits in kind could be extended to member's dependants who were not themselves liable for contributions through appropriate terms and conditions laid down by the self-managed funds of the insured. This kind of insurance protection, which was made available at first by only a few funds, may well have benefited around 24 million citizens or 36 per cent of the Reich's population by 1913 (cf. above, p. 85). The figures for 1950 do not include sickness insurance for old-age pensioners.

Table 1: *continued*

[b] Annual average figures.

[c] For the years after 1955 the ratio of benefits in kind to cash benefits developed as follows: 1955 = 4 : 1, 1969 = 5.7 : 1, 1970 = 10.3 : 1, 1975 10.4 : 1. (Dieter Schewe *et al.* [eds.], *Übersicht über die Soziale Sicherung.* [Figures as at 1 April 1977], Bonn, 10th edn 1977, p. 192).

[d] Figures for 1937.

Sources:

Column 1:	1885–1965	*Bevölkerung und Wirtschaft*, pp. 219 f.
	1982	Der Bundesminister für Arbeit und Sozialordnung (ed.), *Arbeits- u. Sozialstatistik, Hauptergebnisse 1984*, Bonn 1984, p. 106.
Column 2:	1885–1965	*Bevölkerung und Wirtschaft*, pp. 219 f. (calculated).
	1982	*Arbeits- u. Sozialstatistik, Hauptergebnisse 1984*, p. 106 (calculated).
Column 3:	1885–1937	Relevant volumes of *Krankenversicherung der Statistik des Deutschen Reichs.*
	1950, 1965	Calculated on the basis of population figures in *Bevölkerung und Wirtschaft*, p. 91.
Column 4:	1885–1965	*Bevölkerung und Wirtschaft*, pp. 219 f.
	1982	*Arbeits- u. Sozialstatistik, Hauptergebnisse 1984*, pp. 152–4
Column 5:	1885–1914	*Statistik des Deutschen Reichs*, vol. 289, p. 56*.
	1938–82	Calculated from the figures in columns 1 and 4.
Column 6:	1885–1965	*Bevölkerung und Wirtschaft*, pp. 219 f.
	1982	*Arbeits- u. Sozialstatistik, Hauptergebnisse 1984*, pp. 152–4.
Columns 7/8:	1885–1937	Relevant volumes of *Krankenversicherung der Statistik des Deutschen Reichs.*
Column 9:	1885–1914	*Statistik des Deutschen Reichs*, vol. 331, p. 18.
	1938–82	Calculated from the figures in columns 1 and 6.

Table 2. Accident insurance in Germany

	Nos. of insured (000s)[a] 1	No. of persons registered injured or sick[b]		No. of persons receiving pensions or sickness benefits (000s) 4	Expenditure	
		Figures (000s) 2	% of insured 3		Total (millions) 5	Benefit per recipient in RM p.a. 6
1886	3,822	100	2.68	11	10	178
1890	13,680	200	1.46	100	39	202
1895	18,389	310	1.68	318	68	157
1900	18,893	454	2.40	595	101	145
1905	20,243	609	3.00	893	176	151
1910	27,554	673	2.44	1,018	228	160
1914	27,965	705	2.52	1,000	223	178
1920	26,856	592	2.20	912	–	308
1938	33,149	2,007	6.05	659	394	485
1950	25,198	1,382	5.48	667	599	–
1968	24,327	2,513	10.33	1,047	4,061	–
1982	24,967	1,807	7.23	992	12,524	–

[a] Annual average figures. Up to and including 1955 it was possible for the same persons to be provided with insurance cover by several separate agencies administering insurance. According to figures in the relevant volumes of the *Amtliche Nachrichten des Reichsversicherungsamts*, the number of persons insured with more than one agency amounted to approximately 1.5 million in 1895, 1.5 million in 1900 and 1905, 3.4 million in 1910 and 3.3 million in 1914 and 1920. The figures for 1968 and 1982 represent the number of *Vollarbeiter* (full-time employees) in the year, i.e., those working part-time or for only part of a complete year count as only part of a *Vollarbeiter*.
[b] Persons registered as injured and sick with accident or sickness insurance (in accordance with the extension of accident insurance to include occupational diseases in 1925).

Sources:

Column 1:	1886–1950	*Bevölkerung und Wirtschaft*, pp. 220 f.
	1968, 1982	*Arbeits- und Sozialstatistik, Hauptergebnisse 1981*, p. 134; 1984, p. 142.
Column 2:	1886–1910	Relevant volumes of the *Amtl. Nachr. d. Reichsversicherungsamts*.
	1914–38	Petzina *et al.* (eds.), *Sozialgeschichtliches Arbeitsbuch III*, pp. 159.
	1959–82	*Arbeits- u. Sozialstatistik, Hauptergebnisse 1981*, pp. 104, 134; 1984, p. 142.
Column 3:		Calculated from the figures in columns 1 and 2.

Table 2: *continued*

Column 4:	1886–1968	*Bevölkerung und Wirtschaft*, pp. 220 f.
	1982	*Arbeits- u. Sozialstatistik, Hauptergebnisse 1984*, p. 141.
Column 5:	1886–1968	*Bevölkerung und Wirtschaft*, pp. 220 f.
	1984	*Arbeits- und Sozialstatistik, Hauptergebnisse 1984*, p. 144.
Column 6:	1886–1910	Relevant volumes of the *Amtl. Nachr. d. Reichsversicherungsamts*.
	1914–38	Petzina *et al.* (eds.), *Sozialgeschichtliches Arbeitsbuch III*, p. 159.

Table 3. Workers' pension insurance in Germany

	Numbers of insured (000s)[a]	Number of pensions (000s)[b] old age	Number of pensions (000s)[b] disablement	Revenue total (millions)	Revenue % of imp./ fed. govt. supplement	Expenditure (millions) total	Expenditure (millions) of which pensions	Average pension in RM per annum/ DM per annum old age	Average pension in RM per annum/ DM per annum disablement
	1	2	3	4	5	6	7	8	9
1891	11,490	–	–	101	5.9	19	15	123.35	113.38
1895	12,145	–	–	133	12.8	49	41	132.80	123.92
1900	13,015	215	450	187	16.6	104	81	145.54	142.04
1905	13,948	156	858	250	18.8	173	137	159.10	159.45
1910	15,660	114	1,008	307	17.3	219	164	164.31	176.93
1914	16,552	98	1,129	405	15.3	258	200	167.99	200.81
1920	17,500[c]	1,929		–	–	–	–	–	–
1938	–	3,646		2,085	23.6	1,413	1,233	–	–
1950	–	3,232		2,701	20.2	2,399	1,995	60.50	
1965	12,390	5,952		20,521	24.4	20,066	14,428	215.10	
1982	10,920[d]	8,625		89,181	21.0	88,577	72,675	740.77	

a The number of insured is calculated in each case on the total amount of annual weekly contributions divided by the estimated number of weekly contributions, paid annually on a per capita basis. These estimates vary between fifty-two and forty weekly contributions.

b For the years 1891 and 1895 figures are available only for pension awards: in 1891, 132,926 new old-age pensions (for people aged 70 or over before the law came into effect) and 31 disablement pensions were awarded; for 1895, the figures were 30,144 and 55,983 respectively. In 1897 the total number of pensions amounted to 226,275 old-age pensions and 237,416 disablement pensions.

c Figure for 1925 (*Amtliche Nachrichten des Reichsversicherungsamts* 1927, pp. 93f.).

d Figure for 1976.

Table 3: *continued*

Sources:

Column 1: 1891–1914 Born et al. *Quellensammlung*, p. 153.
           1925   *Amtliche Nachrichten des Reichsversicherungsamts 1927*, pp. 93f.
           1965, 1976 Tietz, George, *Zahlenwerk zur Sozialversicherung in der Bundesrepublik Deutschland, Gegenwärtiger Stand, Entwicklung seit 1951, Vergleich mit der Reichsversicherung 1938*, Berlin 1963 ff., 39 Ü (bersicht).

Column 2/3: 1891–1914 Born et al. (eds.) *Quellensammlung*, p. 153.
             1920–65   *Bevölkerung und Wirtschaft*, p. 222.
             1982   *Arbeits- und Sozialstatistik, Hauptergebnisse 1984*, p. 114.

Column 4: 1891–1965 *Bevölkerung und Wirtschaft*, p. 222.
           1982   *Arbeits- und Sozialstatistik, Hauptergebnisse 1984*, p. 124.

Column 5: 1891–1914 Born et al. (eds.) *Quellensammlung*, p. 152 (calculated).
           1938, 1955–70 Tietz, 56 Ü (bersicht).
           1950   *Arbeits- und Sozialstatistische Mitteilungen (ASM)* 28 (1977), p. 259 (calculated).
           1982   *Arbeits- und Sozialstatistik, Hauptergebnisse 1984*, p. 105 (calculated).

Column 6/7: 1891–1965 *Bevölkerung und Wirtschaft*, p. 222.
             1982   *Arbeits- u. Sozialstatistik, Hauptergebnisse 1984*, p. 125.

Column 8/9: 1891–1914 Relevant volumes of *Amtl. Nachr. d. Reichsversicherungsamts*.
             1950   *ASM* 14 (1963), 321.
             1965   Tietz, 1 Ü (bersicht).
             1982   *Arbeits- u. Sozialstatistik, Hauptergebnisse 1984*, p. 118.

Table 4. The number of persons receiving assistance in Great Britain, 1900–38

		Outdoor relief^a						Non-contributory old-age pensions
				Old^b				
Total	Adults	Children	Total	With pension	Sick	Unemployed^c	
1	2	3	4	5	6	7	8
584,311	350,327	158,190	158,843	—	292,660	—	—
622,837	355,032	184,171	138,223	—	282,939	—	607,000
368,792	167,469	138,380	8,621	6,284	104,958	—	785,883
1,356,293	866,475	338,942	143,376	99,231	271,351	163,313	1,373,331
1,327,665	835,442	270,552	225,130	226,756	439,746	512,356	1,789,207

(Row labels, left to right: 1900, 1910, 1920, 1930, 1938)

a Figures in columns 2–6 are for England and Wales only as Scottish figures are not broken down in the same way. The numbers in the categories do not add up to the numbers in the total column as they are not mutually exclusive. Dependants are included; that is, where relief is given to the head of the family, the wife (if any) and children under sixteen living with the head and dependent on him for support are counted. If outdoor relief is given exclusively to a wife or child, the head of the family is also counted as relieved, but other dependants are not.

b The old are over seventy up to and including 1920; in 1930 and 1938 they are over sixty-five.

c Unemployed in England and Wales are added to the Scottish category 'destitute and able-bodied'. The statistics for 1900 and 1910 introduced the categories of able-bodied men 'in want of work' and 'in health'. Of these, 8,000 were receiving assistance in 1900 (of whom 300 received outdoor relief) and 18,100 in 1910 (of whom 3,300 received outdoor relief). Added to this were 24,100 dependants in 1900 (54,100 in 1910). No figures are available for 1920 for the number of maintained poor caused by unemployment. In 1922 the number of unemployed receiving outdoor relief was 744,800 (Williams, *From Pauperism to Poverty*, pp. 183f.).

Source: Parker, 'Welfare', in Halsey (ed.), *Trends*, p. 400 (reproduced by permission of Macmillan, London and Basingstoke).

Table 5. Expenditure on income maintenance: cash grants and insurance benefits in £000s and as % of total yearly expenditure, Great Britain, 1900–38

	Assistance			Insurance benefits						War pensions
	Poor Law outdoor relief	Non-contributory old-age pensions	Unemployment allowances	Sickness, disablement, maternity	Unemployment	Old-age contributory pensions	Widows, orphans and guardians	Workmen's accidents	Compensation industrial disease[a]	
	1	2	3	4	5	6	7	8	9	10
1900	3,166 (97.6%)	—	—	—	—	—	—	78 (2.4%)	—	—
1910	4,084 (30.0%)	7,360 (54.1%)	—	—	—	—	—	2,108 (15.5%)	54 (0.4%)	—
1920	5,416 (3.6%)	20,676 (13.7%)	—	10,089 (6.7%)	8,752 (5.8%)	—	—	4,857 (3.2%)	366 (0.2%)	100,949 (66.8%)
1930	15,616 (6.0%)	36,676 (14.0%)	—	19,303 (7.4%)	101,594 (38.9%)	16,363 (6.3%)	16,890 (6.5%)	5,127 (2.0%)	583 (18.7%)	49,205 (18.7%)
1938	19,380 (7.3%)	44,154 (16.7%)	41,309 (15.6%)	18,599 (7.1%)	51,662 (19.5%)	21,130 (8.0%)	24,305 (9.2%)	4,940[b] (1.9%)	546 (0.2%)	38,428 (14.5%)

[a] Figures refer to the United Kingdom and do not include death benefits.

[b] Figure for 1935/6.

Source: Parker, 'Welfare', in Halsey (ed.), *Trends*, p. 402 (reproduced by permission of Macmillan, Basingstoke and London).

Table 6. Total number of persons receiving indoor and outdoor
relief in England and Wales, 1850–1939[a]

	Indoor		Outdoor		Total (excluding casuals and insane)[b]	Total (all classes)[b]
	(b)	(c)	(b)	(c)		
	1	2	3	4	5	6
1850[d]	123	7.0	886	50.4	—	1,009
1855	121	6.5	776	41.7	—	898
1860	101	5.1	695	35.3	796	845
1865	118	5.7	783	37.5	901	951
1870	141	6.4	838	37.7	979	1,033
1875	129	5.5	616	25.9	745	801
1880	159	6.3	582	22.9	741	808
1885	162	6.0	533	19.8	695	769
1890	166	5.8	530	18.7	696	775
1895	184	6.1	523	17.4	706	797
1900	188	5.9	500	15.7	689	797
1905	240	7.1	547	16.3	787	879
1910	275	7.8	540	15.2	815	916
1914	255	7.0	387	10.6	642	748
1920	181	4.8	298	7.9	479	563
1930	217	5.5	850	21.4	1,067	1,183
1939	149	3.6	928	22.6	1,077	1,208

[a] Up to 1858 the totals in the columns headed 'indoor' and 'outdoor' include all classes of
paupers. From 1859 the totals in columns 1, 3 and 5 exclude the insane (wherever
domiciled) and casuals. They are still included here as part of the total figure in column
6. From 1901 the columns headed 'indoor' and 'outdoor' continue to exclude all casuals
but now only exclude those insane who were institutionalised in county and borough
asylums, registered hospitals and licensed houses.
[b] Mean numbers, in 000s.
[c] Rates per 000 of estimated population.
[d] Years are calculated as ending 31 March of following year.
Source: Williams, *From Pauperism to Poverty*, pp. 158ff.

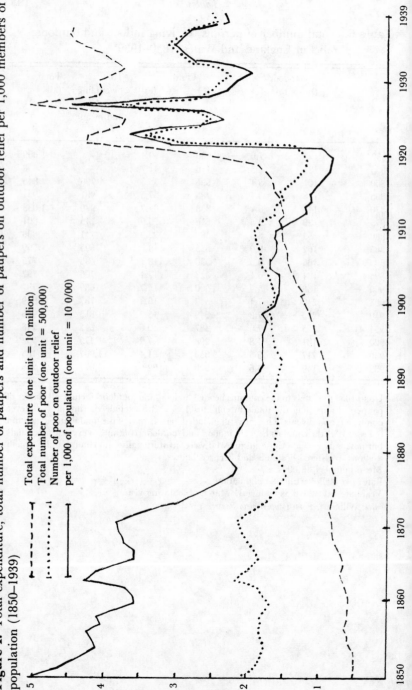

Figure I. Total expenditure, total number of paupers and number of paupers on outdoor relief per 1,000 members of population (1850–1939)

Total expenditure (one unit = 10 million)
Total number of poor (one unit = 500,000)
Number of poor on outdoor relief
per 1,000 of population (one unit = 10 0/00)

Table 7. Paupers aged 70 and over, receiving indoor and outdoor relief, 1890–1930

	70 years of age and over (000s)			Column 3 as % of all paupers	Column 1 as % of col. 3	Column 3 as % of all aged 70+
	Indoor relief	Outdoor relief	Total[a]			
	1	2	3	4	5	6
1890 (1.8)	38.9	144.5	183.4	24.8	21.2	22.9[b]
1900	49.4	152.8	202.2	27.9	24.4	22.8
1903 (1.9)	53.4	156.9	210.3	26.2[c]	25.4	23.7
1906 (1.3)	61.4	168.1	229.5	28.1	26.8	24.5
1910	57.7	138.2	195.9	20.9	29.5	
1911	55.3	93.2	148.4	16.6	37.3	13.9
1912	49.3	9.5	58.9	7.3	83.7	–
1913[d]	49.2	8.6	57.8	7.2	85.1	
1914	48.1	8.9	57.0	7.5	84.3	
1915	47.2	8.5	55.7	7.5	84.7	
1920	38.2	8.6	46.8	8.1	81.6	
1930	45.5	79.8	125.5	10.4	36.3	7.4

[a] The figures do not include the insane in asylums, licensed houses and registered hospitals. Vagrants are excluded 1890–1906 and are only included in column 3 from 1925. The returns for 1900 exclude all insane. There was a huge decrease in pauperism among the aged between 1906 and 1913. Figures for outdoor relief fell by 94.9 per cent, those for indoor relief by 19.8 per cent, resulting in a combined fall of 74.8 per cent. This was a direct result of the Old Age Pensions Act of 1908 which came into operation on 1 January 1911. 122,415 persons in receipt of relief on 31 December 1910 subsequently received old-age pensions.

[b] In this case, the totals are of estimated population aged sixty-five years and over.

[c] Figure for 1 July.

[d] Figures for 1913 are from December.

Source: Williams, *From Pauperism to Poverty*, pp. 207f.

Select Bibliography

Only the most important works on the subject are listed here for further reference. Sources and literature on detailed aspects are to be found in the notes.

General literature

Alber, Jens, *Vom Armenhaus zum Wohlfahrtsstaat: Analysen zur Entwicklung der Sozialversicherung in Westeuropa*, Frankfurt and New York 1982

Bödiker, Tonio, *Die Arbeiterversicherung in den Europäischen Staaten*, Leipzig 1895

Briggs, Asa: 'The Welfare State in Historical Perspective', in *Archives Européennes* 2 (1961), pp. 221–58

Fischer, Wolfram, *Armut in der Geschichte: Erscheinungsformen und Lösungsversuche der 'Sozialen Frage' in Europa seit dem Mittelalter*, Göttingen 1982

Flora, Peter, Alber, Jens, and Kohl, Jürgen 'Zur Entwicklung der westeuropäischen Wohlfahrtsstaaten', in *Politische Vierteljahresschrift* 18 (1977), pp. 707–72

Flora, Peter, and Heidenheimer, Arnold J. (eds.), *The Development of Welfare States in Europe and America*, New Brunswick and London 1981

Flora, Peter, *et al.*, *State, Economy and Society in Western Europe 1815–1975. A Data Handbook in Two Volumes*, vol. 1, *The Growth of Mass Democracies and Welfare States*, Frankfurt, London and Chicago 1983

Herold, Hans, 'Voraussetzungen und Ursprünge der Sozialversicherungen', in *Schweizerische Zeitschrift für Sozialversicherung* 9 (1965), pp. 98–126

Kaiserliches Statistisches Amt, *Die Arbeiterversicherung in Europa nach dem gegenwärtigen Stande der Gesetzgebung in den verschiedenen Staaten. Sonderbeilage zum*

'*Reichsarbeitsblatt*', *Nr. 7, Juli 1910. Zusammengestellt vom Kaiserlichen Statistischen Amte. Abteilung für Arbeiterstatistik*, Berlin 1910

Köhler, Peter A., and Zacher, Hans F., 'Die Sozialversicherung im Europa der Jahrhundertwende', in *Die Sozialgerichtsbarkeit* 28 (1981), pp. 420–32

(eds.), *Ein Jahrhundert Sozialversicherung in der Bundesrepublik Deutschland, Frankreich, Grossbritannien, Österreich und der Schweiz*, Berlin 1981

(eds.), *Beiträge zu Geschichte und aktueller Situation der Sozialversicherung, Colloquium des Max-Planck-Instituts für ausländisches und internationales Sozialrecht*, Berlin 1983

Matthes, Joachim (ed.), *Sozialer Wandel in Westeuropa: Verhandlungen des 19. Deutschen Soziologentages 17–20. April 1979 im Internationalen Congress Centrum (ICC) in Berlin*, Frankfurt and New York 1979

Mommsen, Hans, and Schulze, Winfried (eds.), *Vom Elend der Handarbeit: Probleme historischer Unterschichtenforschung*, Stuttgart 1981

Mommsen, Wolfgang J. (editor in collaboration with Wolfgang Mock), *The Emergence of the Welfare State in Britain and Germany 1850–1950*, London 1981

Rimlinger, Gaston V., *Welfare Policy and Industrialization in Europe, America and Russia*, New York 1971

Tomasson, Richard F. (ed.), 'The Welfare State, 1883–1983', *Comparative Social Research* 6, 1983

Zacher, Georg, *Die Arbeiter-Versicherung im Auslande*, 5 vols., Berlin 1900–08

Zacher, Hans F. (ed.), *Bedingungen für die Entstehung und Entwicklung von Sozialversicherung, Colloquium der Projektgruppe für internationales und vergleichendes Sozialrecht der Max-Planck-Gesellschaft*, Berlin 1979

Zöllner, Detlev, *Öffentliche Sozialleistungen und wirtschaftliche Entwicklung: Ein zeitlicher und internationaler Vergleich*, Berlin 1963

Social insurance in Germany before 1914

Die deutsche Arbeiterversicherung als soziale Einrichtung. Im Auftrage des Reichsversicherungsamts dargestellt für die Weltausstellung in St Louis 1904 [in 5 parts], Berlin 1904

Baron, Rüdeger, 'Weder Zuckerbrot noch Peitsche. Historische Konstitutionsbedingungen des Sozialstaats in Deutschland', in *Gesellschaft: Beiträge zur Marxschen Theorie* 12, Frankfurt am Main 1979, pp. 13–55

Benöhr, Hans-Peter, 'Verfassungsfragen der Sozialversicherung nach den Reichstagsverhandlungen von 1881 bis 1889', in *Zeitschrift der Savigny-Stiftung für Rechtsgeschichte, Germ. Abteilung* 97 (1980), pp. 94–163

'Soziale Frage, Sozialversicherung und Sozialdemokratische Reichstagsfraktion (1881–1889)', in *Zeitschrift der Savigny-Stiftung für Rechtsgeschichte, Germ. Abteilung* 98 (1981), pp. 95–156

Born, Karl Erich, *Staat und Sozialpolitik seit Bismarcks Sturz: Ein Beitrag zur Geschichte der innenpolitischen Entwicklung des Deutschen Reiches 1890–1914*, Wiesbaden 1957

Breger, Monika, *Die Haltung der industriellen Unternehmer zur staatlichen Sozialpolitik in den Jahren 1878–1891*, Frankfurt am Main 1982

Craemer, Rudolf, *Bismarcks Erbe in der Sozialversicherung*, Berlin 1940

Dawson, William Harbutt, *Bismarck and State Socialism: An Exposition of the Social and Economic Legislation of Germany since 1870*, London 1890; reprint edn, New York 1973

Social Insurance in Germany 1883–1911: Its History, Operation, Results. And a comparison with the National Insurance Act 1911, New York 1911; reprint edn, Westport 1979

Dreher, Wolfgang, *Die Entstehung der Arbeiterwitwenversicherung in Deutschland, nach z.T. unveröffentlichten Quellen*, Berlin 1978

Feige, Lothar, *Sozialpolitische Analyse der Organisation von Interessen in der Gesetzlichen Krankenversicherung. Von den Anfängen sozialer Sicherung bis zur Notgesetzgebung 1932 in Deutschland*, Wirtschafts- und sozialwissenschaftliche Diss., Cologne 1980

Freund, Richard, *Armenpflege und Arbeiterversicherung: Prüfung der Frage, in welcher Weise die neuere soziale Gesetzgebung auf die Aufgaben der Armengesetzgebung und Armenpflege einwirkt*, Leipzig 1895

Frevert, Ute, *Krankheit als politisches Problem 1870–1880: Soziale Unterschichten in Preussen zwischen medizinischer Polizei und staatlicher Sozialversicherung*, Göttingen 1984

Fröhlich, Sigrid, *Die soziale Sicherung bei Zünften und Gesellenverbänden: Darstellung, Analyse, Vergleich*, Berlin 1976

Gladen, Albin, *Geschichte der Sozialpolitik in Deutschland: Eine Analyse ihrer Bedingungen, Formen, Zielsetzungen und Auswirkungen*, Wiesbaden 1974

Greißl, 'Wirtschaftliche Untersuchungen über die Belastungen der deutschen Industrie durch die Arbeiter-Versicherungs- und Schutzgesetzgebung', in *Schmollers Jahrbuch*, Neue Folge, 23 (1889), pp. 855–912

Heidemann, Karl, *Bismarcks Sozialpolitik und die Zentrumspartei 1881–1884*, Phil. diss., Göttingen 1929, Herford 1930

Heinz, Hans Michael v., *Entsprechungen und Abwandlungen des privaten Unfall- und Haftpflichtversicherungsrechts in der gesetzlichen Unfallversicherung nach der Reichsversicherungsordnung*, Berlin 1973

Henning, Friedrich-Wilhelm (ed.), *Entwicklung und Aufgaben von Versicherungen und Banken in der Industrialisierung*, Berlin 1980

Henning, Hansjoachim, 'Arbeitslosenversicherung vor 1914: Das Genter System und seine übernahme in Deutschland', in Hermann Kellenbenz (ed.), *Wirtschaftspolitik und Arbeitsmarkt*, Munich 1974, pp. 271–87

Hentschel, Volker: 'Das System der sozialen Sicherung in historischer Sicht 1880 bis 1975', in *Archiv für Sozialgeschichte* 18 (1978), pp. 307–52

Geschichte der deutschen Sozialpolitik (1880–1980), Soziale Sicherung und kollektives Arbeitsrecht, Frankfurt a. Main 1983

Hockerts, Hans Günter, 'Sicherung im Alter. Kontinuität und Wandel der gesetzlichen Rentenversicherung 1889–1979', in Werner Conze and M. Rainer Lepsius (eds.), *Sozialgeschichte der Bundesrepublik Deutschland: Beiträge zum Kontinuitätsproblem*, Stuttgart 1983, pp. 296–323

'Hundert Jahre Sozialversicherung in Deutschland: Ein Bericht über die neuere Forschung', in *Historische Zeitschrift*, 237 (1983), pp. 361–84

Klöhn, Sabine, *Helene Simon (1862–1947): Deutsche und britische Sozialreform und Sozialgesetzgebung im Spiegel ihrer Schriften und ihr Wirken als Sozialpolitikerin im Kaiserreich und in der Weimarer Republik*, Frankfurt 1982

Kleeis, Friedrich, *Die Geschichte der sozialen Versicherung in Deutschland*, 1st edn 1928; reprint edn by Dieter Dowe with an introduction by Florian Tennstedt, Berlin and Bonn 1981

Knaack, Rudolf, and Schröder, Wolfgang, 'Gewerkschaftliche Zentralverbände, Freie Hilfskassen und die Arbeiterpresse unter dem Sozialistengesetz: Die Berichte des Berliner Polizeiprasidenten vom 4. September 1886 und 28. Mai 1888', in *Jahrbuch für Geschichte* 22 (1981), pp. 351–481

Landwehr, Rolf, and Baron, Rüdeger (eds.), *Geschichte der Sozialarbeit: Hauptlinien ihrer Entwicklung im 19. und 20. Jahrhundert*, Weinheim and Basle 1983

Lass, Ludwig, and Zahn, Friedrich, *Einrichtung und Wirkung der Deutschen Arbeiterversicherung*, Berlin 1904

Lederer, Emil, *Die Pensionsversicherung der Privatangestellten*, Staatswirtschaftliche diss., Munich, Tübingen 1911

Lindenlaub, Dieter, *Richtungskämpfe im Verein für Sozialpolitik: Wissenschaft und Sozialpolitik im Kaiserreich, vornehmlich vom Beginn des 'Neuen Kurses' bis zum Ausbruch des I. Weltkrieges (1890–1914)*, 2 vols., Wiesbaden 1967

Müller, Rudi, 'Die Stellung der liberalen Parteien im Deutschen Reichstag zu den Fragen der Arbeiterversicherung und des Arbeiterschutzes bis zum Ausgang des 19. Jahrhunderts', Phil. diss., (MS) Jena 1952

Peters, Horst, *Die Geschichte der sozialen Versicherung*, 3rd edn, Sankt Augustin 1978

Quandt, Otto, *Die Anfänge der Bismarckschen Sozialgesetzgebung und die Haltung der Parteien (Das Unfallversicherungsgesetz 1881–1884)*, Berlin 1938

Ratz, Ursula, *Sozialreform und Arbeiterschaft: Die 'Gesellschaft für Soziale Reform' und die sozialdemokratische Arbeiterbewegung von der Jahrhundertwende bis zum Ausbruch des Ersten Weltkrieges*, Berlin 1980

Reif, Heinz, 'Soziale Lage und Erfahrungen des alternden Fabrikarbeiters in der Schwerindustrie des westlichen Ruhrgebietes während der Hochindustrialisierung', in *Archiv für Sozialgeschichte* 22 (1982), pp. 1–94

Reulecke, Jürgen, *Sozialer Frieden durch soziale Reform: Der Centralverein für das Wohl der arbeitenden Klassen in der Frühindustrialisierung*, Wuppertal 1983

Reuter, Hans-Georg, 'Verteilungs- und Umverteilungseffekte der Sozialversicherungsgesetzgebung im Kaiserreich', in Fritz Blaich (ed.), *Staatliche Umverteilungspolitik in historischer Perspektive: Beiträge zur Entwicklung des Staatsinterventionismus in Deutschland und Österreich*, Berlin 1980, pp. 107–93

Richter, Adolf, *Bismarck und die Arbeiterfrage im preussischen Verfassungskonflikt*, Stuttgart [1934]

Ritter, Gerhard A., *Staat, Arbeiterschaft und Arbeiterbewegung in Deutschland: Vom Vormärz bis zum Ende der Weimarer Republik*, Berlin and Bonn 1980

Rosin, Heinrich, *Das Recht der Arbeiterversicherung. Für Theorie und Praxis systematisch dargestellt*, vol. 1 in three parts, Berlin 1890–1893; vol. 2, Berlin 1905

Rothfels, Hans, *Theodor Lohmann und die Kampfjahre der staatlichen Sozialpolitik (1871–1905): Nach ungedruckten Quellen*, Berlin 1927
'Bismarck's Social Policy and the Problem of State Socialism in Germany', in *Sociological Review* 30 (1938), pp. 81–94, 288–302
'Prinzipienfragen der Bismarckschen Sozialpolitik', in Rothfels, *Bismarck: Vorträge und Abhandlungen*, Stuttgart 1970, pp. 166–81
Rubin, J., *Grundzüge der internen Arbeiterversicherungs-Medizin*. Jena 1909
Sachße, Christoph, and Tennstedt, Florian, *Geschichte der Armenfürsorge in Deutschland: Vom Spätmittelalter bis zum Ersten Weltkrieg*, Stuttgart 1980
Saul, Klaus, 'Industrialisierung, Systemstabilisierung und Sozialversicherung: Zur Entstehung, politischen Funktion und sozialen Realität der Sozialversicherung des kaiserlichen Deutschland', in *Zeitschrift für die gesamte Versicherungswissenschaft* 69 (1980), pp. 177–98
Schmoller, Gustav, 'Vier Briefe über Bismarcks sozialpolitische und volkswirtschaftliche Stellung und Bedeutung', in Schmoller, *Charakterbilder*, Munich and Leipzig 1913, pp. 27–76
Schönhoven, Klaus, 'Selbsthilfe als Form der Solidarität: Das gewerkschaftliche Unterstützungswesen im Deutschen Kaiserreich bis 1914', in *Archiv für Sozialgeschichte* 20 (1980), pp. 147–93
Spree, Reinhard, *Soziale Ungleichheit vor Krankheit und Tod: Zur Sozialgeschichte des Gesundheitsbereichs im Deutschen Kaiserreich*, Göttingen 1981; trans. edn *Health and Social Class in Imperial Germany*, Leamington Spa 1987
Stollberg, Gunnar, 'Die gewerkschaftlichen zentralisierten Hilfskassen im Deutschen Kaiserreich', in *Zeitschrift für Sozialreform* 29 (1983), pp. 339–69
Stolleis, Michael, 'Hundert Jahre Sozialversicherung in Deutschland, Rechtsgeschichtliche Entwicklung', in *Zeitschrift für die gesamte Versicherungswissenschaft* 69 (1980), pp. 155–75
Syrup, Friedrich, *Hundert Jahre staatliche Sozialpolitik*, 1839–1939, ed. by Julius Scheuble and Otto Neuloh, Stuttgart 1957
Tennstedt, Florian, 'Quellen zur Geschichte der Sozialversicherung', in *Zeitschrift für Sozialreform* 21 (1975), pp. 225–33, 358–65, 422–7
'Sozialgeschichte der Sozialversicherung', in Maria Blohmke (ed.), *Handbuch der Sozialmedizin*, Stuttgart 1976, vol. 3, pp. 385–492
Soziale Selbstverwaltung: Geschichte der Selbstverwaltung in der Krankenversicherung von der Mitte des 19. Jahrhunderts bis zur Gründung der Bundesrepublic Deutschland, vol. 2, Bonn 1977
'Sozialwissenschaftliche Forschungen in der Sozialversicherung', in *Kölner Zeitschrift für Soziologie und Sozialpsychologie, Sonderheft* 19 (1977) of *Soziologie und Sozialpolitik*, ed. by Christian v. Ferber and Franz-Xaver Kaufmann, Opladen 1977, pp. 483–523
Sozialgeschichte der Sozialpolitik in Deutschland: Vom 18. Jahrhundert bis zum Ersten Weltkrieg, Göttingen 1981
'Vorgeschichte und Entstehung der Kaiserlichen Botschaft vom 17. November 1881', in *Zeitschrift für Sozialreform* 27 (1981), pp. 663–710
Vom Proleten zum Industriearbeiter: Arbeiterbewegung und Sozialpolitik in Deutschland 1880 bis 1914, Cologne 1983

'Die Errichtung von Krankenkassen in deutschen Städten nach dem Gestetz betr. die Krankenversicherung der Arbeiter vom 15. Juni 1883', in *Zeitschrift für Sozialreform* 29 (1983), pp. 297–338

Ullmann, Hans-Peter, 'Industrielle Interessen und die Entstehung der deutschen Sozialversicherung 1880–1889', in *Historische Zeitschrift* 229 (1979), pp. 574–610

Umlauf, Joachim, *Die deutsche Arbeiterschutzgesetzgebung 1880–1890: Ein Beitrag zur Entstehung des sozialen Rechtsstaates*, Berlin 1980

Verhein, Heinrich, *Die Stellung der Sozialdemokratie zur deutschen Krankenversicherungsgesetzgebung und ihr Einfluss auf dieselbe*, Phil. diss., Halle-Wittenberg 1914, Halle 1916

Vogel, Walter, *Bismarcks Arbeiterversicherung: Ihre Entstehung im Kräftespiel der Zeit*, Brunswick 1951

Volkmann, Heinrich, *Die Arbeiterfrage im preussischen Abgeordnetenhaus 1848–1869*, Berlin 1968

Wattler, Theo, *Sozialpolitik der Zentrumsfraktion zwischen 1877 und 1889 unter besonderer Berücksichtigung interner Auseinandersetzungen und Entwicklungsprozesse*, Phil. diss., Cologne 1978

Wickenhagen, Ernst, *Geschichte der gewerblichen Unfallversicherung: Wesen und Wirken der gewerblichen Berufsgenossenschaften*, 2 vols., Munich and Vienna 1980

Wolff, Hertha, *Die Stellung der Sozialdemokratie zur deutschen Arbeiterversicherungsgesetzgebung von ihrer Entstehung bis zur Reichsversicherungsordnung*. Rechts- und staatswissenschaftliche diss., Freiburg 1933

Zahn, Friedrich, 'Arbeiterversicherung und Armenwesen in Deutschland (unter Mitberücksichtigung der neuen Reichsversicherungsordnung)', in *Archiv für Sozialwissenschaft und Sozialpolitik* 35 (1912), pp. 418–86

Social reform and social insurance in Britain before the First World War

Askwith, Lord, *Industrial Problems and Disputes*, London 1920; reprint with an introduction by Roger Davidson, Brighton 1974

Bartrip, P. W. J., and Burman, S. B., *The Wounded Soldiers of Industry: Industrial Compensation Policy, 1833–1897*, Oxford 1983

Beveridge, W. H., *Unemployment: A Problem of Industry* (1909, 1930), new edn, New York 1969

Bend, William A., *Health and the State*, London 1917

Booth, Charles, *Life and Labour of the People in London*, 2 vols., London 1892

Briggs, Asa, *Social Thought and Social Action: A Study of the Work of Seebohm Rowntree, 1871–1954*, London 1961

Brown, Kenneth D., *Labour and Unemployment, 1900–1914*, Totowa, NJ, 1971

Bruce, Maurice, *The Coming of the Welfare State*, London 1961

The Rise of the Welfare State: English Social Policy, 1601–1971, London 1973

Bunbury, Sir Henry N. (ed.), *Lloyd George's Ambulance Wagon: Being the Memoirs of William J. Braithwaite, 1911–1912*, commentary by Richard Titmuss, London and Southampton 1957

Burrow, J. W., *Evolution and Society: A Study in Victorian Social Theory*, Cambridge 1966

Clarke, P. F., *Lancashire and the New Liberalism*, Cambridge 1971
Liberals and Social Democrats, Cambridge 1978

Collins, Doreen, 'The Introduction of Old Age Pensions in Great Britain', in *Historical Journal* 8 (1966), pp. 246–59

Crowther, M. A., *The Workhouse System, 1834–1929: The History of an English Social Institution*, London 1981

Davidson, Roger, 'Llewellyn Smith, the Labour Department and Government Growth, 1886–1909, in Gillian Sutherland (ed.), *Studies in the Growth of Nineteenth-Century Government*, London 1972, pp. 227–62

Emy, H. V., *Liberals, Radicals and Social Politics, 1892–1914*, Cambridge 1973

Evans, Eric J. (ed.), *Social Policy, 1830–1914: Individualism, Collectivism and the Origins of the Welfare State*, London 1978

Fraser, Derek, *The Evolution of the British Welfare State: A History of Social Policy since the Industrial Revolution*, 2nd edn, London 1984
(ed.), *The New Poor Law in the Nineteenth Century*, London and Basingstoke 1976

Freeden, Michael, *The New Liberalism: An Ideology of Social Reform*, Oxford 1978

Gilbert, Bentley B., *The Evolution of National Insurance in Great Britain: The Origins of the Welfare State*, London 1966

Gosden, P. H. J. H., *The Friendly Societies in England, 1815–1875*, Manchester 1961
Self-Help: Voluntary Associations in the 19th Century, London 1973

Halsey, A. H. (ed.), *Trends in British Society since 1900: A Guide to the Changing Social Structure of Britain*, London and Basingstoke 1972

Harris, José, *Unemployment and Politics: A study in British Social Politics 1886–1914*, Oxford 1972
William Beveridge: A Biography, Oxford 1977

Hay, J. R., *The Origins of the Liberal Welfare Reforms, 1906–14*, London and Basingstoke 1975
'Employers and Social Policy in Britain: the Evolution of Welfare legislation, 1905–1914', in *Social History* 2 (1977), pp. 435–55
(ed.), *The Development of the British Welfare State, 1880–1975*, London 1978

Heclo, Hugh, *Modern Social Politics in Britain and Sweden: From Relief to Income Maintenance*, New Haven and London 1974

Hennock, E. P., 'Poverty and Social Theory in England: The Experience of the Eighteen-eighties', in *Social History* 1 (1976), pp. 67–91

Hennock, Peter: 'Arbeiterunfallentschädigung und Arbeiterunfallversicherung: Die britische Sozialreform und das Beispiel Bismarck', in *Geschichte und Gesellschaft* 11 (1985), pp. 19–36

Hollenberg, Günter, *Englisches Interesse am Kaiserreich: Die Attraktivität Preussen-Deutschlands für konservative und liberale Kreise in Grossbritannien, 1860–1914*,

Wiesbaden 1974

Jones, Gareth Stedman, *Outcast London: A Study in the Relationship between Classes in Victorian Society*, Oxford 1971

Martin, E. W. (ed.), *Comparative Development in Social Welfare*, London 1972

Marwick, Arthur, 'The Labour Party and the Welfare State in Britain, 1900–1948', in *American Historical Review* 73 (1967/68), pp. 380–403

Mowat, Charles Loch, *The Charity Organisation Society, 1869–1913: Its Ideas and Work*, London 1961

Pelling, Henry, 'The Working Class and the Origins of the Welfare State', in idem, *Popular Politics and Society in Late Victorian Britain*, London 1969, pp. 1–18.

Roberts, David, *Victorian Origins of the British Welfare State*, New Haven 1960

Rose, Michael E. (ed.), *The English Poor Law, 1780–1930*, Newton Abbot 1971
   The Relief of Poverty, 1834–1914, London and Basingstoke 1972

Rowntree, B. Seebohm, *Poverty: A Study of Town Life*, 1st edn, London 1901; reprint of the 1922 edn, New York 1971

Searle, G. R., *The Quest for National Efficiency: A Study in British Politics and Political Thought, 1899–1914*, Oxford 1971

Semmel, Bernard, *Imperialism and Social Reform: English Social-Imperial Thought, 1895–1914*, London 1960

Simey, T. S., and Simey, M. B., *Charles Booth: Social Scientist*, Oxford 1960

Thane, Pat (ed.), *The Origins of British Social Policy*, London 1978
   The Foundations of the Welfare State, London and New York 1982

Treble, J. E., 'The Attitude of Friendly Societies towards the Movement in Great Britain for State Pensions, 1878–1908', in *International Review of Social History*, 15 (1970), pp. 266–99

Treble, James H., *Urban Poverty in Britain 1830–1914*, New York 1979

Watkin, Brian (ed.), *Documents on Health and Social Services 1834 to the Present Day*, London 1975

Webb, Sidney, and Webb, Beatrice, *English Poor Law History, Part II: The Last Hundred Years*, 2 vols., London 1929; reprint edn by W. A. Robson, London 1963 (vols. VIII and IX of the Webbs' study of English local government)

Williams, Karel, *From Pauperism to Poverty*, London 1981

Index

Names

Subject